ONE HUNDRED
INDIAN FEATURE FILMS

GARLAND REFERENCE LIBRARY
OF THE HUMANITIES
(VOL. 915)

ONE HUNDRED INDIAN FEATURE FILMS
An Annotated Filmography

Shampa Banerjee
Anil Srivastava

GARLAND PUBLISHING, INC. • NEW YORK & LONDON
1988

Library of Congress Cataloging-in-Publication Data

Banerjee, Shampa.
   One hundred Indian feature films: an annotated filmography /
Shampa Banerjee, Anil Srivastava.
      p.   cm. — (Garland reference library of the humanities; vol.
915)
   Includes index.
   ISBN 0–8240–3647–6 (alk. paper)
   1. Motion pictures—India—Catalogs.   2. Motion pictures—India—
Bibliography.   3. Motion pictures—India—Plots, themes, etc.
I. Srivastava, Anil, 1945–   II. Title.   III. Series.
PN1993.5.I8B27 1988
016.79143'75'095—dc19   88-22716
                                                           CIP

This book was written and edited on a Macintosh computer using Microsoft Word
and printed on a QMS PS Jet+ laser printer.

Printed on acid-free, 250-year-life paper
Manufactured in the United States of America

CONTENTS

Preface   vii

Introduction   1

The Films   9

Indexes   189

PREFACE

THIS BOOK originated as a project under the National Film Heritage programme at the Centre for Development of Instructional Technology in Delhi, along with the efforts to build up a collection of Indian cinema at the United States Library of Congress. Many of the films encapsulated within these pages are available with the Library of Congress in Washington, D.C., along with a large number of film scripts in microfiche form. The National Film Heritage has now become an independent activity being pursued by the authors together with others who believe "that moving images are an expression of the cultural identity of peoples, and because of their educational, cultural, artistic, scientific and historical value, form an integral part of a nation's cultural heritage."

One Hundred Indian Films attempts to bring together a representative selection from the first talkies to the present day. How far it succeeds in doing so is questionable, for the choice of the entries, though they emerged initially out of the suggestions of a panel of advisers, finally had to depend on accessibility to information on the films. There are obvious gaps—for example, there are no films of M.G. Ramachandran, the late Chief Minister of Tamil Nadu, who was a swashbuckling hero in Tamil cinema for many glorious years, nor of Akkineni Nageswara Rao from Andhra Pradesh, and Uttam Kumar and Suchitra Sen from Bengal—just to mention a few of the missing names. The balance between serious cinema and popular successes is a difficult one to maintain, no less than that between the directors, artistes, music makers, and the entire magical band that participate in the adventure of film making. In a country where documentation on the cinema has been sporadic and unorganized, no selection of a hundred from nearly eighty highly prolific years of Indian talkies, can possibly do justice to all the films that deserve similar attention. This book will also not contain information on the two most important films of the present year—Tinnu Anand's *Shahenshah*, an absurd extravaganza which has reaffirmed the tremendous impact of the Bachchan factor on the Indian film industry; and *Anantaram*, a quiet, subterranean experiment in separate realities by the most original and artistic of our younger directors, Adoor Gopalakrishnan.

The process of collecting information on the one hundred films has not been an easy one, for information on Indian cinema, where it exists, often does so in a fragmentary form. Perfection and complete authenticity can be aspired for, but not achieved. There are no means of checking out every single fact about a particular entry. The date of a film, for example, can be either the release date or the date on the censor certificate. There can be vast difference between the two when a film takes a long time to find a distributor. Names in the credits are sometimes also in English, but the spellings may differ; or the same producer may at one time display a technician's full name, and at another, only the initials. Even the running time of the films is not necessarily a constant factor. For example, a whole sequence was removed from Satyajit Ray's *Aparajito* after the film was passed by the Censor Board. References to events associated with the films can be equally confusing, reflecting as they do the subjective viewpoints of the writers. The English language titles of the films too present a problem. Effort has been made to use, wherever possible, the official English version of the name. Where there is none in existence, a translation has been provided instead.

This book would not have been possible without the initiative and continued support of P.K. Nair, Director of the National Film Archive of India in Pune, who not only provided viewing facilities for and stills from films in his collection but was also a continuous source of information and verification while preparing the manuscript. In consultation with him, an initial list of films was drawn up and sent to almost ninety film critics and scholars for their comments and suggestions. We are specially grateful to Jugu Abraham, Bindu Batra, Chidananda Das Gupta, Nasreen Kabir, Amit Khanna, Pradip Krishen, S. Krishnaswamy, Hameeduddin Mahmood, Jag Mohan, Kironmoy Raha, Raghunath Raina, T.M. Ramachandran, and Pandit Shimpi who took time off from their busy schedules to suggest significant alterations to our initial list.

April 1988   SHAMPA BANERJEE
                                                    ANIL SRIVASTAVA

INTRODUCTION

IN 1901, exactly five years after an envoy from Lumière Brothers had stopped over in Bombay *en route* to Australia, with their "living photographic pictures," Harishchandra Sakharam Bhatvadekar, an owner of a photographic studio in Bombay, made what would now be described as the first Indian newsreel, describing the return of an Indian scholar from Cambridge. Enthused by the *cinématographe*, Bhatvadekar had ordered a motion picture camera from London at the princely cost of 21 guineas five years ago. With it he shot subjects like a wrestling match, or the training of circus monkeys. Eventually he bought a projector and started exhibiting imported films along with his own productions.

The boom had begun. Travelling missions from Europe and America, often doubling as sales agents, helped eccentric Indian adventurers to import films, projectors and other equipment. What began as an accessory to magic shows and stage performances was soon to have an immense and longstanding impact on the social and economic forces governing a heterogenous mass of people whose common political identity as Indians was only a fairly recent phenomenon of history.

The silent film was ideally suited to a country which today officially recognizes fifteen languages besides English within its wide geographical boundaries. The mythologicals with which Dada Saheb Phalke won his place in the sun would thematically be of contemporary interest even today in a country that has absorbed the religion of the ancients into its cultural and social life. That is to say, their popularity was assured even in the brand new and uncertain profession of film making. The magical hold that the cinema has over the popular mind, has allowed it to cross many hurdles with ease, including that of a babble of tongues. With the first Indian talkie, *Alam Ara*, in 1931, a flood of sound engulfed the screen, and plunged into silence the hitherto noisy and highly participatory audience of the soundless era. At the same time, the nascent industry moved onto a period of transition. For a while the studios that represented entrepreneurship in production as well as exhibition of films flourished not only as business enterprises but also as training grounds for technical staff and artistes who were still grappling with the unfamiliar medium that was not much like, yet not so unlike the traditional stage. Men behind the cameras were swiftly adjusting to the sudden mobility and freedom of the new angle of vision. The people who faced the cameras, soon discovered that the high-pitched flamboyance of live drama had to be tempered to suit the intimacy of the sound screen.

The situation was quite the same everywhere else in the world. Salaried actors and actresses found the world at their feet, and quickly realized that their future lay outside the studios. The star system was born, the first nail in the coffin of the studios. With the war shortages, and individual producers springing up all over the country, the monopoly of the studios collapsed. Yet the war years were conspicuous for the increased returns at the box-office, with a large section of the rural population moving to the cities and towns along with an artificial economic inflation.

The idealism, nationalistic fervour and growing social consciousness of the years preceding the war were reflected in many productions. Indian cinema which had had its successful initiation with popular mythologicals, had by now embraced a much wider field of interests. It had also consolidated itself as an economically stable industry, and the highly unstable character of the professions encompassed by it had come to be looked upon as a romantic adventure. Surviving the problems of the war years, the Indian film industry emerged as an important source of revenue immediately after the country gained its independence, even as homeless refugees flocked in from the new frontiers of the fragmented Punjab and Bengal, and communal riots shook the foundations of the land. The new government, yet unable to take "entertainment" seriously, introduced fresh levies and taxes, centralized censorship, compulsory exhibition at a price of the films of the newly set up Films Division, and high import duties even for prints being brought back after a successful run outside the country. The now organized leadership within the film industry recovered quickly from their state of shock and threw themselves into a prolonged battle for survival. Even so, as India entered the era of independence, she emerged as the second largest producer of feature films in the world.

* * * * *

THE CINEMA WAS big business, and the two largest centres were Bombay and Madras. Calcutta, so far the accepted haven of culture, had produced its own pioneers. But exhibitors like Madan and producers like B.N. Sirkar were already part of an illustrious past by the early fifties. With the market in East Bengal virtually out of bounds, Bengali cinema became a regional offshoot of the main industry. The highest paid stars were in Bombay. They still are. But what happened to the films themselves? The reformist zeal of the pre-war years was slowly and inevitably giving way to the immediate emotional needs of the new nation. Even if India did not have to face a full-scale world war, as a British colony it felt the severe economic backlash. With independence came partition and a new rootless generation. While the government grappled with social and economic reforms, the people faced a crisis of survival. The cinema became the new opium of the masses. Fantasy, folk lore, religion, social drama and romance were the dominant themes. Bombay evolved the "formula film," the right mix of each element that produced the loudest applause or the wettest handkerchiefs. The blacks and whites were clearly demarcated and after a few exciting fights and chases, good invariably triumphed over evil.

It could have become extremely boring for the film historian, but for the fact that within this strongly entrenched value system with its simplistic answers to life's problems, grew a new set of giants. The new generation was aware that the industry was now too well established to quietly accept brash adventurers.

A film was still a gamble, but it now incorporated a certain element of professionalism, an understanding of what sold in the market, without which no film maker could survive. Bimal Roy, Guru Dutt and Raj Kapoor made their films within the familiar constraints of the industry. Yet they could afford to be different in their themes, their treatments, even in their values, and still be accepted by the audience. Today they are cult figures, recalled with stirring nostalgia, not only in India, but in the divergent cultures of the West as well.

In the South the film industry had initially taken off with considerable dependence on the studios of Bombay and Calcutta and their experienced technicians. However, in 1934, Srinivasa Cinetone Studios produced the first Tamil talkie in Madras, *Srinivasa Kalyanam*, and within a year there were thirty-five local productions in the language. By 1937 there were nine studios in Madras, one at Salem, and two at Coimbatore. During the next fifteen years or so, the South Indian film industry flourished mainly from Madras, gradually taking control of films from language groups other than Tamil. Different language versions of the same film were mostly shot simultaneously. Having started their careers slightly later than the studios in the North and the East, the studios of the South survived marginally longer, by changing their character to suit the times, and by allowing an influx of free-lancers within their strictly patriarchal walls. As in the North, mythologicals, lives of saints and social dramas with reformist themes were the standard fare in the early days. The late thirties also saw the rise of the stunt films with the usual strong man or woman as a redeemer of the oppressed poor. But it was not till the late forties that South Indian cinema showed signs of being a formidable contender to the Northern markets.

S.S. Vasan in his Gemini Studios produced *Chandralekha* in Tamil as well as Hindi in 1948. With huge spectacular sets, and every popular element from songs and dances to swordplay, the film also had a mammoth promotion campaign and proved to be an unqualified success. By the fifties, the scene in the South, especially in Madras, was completely dominated by the local political developments. The DMK (Dravida Munnetra Kazhagam) party leader, C.N. Annadurai was the first to utilize the propagandist potential of the film medium to consolidate his own position in the State, and the two Chief Ministers who followed him have also been essentially film personalities who have successfully used the cinema to draw upon local support. Incidentally, N.T. Rama Rao, an extremely popular star from the South and a pioneer of the Telugu film industry, is today the Chief Minister of Andhra Pradesh and a leader of the Opposition, while some of the phenomenal successes of Hindi cinema have recently joined the ruling party.

* * * * *

THE FIFTIES SAW a different kind of movement in the now neglected Bengali film scene. Bengal, which had seen a resurgence of interest in traditional culture through the efforts of the left-wing Indian Peoples Theatre Association (IPTA), found a new direction in Nemai Ghosh's *Chhinnamul*, made in 1951 with a cast which included artistes from the IPTA. Though it was a landmark in the history of Indian cinema as the first neo-realist Indian film, and was highly acclaimed by the veteran Soviet director V.I. Pudovkin, it remained unknown. Its real achievement, however, lay in the first breakthrough it provided for serious cinema. One of its actors was Ritwik Ghatak who was soon to emerge as one of the major figures of Indian cinema.

Ghatak's first film, *Nagarik*, made in 1952-3, was never shown to the public, and it was not till 1958, with *Ajantrik*, that he would make his mark as a director of importance. In the meanwhile realistic and serious cinema took its first major stride with *Pather Panchali*, and Satyajit Ray became an international phenomenon. *Pather Panchali*, with its documentary realism, became an astounding success with the Bengali public even though it had nothing at all in common with what the audience had been viewing so far on the screen. It remains today perhaps one of those inexplicable facts of history where an audience fed on fairy tales found themselves emotionally stirred by the real joys and sufferings of a rural family of an earlier generation, in a Bengal yet untouched by famine and war, and the historic upheavals of the later years.

While films of Ray and Ghatak achieved the status of the classic, Mrinal Sen, also from Bengal, ushered in a whole new culture of youthful experimentation with his *Bhuvan Shome*, made in Hindi in 1969 on a shoe-string budget. Sen had already established himself as a serious filmmaker, with eight previous films to his credit. But between Ray's *Pather Panchali* and Sen's *Bhuvan Shome*, the Indian film industry continued in the direction that it had chosen years ago. Films from Bombay and Madras flooded the market and were avidly watched by cinema goers all over the country. With the coming of colour, productions were more expensive and the producers had more at stake. On the celluloid screen lovers continued to jiggle around trees and roll on the grass singing to the accompaniment of disembodied music. Tough villains were vanquished by heroes of lesser physique and "fight masters" and "dance directors" had a field day. Even V. Shantaram, the doyen of Hindi cinema and a founder of the famous Prabhat Studios in Pune, produced under his own banner *Jhanak Jhanak Payal Bajey* in 1955, a dance extravaganza far removed from his earlier reformist themes, which was the first film in India to be produced in Technicolor. Elements of Hollywood musicals were so well integrated in the mainstream Hindi cinema, that even directors like Raj Kapoor and Guru Dutt relied heavily on the musical component of their films for popular support.

The sixties, however, saw the creation of three new institutions which were to have a far-reaching impact on Indian cinema. The film society movement in India had already come into being in the early forties with the Bombay Film Society. In 1947 the Calcutta Film Society had been formed by Chidananda Dasgupta and Satyajit Ray. Starting with many restrictions and constraints, the movement nevertheless built up its own momentum with the enthusiastic support of youthful film buffs in the metropolitan cities. In later years the movement was to penetrate the remotest small town in the country. There is no doubt that the interest in serious cinema was growing, even if it was limited to a small band of intellectuals in this vast country. The first International Film Festival of India was held in 1952 in Bombay, but a long gap of nine years was to follow before the second such festival could be held, by which time the film societies had got over their initial teething troubles and occasional periods of stagnation to become once again a growing force.

It is in this atmosphere of increasing awareness about the cinema as an art that the Film Institute of India was established in 1961. Within three years time came the National Film Archive of India. The Film Finance Corporation, a government owned organization, had already started taking its first cautious steps in 1960. Though one of its first beneficiaries was the veteran mainstream director V. Shantaram, for his remake of the Shakuntala story in colour, the Corporation did manage to provide assistance to a number of new and young directors in later years whose films were not the kind that would attract the interest of financiers from the established film industry. Shifting its policy to favour low-budget experimental films in the late sixties, the Corporation suddenly hit a gold mine in Mrinal Sen's *Bhuvan Shome*. Made in Hindi, the film was a total departure from the popular cinema, and yet it scored a box-office success and won national and international awards.

* * * * *

THE NEW INDIAN CINEMA, as it started to be called, was gaining in strength through the sixties and seventies with young talents appearing in different regions of the country, many of them having trained in the Film Institute which had also added on a television wing and now called itself the Film and Television Institute of India. But in spite of the established film society movement in the country, serious Indian cinema did not find distribution within the country, where the popular cinema continued to hold the audience in thrall. The old themes based on a confrontation between good and evil, had not changed over the years; but within the same framework new sensationalist elements had been added. By the seventies, violence and sex had come to be accepted as integral to popular cinema. The tradition bound society where films were family entertainment could not allow obvious demonstration of sex. A flower or a child would appropriately appear and foil an imminent kiss between lovers. And yet the suggestive quality of the relationships, characters and clothes, would provide far more titillation than would an average film from the West. Without a social taboo attached to it, violence on the Hindi screen became an essential part of "entertainment," and directors and script-writers became more and more inventive about brutality and cruelty which were acceptable as long as they were indulged in by the baddies, or the hero was merely retaliating against gross injustice. The phenomenal rise of Amitabh Bachchan as a star was based on his "angry young man" image, a hero more sinned against than sinning, and inevitably, an area of grey began to emerge in the old value system propagated by the popular cinema. Good and evil still remained opposed to each other, only their methods of operation were fast becoming indistinguishable.

As an industry the popular cinema had never seen better days. These were the magical years of the "multi-starrers," of huge box-office successes, of major gambles which paid off. Simultaneously, the mainstream directors were becoming more professional in their story-telling, the films were achieving a technical polish and pace which defied their unusual length, and the stars gave the best performances of their lives. The curry-Western, *Sholay*, was a block-buster to end them all, and till today remains a phenomenon that has not been repeated. On the other end of the spectrum, the mythologicals were coming back with new force. *Jai Santoshi Ma* brought out of obscurity a little known goddess of the Hindu pantheon and gave her a mass following overnight. Today all over the country women fast on Fridays to appease this rejuvenated divinity. It is a tangible measure of the influence that the popular cinema wields over the lives of the vast majority of people in India.

It was as if to counter the fast growing strength of the established commercial cinema that a new set of films appeared in the eighties. These have been variously named the "middle cinema" or the "parallel cinema." What they do stand for is conscious artistic awareness coupled with some concessions to so-called popular tastes. Presumably, the directors started with the concept of meaningful cinema, and then went on to make them acceptable to the largest possible audience, unlike the very personal statements of the previous decade which remained mostly in their cans, unheralded and unsung. Chronologically one might date the beginning of this form of cinema from *Ardh Satya*, the second film by Govind Nihalani, who began his career as a cameraman. But the shift from the obscure art cinema had already started with Shyam Benegal's *Ankur* and M.S. Sathyu's *Garam Hava*, films that told a straight-forward tale, but a serious one with a bearing on real problems in the lives of real people. But it was *Ardh Satya* that established the genre and made it acceptable to the same audience that demanded the fairy tales that the mainstream cinema willingly provided them with.

It was followed by other similar efforts, some successful, some not so successful, but none of them were rejected outright by the public. The new atmosphere created by these films provided the opportunity for Mahesh Bhatt, a mainstream director, to make films on non-formula themes but with the dramatic flamboyance of popular cinema, which were immediate box-office successes. It also allowed Jabbar Patel, a theatre personality from Pune in Maharashtra, to produce a film like *Simhasan* in Marathi, a political thriller and a black comedy in disguise, which became a rage among the regional audience. In the South, similar change was ushered in by Bharathi Rajaa in his Tamil films, which, along with their usual technical excellence, presented a new kind of story with relatively real characters who spoke a language that was colloquial and therefore easier to identify with.

In the meanwhile the "multi-starrers" have been dying a slow but natural death. The sudden influx of television, which in itself was not considered much competition for mainstream cinema, soon led to large-scale video piracy of popular films. Although it worried the old guards, many of the younger stalwarts of the industry found in video a new opening up of their markets. Doordarshan, the government-owned Indian television, has commercialized much of its programmes, and the corporate sponsors need experienced people to handle the serials that become indirect vehicles for product advertising. After a brief period of adjustment, the film industry has now come forward to join the latest bandwagon.

In 1971 India became the largest film producing country in the world, a position that she still maintains. Today a group of fresh young faces are busy ousting the established stars of the last decade. Young directors are on the rise in the industry, while the older ones are becoming more conscious of the need to resort to further innovations within their established formulas. With a growing audience for non-formula films as well, the middle cinema is providing the impetus for fresh themes, a more realistic approach and a conscious effort at artistry. The serious cinema, with a few notable exceptions like Adoor Gopalakrishnan and G. Aravindan from the South, has lost its intensely personal character, and is more amenable to mass viewing. The changing atmosphere is a palpable reality. It is also a matter for hope.

The Films

THE FILMS

AADMI AUR AURAT (Man and Woman)
colour, 56 minutes, Hindi, 1984

Production: Doordarshan/ Direction and screenplay: Tapan Sinha/ Story: Prafulla Roy/ Camera: Kamal Nayek/ Music: Ashish Khan/ Art Direction: Kartick Bose/ Editing: Subodh Roy/ Sound: Satyen Chatterjee
Cast: Amol Palekar, Mahua Roy Chowdhury

A YOUNG village girl, with a shapeless bundle in her arms, waits on the highway for a bus into town. When the bus finally comes, it is impossibly overcrowded, and the men waiting with her, decide to take a short cut through the hills into town. The girl follows at a distance as the group find their way through the forested, undulating land. Bansi, the poacher, walks with the men, and yet a few steps behind. He is a loner, a tough youth who earns a living by helping the landlords hunt game, and the difficulties of the route hold no fears for him. He turns back to look at the girl and finds that she is falling behind. The other men say they do not know her at all. Bansi grins as she shies off like a nervous filly every time he stops.

A slow drizzle begins to fall. The group of men hasten their steps and are soon hidden from view. The girl looks ill, and stops near a boulder to catch her breath. Bansi decides to approach her. Maybe she is playing a little game. But she looks genuinely scared when he comes closer, and he realizes that she is pregnant. In his simple, harsh existence, there are some things that Bansi has learnt to respect. Now he talks to the girl kindly, and when he learns that her destination is the hospital at Vakilganj, he decides to help her get there. Her husband has taken a loan to send her to the hospital, she says haltingly, so now he must work on the moneylender's field to pay it off.

But the road is arduous, and the weight in her stomach seems to grow with each step. Bansi talks of his life in the forest, of exotic tiger hunts, to keep her going. When she collapses, he carries her on his strong shoulders, till he too is tired. Then he makes her a bamboo stretcher and drags her along, keeping her awake with his stories and his force of will. When the girl is nearly unconscious, and Bansi panics, a forest guard helps him to carry the makeshift stretcher to the river that they must cross. It is actually a shallow stream, now swollen with rain. Determined to save her life, Bansi manages to drag her across the swirling currents, imploring her to keep awake, forcing her out of her stupor. Once across, a bullock cart carries them to the hospital. At the hospital he is casually told there is no room for another patient, but Bansi threatens and cajoles till he gets his way.

Bansi goes to meet the landlord whom he was supposed to escort on a hunt. But he has reached late and the hunt has been postponed. Next morning, on his way back home, he stops at the hospital. The girl has given birth to a baby boy, they tell him. He goes to see her, and asks her husband's name, so that he may give him the news. "Anwar Hossain," says the girl. For a brief moment it startles him. He, a god-fearing Hindu, has saved the life of a Muslim woman. Then he smiles. "I'll tell him about the baby," he says. The girl raises her frail arms. "I shall always pray to Allah for you," she says.

THOUGH IT won the award for the best film of the year on national integration, *Aadmi aur Aurat,* originally made for Indian television, focuses on something much larger than religious separatism. The incredible journey of Bansi and the girl becomes a metaphor for human compassion and courage. That he is a staunch Hindu seems an accidental factor, to be dismissed just as Bansi himself dismisses it at the end of the film. The visual beauty and the simplicity of its style is a common trait in the films of Tapan Sinha, who started his career as a filmmaker with *Ankush,* made in 1953. His training in the language of the cinema, however, had started earlier, with a long stint as a sound recordist at the famous New Theatres studio in Calcutta. With his variety of themes and his obvious talent for visual story-telling, Tapan Sinha has been for many years, the link between the artistic and the popular cinema of Bengal. Fitting into neither slot, he has entertained both the critics and the ordinary film viewer with equal success. Though most of his films are made in Bengali, there have been Hindi remakes as wells as originals in his repertoire. In 1985, as homage to the veteran director, a retrospective of his films was held during the Tenth International Film Festival of India.

AAKROSH (Cry of the Wounded)
colour, 144 minutes, Hindi, 1980

Production: Krsna Movies Enterprises/ Direction and Camera: Govind Nihalani/ Story and Screenplay: Vijay Tendulkar/ Music: Ajit Varman/ Art Direction: C.S. Bhatti/ Editing: Keshav Naidu
Cast: Naseeruddin Shah, Smita Patil, Om Puri, Arvind Deshpande, Mohan Agashe, Achut Potdar, Nana Palsikar, Bhagyasree Kotnis, Mahesh Elkunchwar

LAHANYA BHIKU, an illiterate tribal, is accused of killing his wife. For his defence, the court appoints a young upper-caste lawyer, Bhaskar Kulkarni. This is Kulkarni's first major independent case, and he is anxious to win it. But Lahanya refuses to cooperate. He refuses to speak. Exasperated and intrigued by Lahanya's seemingly stupid and stubborn silence, Kulkarni decides to investigate on his own the truth behind the case. He soon discovers that there are hidden complexities that cannot be resolved easily. He is threatened by strangers, but helped by a young leftist social worker who takes him to the tribal village. But here too, Kulkarni meets with obstinate silence, mingled with a long history of fear and distrust. Probing further, Kulkarni learns that Lahanya has been falsely accused. His wife was raped and murdered on a night of obscene revelry by a combine of local officials, politicians and businessmen. They form the power elite beyond the reach of the law. The police protect them, not their victims.

Kulkarni's involvement with the case gradually changes from a professional to a social commitment. It brings him in conflict with his mentor, Dussane, who himself comes from tribal stock but has had the privilege of a middle-class education. Dussane values his hard-earned social and professional status, and though aware of the truth, chooses to keep silent, reacting with mixed feelings to the late night telephone calls that regularly aim at him a stream of invective and threats.

But all Kulkarni's determination cannot save Lahanya. His only supporter, the social worker, disappears suddenly, presumably eliminated by the forces he fought against. At his father's funeral which the shackled Lahanya is allowed to attend, the young tribal breaks his bonds and hacks down his helpless sister. As long as his father was alive, Lahanya's silence could perhaps protect the family from persecution. Now alone in the world, his young sister too would be an inevitable prey to the same exploitative system. Lahanya breaks his long silence with a last cry of anguish—his final protest. Bewildered by the turn of events, Kulkarni attempts to come to terms with his own helplessness in a society where the corrupt are protected and justice is a pawn in the hands of the powerful.

"NIHALANI ranges between the documentarist's observation and a sense of theatrical presentation, a film technician making fiction out of reality," says filmmaker Shama Habibullah. The comment is specially meaningful, for it explains the dual role that Govind Nihalani plays in his first film, as cameraman and director. Nihalani, who has been an important contributor to the parallel cinema in India ever since *Aakrosh*, has had a long and successful career as a cameraman. His association with filmmaker Shyam Benegal not only sharpened his camera vision, but honed his intellectual perceptions of contemporary Indian reality. Perhaps it also helped him to realize that "art" and "commercial" cinema are not permanently opposed in their artistic viewpoint. His second film, *Ardh Satya*, examining the brutalizing of a young police officer, was an unusual box-office success, and established the viability of serious themes for the popular market.

What Benegal did for Shabana Azmi, Smita Patil and Naseeruddin Shah, Nihalani did for Om Puri who, in the role of Lahanya, emerged as one of the most powerful screen actors of the parallel cinema. The lean, rugged, unglamorous Puri with his strange eyes haunted with memories of happiness and forebodings of death, carries the film silently and inexorably towards its explosive climax. *Aakrosh* also demonstrates Nihalani's strong dramatic sense transmuted into cinema. Most of his actors in the film came from the Hindi and Marathi stage, while the young social worker was played by Mahesh Elkunchwar, himself a playwright, one of whose plays Nihalani was to use later for his film, *Party*. The story and screenplay for *Aakrosh* were written by Vijay Tendulkar, a much revered playwright and director of the Marathi stage who has worked as a scriptwriter for many successful filmmakers within the parallel cinema movement, and has also produced a television series based on a young urban middle-class woman's experiences as a divorcee. Nihalani has recently made a rather controversial television serial on the partition of India, based on a well-known novel by Bhisham Sahni.

ACHAMILLAI ACHAMILLAI (Fearless)
colour, 160 minutes, Tamil, 1984

Production: Kavithalayaa Productions (P) Limited/ Direction, story, screenplay and dialogue: K. Balachander/ Camera: B.S. Lokanath/ Music: V.S. Narasimhan/ Lyrics: Vairamuthu/ Art Direction: Mohanam/ Editing: N.R. Kittoo/ Sound: S.P. Ramanathan
Cast: Saritha, Rajesh, Delhi Ganesh, Pavithra, Ahalya, Prabhakar, Vairam Krishnamoorthy, Veeraiah, Charley

THENMOZHI, a worker in a fibre factory, lives with her blind father, an ex-freedom fighter, in a village nestling among the southern hills. She is attracted to Ulaganathan, a young idealist from a lower middle-class background, who works in a local saw mill, and is highly respected in the community for his moral integrity and selflessness. Ulaganathan's father approves of their friendship and sets an auspicious date for their marriage—Independence Day. The young couple devote themselves to social work, but soon Ulaganathan's influence over his community makes political parties vie with each other in their efforts to woo him. Thenmozhi believes that her husband's high moral standards will not allow him to become a victim of unscrupulous politicians. But the greed for power eventually overcomes Ulaganathan's resistance, and he joins one of the parties when promised a ministership.

The process of disintegration has begun and Ulaganathan makes one compromise after another, refusing to heed the warnings of his wife and father who soon become marginalized in his home. For Thenmozhi his brutalization is complete when she learns that in order to force a man to vote for him, Ulaganathan has hired local ruffians to molest the man's wife. When she remonstrates, she is crudely told to keep to her place. Thenmozhi goes to her father's home to deliver her first child. Meanwhile Ulaganathan wins the election, but when neither party gains a clear majority, defects to the rival party and gets a palatial house as part of his pay off.

When Thenmozhi returns with the child, she is revolted by Ulaganathan's behaviour and refuses to share his bed. To retaliate, Ulaganathan brings Alangaram into the house as his mistress, and she and her mother gradually take over the running of the household. Unwanted and repeatedly humiliated, Thenmozhi leaves home. Subsequently she loses her child in an accident. The final blow falls when she hears that her husband is "arranging" a communal riot to silence his critics in the community. She tries for the last time to talk to him, but Ulaganathan justifies himself by saying that political murders cannot be judged by common ethics. The next day is Independence Day. A new statue of Mahatma Gandhi is unveiled; Ulaganathan stands on the dais and talks of sacrifices made by him and his party for the people. Listening to him, Thenmozhi can only hear the brutal words with which he had justified his misdeeds to her. She goes to him carrying a garland. As she puts it round his neck, she draws a knife hidden among the flowers and stabs Ulaganathan to death.

K. BALACHANDER is a highly successful and prolific director of popular Tamil cinema, who has also directed films in Malayalam, Telugu and Hindi with equal success. Many of his films have won national and regional awards, and he has a large following among the film critics in the South. Not unlike the popular cinema from Bombay, Balachander's films come with the spit and polish of technical excellence, and his themes are often even more dramatic. Not for him the ordinary romance threatened by ordinary villains, or the confrontation between common or garden varieties of good and evil. Social purpose is writ large on his productions, and is used as the justification for his popularity. That he is considered a major director in his region is an established fact. Yet his films disclose basic crudities that are irreconcilable with his lofty purpose. Whether it is his Hindi blockbuster, *Ek Duje ke Liye,* a song and dance romance ending in tragedy between a South Indian boy and a Punjabi girl (unusual, never-before theme!), or a drama of political corruption as in *Achamillai Achamillai,* the overlay of crudity takes away from the basic validity of the narrative.

Achamillai Achamillai has a wealth of obvious symbolism: Thenmozhi's brother, born on the day of the country's independence, is named after it Swatantram (independent); yet he is a deformed midget who is all sound and fury, and willingly accepts a bribe from his corrupt brother-in-law. To establish Ulaganathan's personal degeneration, his bringing a mistress home is not enough. The breeze blows the curtain aside, and the audience and Thenmozhi must witness the hefty Ulaganathan lying naked to the waist, being massaged by the fair feet of Alangaram. Even Thenmozhi's blind father, an ex-freedom fighter, is bought by Ulaganathan who promises to pay for an operation to restore his sight (more irony!). The quick transformation of the devoted and honest social worker into a ruthless political monster actually seems to imply that the man had no conscience in any case to begin with. Yet Balachander's film seemed convincing enough to his vast audience and critics found revolutionary undertones at Thenmozhi's knife point. Balachander undoubtedly remains a phenomenon in the world of morally self-righteous kitsch.

ACHHUT KANYA (The Untouchable Girl)
b&w, 143 minutes, Hindi, 1936

Production: Bombay Talkies/ Direction: Franz Osten/ Story: Himanshu Rai/ Screenplay and lyrics: J.S. Casshyap/ Camera: Joseph Wirsching/ Music: Saraswati Devi/ Art Direction: Karl von Spreti/ Sound: Savak Vacha
Cast: Ashok Kumar, Devika Rani, P.F. Pithawala, Pramila, Kusum Kumari, Anwar

KASTURI IS a beautiful Harijan girl, the daughter of Dukhia, the pointsman at the level-crossing. Her closest friend is Pratap, the shy, handsome son of Mohanlal, the village grocer who is a Brahmin. Though tongues wag in the village about this unnatural friendship between a casteless untouchable girl and a boy from the highest Hindu caste, the young people can ignore what they say, for their fathers are friends too. The most raucous critic is Babulal, the village quack, who actually has another axe to grind. His pills and potions are not as effective as the medicines Mohanlal often prescribes.

Even as their feelings transform into love, brought up in an environment of strict social norms of behaviour, Kasturi and Mohanlal accept without any real protest the fact that they have no future together. Social taboos ultimately separate them. The villagers, hearing that Mohanlal has even eaten food cooked by an untouchable, are up in arms against both families. They are even more incensed when they learn that because Dukhia is ill, Mohanlal has decided to bring him to his own home, to look after him. Mohanlal is accused by the upper-caste community of destroying their religion.The confrontation becomes a full-scale riot when Mohanlal refuses to throw out Dukhia. A mob loots his shop and sets his home on fire. When Mohanlal is injured, the fever-racked Dukhia rushes out to stop a mail train so that he may bring a doctor back from the junction.The railway authorities promptly dismiss him for this irresponsible act, and an untouchable youth Manoo, the son of an old friend, is employed in his place. Manoo insists on sharing his home with Dukhia and Kasturi.

Pratap is soon married to Meera who feels neglected by him, for he finds it difficult to return her affections. His thoughts are always with Kasturi who is given in marriage to Manoo. A dutiful wife, Kasturi welcomes Manu's estranged first wife, Kajri, to their home even though Manoo will not have her back. Kajri and Meera both feel that Kasturi is the source of all their unhappiness. Between them they hatch a plot which goes tragically astray. Pratap has a small stall in a nearby village fair, where he meets Kasturi after a long interval. Kasturi had come to the fair with Kajri and Meera, but now finds that she has been abandoned by them. Pratap gives her a ride back home in his cart. All this while, afraid of their feelings, they had wisely kept out of each other's way. Now the chance encounter brings back for both of them memories of their time together. Meanwhile Manoo is told that Kasturi has left him for Pratap. In a wild rage, Manoo sets out to kill Pratap. They meet on the railway tracks as a train approaches the level-crossing. Locked in battle, both the Brahmin youth and his untouchable antagonist are unaware of danger. Kasturi, in desperation, tries to halt the onrushing train. She dies to save the man she loved and the man she had married.

HIMANSHU RAI, who had already behind him successful international coproductions, started Bombay Talkies Limited in 1934. A studio with the most modern equipment was built under his personal supervision, and Franz Osten, director of three of his earlier ventures, *The Light of Asia, Shiraz,* and *A*

Throw of Dice, joined the staff along with some other technicians from Germany and England. Rai and his beautiful, talented wife, Devika Rani, initiated a trainee programme, and within a few years had collected a group of talented young Indians, who subsequently became some of the most famous personalities of the Bombay film industry. Actor Ashok Kumar started his career there as a laboratory assistant, and Raj Kapoor as a clapper boy. Among other well-known names were actor Dilip Kumar, producer S. Mukherjee and writer K.A. Abbas. The organization was known for its egalitarian values. There were no caste or class barriers and no job was too low for anyone.

The appeal of *Achhut Kanya* may be limited today to the sensitive performances of Ashok Kumar and Devika Rani in the main roles, and not the least to the obvious charm of their screen personalities. Other than its historical importance, the film may seem too long, and often too contrived; but it carries the stamp of Bombay Talkies productions with its well-constructed plot, its clever use of the popular yearning for doom that had made *Devdas* from New Theatres famous a year earlier, and its condemnation of orthodox and outdated social and religious codes. Those were days when ostracism of the untouchables and the barriers of caste were supported by the law; while the leaders of the Indian National Congress were crying themselves hoarse about the need to reform Hindu society. Bombay Talkies stood at the crossroads of history and pointed at a new direction, towards more enlightened social values. It embodied an idealism that was lost once the studio system was swept away by the same forces of change that had overtaken the film industry in the West.

ADAMINTE VARIYELLU (Adam's Rib)
colour, 142 minutes, Malayalam, 1983

Production: St Vincent Movies/ Direction and Story: K.G. George/ Screenplay: K.G. George, K. Ramachandran/ Camera: Ramchandra Babu/ Music: M.B. Srinivasan/ Lyrics: O.N.V. Kurup/ Art Direction: G.O. Sundaram/ Editing: M.N. Appu/ Sound: Devadas
Cast: Suhasini, Sreevidya, Soorya, Rajam K. Nair, Gopi, Venu Nagavalli, Mammooti, Thilakan

VASANTHI, a young working woman and mother, looks after her job, her household, her child and her errant, drunken husband in a typical suburban home. Ever since the death of her father-in-law, Vasanthi's mother-in-law has relegated all responsibility to the younger woman and found a convenient escape from drudgery. Unloved, uncared for, physically run down, Vasanthi slowly loses her perspective as her days merge one into another. Her middle-class upbringing has only prepared her for obedience. But her instincts revolt against the soul-destroying monotony and her enforced sexual submission to a loveless marriage. At first she just feels tired. Then she slowly loses interest in her job. She stays at home mechanically following the daily routine till her mind loses its grip on reality. Her delusions are initially looked upon with suspicion, then with fear. Intimidated and assaulted by her husband, Vasanthi finds solace in her imaginary world. They take her away to a mental institution. At the gate Vasanthi turns back with a smile. It is a happy smile of a woman long imprisoned, walking towards freedom.

Alice is married to Mammachen, an unscrupulous government contractor, who has risen in his career by using his wife's physical charms. Now deeply involved in making more and more money, he has no time for her or their teenage children. Alice is bored and apathetic towards both her home and her social commitments. The occasional appearance of old business acquaintances only reminds her of her past humiliations. She attempts to find fulfilment in an affair with an architect, but the young man values his career too much to risk Mammachen's wrath. Her husband's open objection to the affair finally leads her to think of divorce. Meanwhile, her young daughter runs away and is discovered in a hotel room with a boy. She is rescued in time. Not so her mother. When her parents and the church refuse to accept the divorce, Alice, permanently confined to a life of ennui and despair, makes her last active choice for freedom—the choice of death.

Ammini is a housemaid in Alice's home. Sixteen years old and an orphan, she has yet imbibed all the knowledge of the world. When Alice's daughter gets her first menstrual period, it is Ammini who provides her support. When Mammachen wants a little diversion, it is Ammini who must silently offer her body. Alice is aware of her husband's indiscretions, but feels revolted when Ammini gets pregnant. Mammachen's hired ruffians swiftly remove Ammini from their home and send her to a government hospital when the baby is due. Once out of the hospital, she leaves her baby at a stranger's doorstep and goes on the streets. Inevitably she is picked up by the police and put in a rescue home where many Amminis meekly sit at their sewing machines daily, learning a respectable profession so that the world may take them back. The helpless surrender in those dull faces goads Ammini into a fantastic leap across reality. She opens her prison doors, and with her sisters in plight, breaks through the barrier of the camera crew to rush to freedom.

TRAINED AT the Film and Television Institute of India, K.G. George's first feature film, *Swapnadanam,* made in 1975, won the National Award for the best regional film. Since then he has not looked back. George's films have repeatedly discussed social and personal degradation of women with compassion and anger. His work belongs to the fairly successful parallel cinema movement in the country, which is slowly making inroads into and widening the scope of popular cinema, making serious themes acceptable even by box-office terms. In *Adaminte Variyellu,* Vasanthi, Alice and Ammini, three women from different walks of life, share a common predicament in their efforts to come to terms with the fundamentally exploitative nature of their relationship with men and society. The freedom they search for and receive is influenced by their own individual environment. Vasanthi and Alice can only take their unconscious rebellion to the point of self-destruction. It is left to Ammini, with her primeval instincts for survival, with her indisputable place among the sisterhood of the deprived, to open the doors. That her freedom has been actually visualized and composed by the camera crew waiting outside the gates of the rescue home, that it spills over beyond their frame to a time and place where the real and the fantastic meet, does not take away from the essential truth of Ammini's action. Yet it is a sad reminder that reality does not change: a newspaper report would send Ammini back to her prison in no time at all.

ADI SHANKARACHARYA
colour, 130 minutes, Sanskrit, 1983

Production: National Film Development Corporation Ltd/ Direction and screenplay: G.V. Iyer/ Camera: Madhu Ambat/ Music: M. Balamurali Krishna/ Art Direction: P. Krishnamoorthy/ Editing: V.R.K. Prasad
Cast: S.D. Banerjee, M.V. Narayana Rao, Manjunath Bhat, Leela Narayana Rao, L.V. Sharada, Bharat Bhushan, T.S. Nagabharana, Shrinivasa Prabhu

SHANKARA, a little Brahmin boy in 8th century Kerala, grows up in his village home among the sonorous chants of ancient hymns and traditional Brahmin rituals. When his father dies, Shankara confronts the phenomenon of death and attempts to understand its significance. From then onwards, death becomes his companion in life's pilgrimage. His second companion is knowledge. After the initiation ceremony when he is given the holy thread of the Brahmins, Shankara enters the first prescribed stage of life, and lives in the hermitage of his guru, memorizing the Vedic texts, and begging alms as a young mendicant. The next stage of life is that of a householder; but Shankara, still troubled by the mysteries of existence, is reluctant to fulfil his familial duties through marriage. Instead, he begs his mother to permit him to take the monastic vows, and promises that he will visit her before she dies. In the course of his wanderings, good and evil, joy and sorrow, wisdom and ignorance, all cross his path. In his search for the truth that lies beyond the temporal world, Shankara goes to the banks of the Narbada, where lives the great teacher, Govinda. The guru recognizes the innate wisdom of the young scholar, and aware of the distortions creeping into orthodox Hinduism, entrusts Shankara with the task of writing a new commentary on the Vedic texts. These are the times when the old texts are full of contradictions and inconsistencies, and ritual is gaining a stronghold in the practice of the religion.

The mysteries of existence reveal their inner truth to Shankara at last, and he becomes a teacher, entering the fourth stage of life, that of the *sanyasin*, the ascetic. He goes from Kerala's green countryside, through the Central Indian desert lands, to the snow-clad peaks of the Himalayas. In Benares, the city of Hindu learning, the king comes to pay him homage. All through his travels, the learned seek him out, the ignorant follow him to receive his wisdom. Shankara is immune to all the adulation he receives. One day an untouchable crosses his path. "Keep off!" cry his disciples in horror. The untouchable answers with a riddle. "Who should keep off?" he asks. "My body, or my inner self?" In front of the shocked eyes of his disciples, Shankara touches the feet of the man. "He who gives me this truth is my greatest teacher," he says.

Shankara uses his brilliant logic to preach that knowledge lies at the root of salvation. He establishes the validity of his own philosophy through long debates and discourses with the greatest teachers in the land. He creates his own monastic order, and monasteries are established where followers of Shankara's faith can preach and study. But Shankara himself wanders as before, carrying only his staff and his begging bowl. He defies the Brahmin community who will not allow him to perform his mother's funeral rites since he is an ascetic. For him the rituals of Hinduism are as much illusions as the human body and the entire physical world. When he is only thirty-two years old, Shankara rises from his sickbed to bathe in the river; then, taking leave of his sorrowing disciples, he walks away alone towards the majestic, snow-covered mountain peaks. He knows the time has come for that final union of his human soul with the *Brahman*, the one eternal, unchanging reality and the true goal of all existence.

SHANKARA, known to later generations as Adi Shankaracharya (literally, the first teacher Shankara), was a philosopher and theologian of the 8th century and the most renowned exponent of the Advaita Vedanta school of philosophy. There are various versions of his biography, and more than three hundred works in the Sanskrit language, commentative, expository and poetical, are attributed to him; but it is difficult to authenticate most of the claims. Shankara's philosophy basically preaches the unity of all existence: it is only by overcoming the illusion of plurality that man will recognize the fundamental unity of the universe. An old Indo-Aryan language, Sanskrit was the classical literary language of the Hindus of India. Though it is the parent language of several tongues spoken in India today, in its day it was used mainly for official, religious and literary purposes—a written language and one of scholarly debate, never to be used as a common medium of intercourse. Iyer's justification for its use in the film is that the complexities and abstractions of philosophical thought could only come alive in the ancient language.

Ganapathy Venkataramana Iyer, known as "the barefoot director" (he literally scorns shoes), in his spotless white *dhoti* and *kurta* and sporting a flowing beard, could pass for a saint himself, but for his rather wicked, penetrating gaze. He openly professes to have known all the worldly sins (which probably include the potboilers he produced for the Karnataka audience for years), before becoming a humble disciple of the new cinema. After Rama Reddy's *Samskara* created a tremendous stir in 1970 in the intellectual circles all over India, Iyer took his first step in establishing his new persona by producing *Vamsa Vriksha,* directed by Girish Karnad and B.V. Karanth the next year. Without getting involved in a debate on the merits and demerits of the Advaita philosophy and how Iyer interprets them, it can be affirmed, however, that his *Adi Shankaracharya* is a tale of a gentle, compassionate and humble man whose knowledge, strength of conviction and intellectual powers made him one of the greatest thinkers of all times. To the extent that Iyer relates the saint's variegated life, he does so with great charm and spontaneity. The only film ever to be made in Sanskrit, it won the National Awards of the year for the best feature film, camera, screenplay and sound. Not unnaturally, Iyer went on to make a second feature on the life of another Indian philosopher and a television serial on Lord Krishna.

AGNISNAAN (Ordeal)
colour, 172 minutes, 1985, Assamese

Production, Direction, Story and Screenplay: Dr Bhabendra Nath Saikia/ Camera: Kamal Nayak/ Music: Tarun Goswami/ Editing: Nikunja Bhattacharya/ Sound: Pijush Kanti Roy
Cast: Malaya Goswami, Biju Phukan, Arun Nath, Kashmiri Barua, Sanjib Hazarika, Anandamohan Bhagawati, Arun Guha Thakurta, Nilu Chakravarty, Indra Bania, Ashok Deka

ASSAM IN the late thirties. Ghanakanta, an old and respected landowner, has handed over his ancestral property to his two elder sons, Ratnakanta and Mohikanta, both of whom have families of their own. The youngest son, Bhadrakanta, is still unmarried and without a livelihood. Mohikanta, who has substantially added to his share of the property by setting up a rice mill in the village, has a spacious home which he shares with his old parents. Bhadrakanta too stays there most of the time. The household is run by Mohikanta's wife, Menoka, a quiet, charming woman, and mother of four young children. Mohikanta, who has adopted the dissolute lifestyle of a decadent aristocracy, is a drunkard and a womanizer. Suddenly there is gossip in the village that Mohikanta is to take another wife, Kiran, a young girl from a poor family in a neighbouring village. Menoka is deeply shocked but can do nothing to deter him, nor can the rest of the family. She even accepts Kiran with stoical affection. But Bhadrakanta, the youngest brother is revolted by the turn of events; so is his friend, Madan, the village thief who has been bailed out many a time through Menoka's intervention. Madan decides to rob Mohikanta with the help of Menoka's eldest son, Inder. It is an act of mute revenge, but Menoka, though touched by Madan's concern, dissuades him when she finds out about his plan. On a sudden impulse, Menoka asks Madan to meet her one night. But a storm rages outside that night, and though Madan waits, Menoka does not go to him.

Mohikanta's mother dies suddenly while visiting her eldest son, Ratnakanta. Kiran is pregnant and goes to her mother's home for a few months. Deeply resenting her husband's behaviour, Menoka keeps her tryst with Madan who submits to the relationship without really understanding Menoka's motivation. Mohikanta, aware of Madan's hostility, tries to win him over by making him an overseer in the rice mill. Madan's thieving days are over. But with Kiran away, Menoka finds it increasingly difficult to fend off her brutish husband, and turns to Madan, her loyal, silent admirer, and now her lover in the darkness of the bamboo grove. Then one night she tells Madan that she will not see him alone any more. For Madan the end of the affair is as bewildering as the beginning.

Kiran comes back with a baby girl. Menoka takes over the responsibility of rearing the child, till one day she too is discovered to be pregnant. Mohikanta, whom Menoka has persistently avoided since he married Kiran, is now consumed with jealousy. He starts seeking out his neglected children, drinking alone in the mill and agonizing over Menoka's betrayal. Finally, he calls Menoka to the mill one day, and asks for an explanation. Dignified, yet rebellious, Menoka refuses to disclose who has fathered her child. She tells him instead of her own humiliation and deprivation, of her disillusionment with the role of a loyal wife that she is supposed to play while Mohikanta indulges himself with Kiran. From now on, she says, Mohikanta will have to live with the fact of her infidelity. To condemn her publicly will mean admitting his own humiliation and defeat. If he can bring himself to do that, Menoka will face the world without shame. She has had her revenge.

A PHYSICIST by profession, Bhabendra Nath Saikia is one of the major contemporary writers of Assam, a hill state in the north east of India. He has won national awards both for his writing and his films, the first of which, *Sandhyaraag*, he made in 1977. *Agnisnaan* is based on one of his own novels. The most striking feature of the film, not surprisingly, is its narrative. Based in the orthodox milieu of the thirties, the story progresses with determined inevitability towards its unusual climax. If it begins as a faithful period picture, it ends as a woman's film, making a forceful plea against the continuing male hypocrisy of another age. The silent, submissive Menoka grows in stature, absorbing her rebellion into her innermost being in the form of her unborn illegitimate child. Madan, whose seed grows within her, is only incidental in her grand design, a mere man who takes on her discarded mantle of submission. The reversal is complete when Menoka faces her husband, no longer afraid, unashamed and in control of her own existence. In spite of its powerful story, or perhaps because of it, *Agnisnaan* is less of a film than a novel visualized. Saikia's skills lie in the pen, not in the camera. But the narrative overtakes the form to sweep the viewer along with it to a culmination as old as it is contemporary in Indian society today.

AGRAHARATHIL KAZHUTHAI
(A Donkey in a Brahmin Village)
b&w, 95 minutes, Tamil, 1977

Production: Nirmithi Films/ Direction: John Abraham/ Screenplay: Venkat Swaminathan/ Camera: Ramachandra Babu/ Music: M.B. Sreenivasan/ Art Direction: Lawrence Gaulbert/ Editing: Ravi
Cast: M.B. Sreenivasan, Swathy, Sreelalitha, Gopali, Raman Veeraraghavan, Narasimhan, Thilairajan, Krishnaraj, Rajan

RETURNING HOME from college one day, Professor Narayanaswami finds a baby donkey at his doorstep. Its mother, mercilessly teased till she retaliated, had been promptly chased and beaten to death by the local people. The professor, a confirmed bachelor, feels drawn to the lonely little animal, and decides to give it a home. But there are practical problems. The arrangement disturbs his daily help, who refuses to clean up the filth the donkey produces in the professor's room after a night's sleep. News of his new pet spreads to the college. The students have a good laugh, draw long-eared pictures of the professor on the walls, and even drag a real life replica into the college one day. The professor has no objection to the boys having some fun at his expense. But the principal thinks otherwise, and Narayanaswami decides to take the donkey to his village home.

In the Brahmin village where Narayanaswami's parents live, his pet is left in the care of a young deaf-mute girl, Uma. The professor comes home occasionally, and hears the neighbours complaining about the donkey. His father is most unhappy, because it is he who gets blamed when naughty Brahmin boys let the donkey loose, at a solemn religious ceremony, or when a bridegroom's family have come to choose a bride, or where an old neighbour is performing his father's funeral rites. There are further complications when the professor's brother Venkittu is transferred to the area, and comes home to stay. Venkittu's childless and unhappy wife takes it out on the donkey. Narayanaswami hands it over to Uma, along with some money for its keep. Uma, in the meanwhile, has given in to the overtures of a young village labourer, and is pregnant. When the professor visits the village again, he learns that one of the village priests one day stepped on some dung on the temple steps, kicked the donkey, and in the process, slipped and fell down the stairs. And then comes the final indignity. Uma has a stillborn baby in the night. In the morning both the donkey and the baby vanish, and a priest discovers the dead baby in front of the door of the temple. The only solution to this menace, suggests Venkittu to his fellow-Brahmins, is to kill the donkey. The donkey is duly killed. Uma is disconsolate. Then one night, a band of gypsys come and make strange predictions: All good things will happen now, they say, but the village will be destroyed.

One of the naughty village boys pounces on Narayanaswami when he comes next, to tell him of the strange happenings. All the villagers have seen the ghost of the little donkey up on the hill! An eighty-year-old paralytic has started walking again, the village headman's long-lost son has come home, and Venkittu's wife is pregnant! The villagers now want to erect a temple and deify the donkey! Narayanaswami wordlessly expresses his sympathy to the lonely Uma, then consoles himself by reading a stirring verse on fire that cleanses, exalts and destroys. The face of Uma comes to his mind, the gentle, plain face wild with divine anger. Transported to fantasy, the mild professor joins Uma on the hill where the skull of the donkey lies. The villagers who killed the animal, now simulate its death in a ritual dance till night falls, the skull catches fire, and the whole village is engulfed in flames. The lines of the poem are a disembodied voice: "Like you, Fire, let our wisdom shine."

AGRAHARATHIL KAZHUTHAI is an unusual film. Though it won the National Award for the best Tamil film in 1978, it has hardly ever been shown to the public. For one thing, the film's anti-Brahmin stance would not endear it to many in southern India, where educated Brahmins are still in a position of power, and the caste system is an important social institution. For another, though it has an undercurrent of humour, the film is a satire, and hardly the stuff for mass consumption in a country where the essential ingredients of cinematic entertainment remain young love, song and dance, fights and the chase. No brief synopsis can do justice to the innovative narrative style of the film, juxtaposing events in time, and framing each prank of its four-legged protagonist within the boundaries of a new complaint, repeated in the same style, every time the professor comes home. The repetitive structure, handled with such expertise, lends itself to the quiet humour of the story, and carries the unsuspecting audience to the startling finale of anger and pain, of rebellion against stupid superstition, social hypocrisy and injustice. Fire, all-cleansing and all-consuming, becomes the ultimate equalizing force, transforming the ridiculous into the sublime.

AJANTRIK (Pathetic Fallacy)
b&w, 102 minutes, Bengali, 1958

Production: L.&B. Films International/ Direction and Screenplay: Ritwik Ghatak/ Story: Subodh Ghosh/ Camera: Dinen Gupta/ Music: Ali Akbar Khan/ Art Direction: Ravi Chatterjee/ Editing: Ramesh Joshi/ Sound: Mrinal Guha Thakurta, Satyen Chatterjee
Cast: Kali Banerjee, Gyanesh Mukherjee, Satindra Bhattacharya, Gangapada Basu, Tulsi Chakravarty, Dipak, Anil Chatterjee, Kajal Gupta, Sita Mukherjee

IN A SMALL TOWN in Bihar in the 50s, Bimal, a taxi-driver, showers all his love on his dilapidated 1920 Chevrolet, Jagaddal. He is laughed at by everyone except a street urchin, who with his child's mind, can sense what Bimal knows for a certainty, that Jagaddal is no mere machine. Jagaddal has a mind of her own. Ridicule from a passenger makes her stop in her tracks in pouring rain. When Bimal shows gentle concern for an abandoned young woman, Jagaddal sputters and jolts with jealous rage. She swivels her large eyes, her headlamps, to watch the view on a hill road while Bimal listens with rapture to the tribal songs floating up in the breeze. When Bimal pours water into her radiator, she gurgles happily, her thirst quenched.

But Jagaddal's days are numbered; even Bimal gets annoyed with her erratic behaviour, yet he cannot accept that Jagaddal is old and dying. Has he betrayed her somehow, this friend who feeds him in these troubled times? To make amends for his occasional impatience, Bimal decides to spend his life's savings to rejuvenate her. Gour Mistry, the mechanic, one of his few friends, watches his obsession with the car with growing concern. Seeing him fritter away his hard-earned money on a condemned piece of machinery, even the little street urchin pleads with him to abandon the project. But Bimal doggedly waits for the last lick of paint to dry before he takes Jagaddal out on a test run. Everyone is speechless with wonder when he proudly drives into the taxi-stand again. The trial drive begins well, but soon the old jalopy is in trouble again. When she stalls on a hill road, Bimal, frustrated and angry, piles the car with boulders from the way side to punish her. Jagaddal starts moving, then lurches violently and reels back downhill. When it finally stops, in a rage Bimal drives his fist through the windscreen.

Bimal finally accepts Jagaddal's fate. When she is sold to a scrap dealer for next to nothing, he bids farewell to his beloved companion: "Go, dear friend," he says. "You've fed and clothed me long enough. After all you can't do it forever." In pieces now, Jagaddal is hauled away on a cart. She gives Bimal a last naughty wink as her headlamps catch the sun's rays. The cart trundles away, but suddenly Bimal hears the familiar sound of Jagaddal's horn. He rushes out to find a child playing with the discarded horn. Bimal smiles at the child through his tears.

THOUGH RELEASED as a first film when Satyajit Ray was already established in Bengali and world cinema, this was actually Ghatak's second effort. An eccentric genius, writer, actor, activist and rebel, Ghatak had tried his hand at filmmaking a little before Ray began his first film. *Nagarik,* completed in 1953, was never released to the public, but is one of the first Bengali films to use day-to-day realism, an unglamorous story and a virtually unknown cast. The difference between *Nagarik* and *Ajantrik,* however, is the difference between an amateur and an experienced craftsman. Based on a short story which was hardly the stuff for popular entertainment, *Ajantrik* was appreciated by the regional critics, establishing Ghatak as a serious filmmaker, and the only one in Bengal to be considered a worthy rival for Satyajit Ray.

Filmmaker Kumar Shahani, one of Ghatak's star pupils from the Pune Film Institute, wrote on *Ajantrik* : "The film humanizes the car but draws attention to the fallacy of investing an inanimate or a natural object with human feeling. He achieves this objectification by comic, picaresque treatment. Moreover, he shows the very source of animistic belief in the excellent tribal sequence in the film. Unlike the films of other Bengali directors, working directly from the nineteenth century novel, the transference of human pathos to nature, takes place only in the minds of the characters, not in the organization of the director. After demonstrating the romantic extension of a character's sentiments into nature, Ritwik Ghatak immediately counterpoints it with his distinctive 180 degree panoramics on empty landscapes. Nature, in the end, is grandly indifferent to human joy or sorrow." [*Filmfare,* 1976]

Ghatak's films received very little popular attention during his lifetime. Of his many film ideas, scripts and stories, he gave complete shape to only eight, and of them seven were released for public viewing over a period of two and a half decades. Though a contemporary of Ray, the influences that formulated Ghatak's world view came from an entirely different milieu, and were rooted in his own childhood in undivided rural Bengal. "If one talks about influences," said Ray in a memorial lecture after Ghatak's death in 1976, "I think one can find some influence of Soviet films on Ritwik's works. But that influence does not mean imitation, because the main virtue of Ritwik was his distinctiveness, his originality, and this he maintained till the end. He had in him this influence of Soviet films, and of theatre in the dialogue, content and conclusions of his films. And these two elements were based on what was very much rooted in the soil of Bengal. Ritwik was a Bengali director in heart and soul, a Bengali artiste—much more of a Bengali than myself. For me that is the last word about him, and that is his most valuable and distinctive characteristic." [Quoted in *Ritwik Ghatak,* Directorate of Film Festivals, 1982.] Ghatak was much admired as a theoretician of the cinema as well as a craftsman by his students during his short stint in the Film and Television

Institute of India, but the significance of his contribution to cinema was not recognized till years after his death.

AKALER SANDHANEY (In Search of Famine)
colour, 115 minutes, Bengali, 1980

Production: D.K. Films/ Direction and screenplay: Mrinal Sen/ Story: Amalendu Chakravarty/ Camera: K.K. Mahajan/ Music: Salil Chowdhury/ Art Direction: Bansi Chandragupta/ Editing: Gangadhar Naskar
Cast: Dhritiman Chaterji, Smita Patil, Sreela Majumdar, Gita Sen, Dipankar De, Rajen Tarafdar, Radhamohan Bhattacharya, Devika Mukherjee, Jochhan Dastidar, Sajal Roy Chowdhury, Reba Roy Chowdhury, Umanath Bhattacharya

IN 1980, a progressive young film director, with faith in his medium as a weapon for social change, comes to a Bengal village with his crew to recreate on film the Great Bengal Famine of 1943. They stay in a dilapidated old mansion which has seen better days, where one corner of the great house still shelters one of the seventeen owners of the property, an impoverished and paralysed old man and his wife. The shooting begins, but is stalled by unseasonal clouds. On a rainy day the unit sit indoors and play a game, identifying from photographs of famine-stricken people the time they belonged to; a difficult game, for the picture of hunger remains the same through history.

The old man dies. The supporting actress, Devika, leaves in a huff after a quarrel. Durga, a local girl working for the unit, recognizes her daily anguish watching the heroine Smita enact a sequence where she is humiliated by her husband who suspects her of selling her body for a handful of grain. Meanwhile, the sumptuous meals served to the unit send the prices of foodstuff soaring in the village. An old peasant accuses them of searching for an old famine and starting a new one in the process. There are other such acts of intrusion. The villagers become hostile when they learn that the director is searching for a local girl to play Devika's role: a woman who takes to prostitution for survival. Disturbed by the reflection of her own life in the film, Durga refuses to work for the unit any more. As the hostility grows, to secure their safety in the village, the unit decide to ask for police protection. But the village schoolmaster, a venerable old man, finally dissuades them and convinces them to go back to the city.

Silence descends as the film unit leave the village. The widow of the old man stares desolately out of the window of the empty mansion, while Durga stands looking into her personal darkness. Her child will soon die, her husband will leave her. Only she will remain, a living face of famine in the world of 1980.

ALONG WITH asserting the historical continuity of a more than forty-year-old famine through a juxtaposition of the real and the fictional, Sen in *Akaler Sandhaney* reassesses the role of the artiste in the context of the reality he desires to portray. "I at least have reached a point," says Sen in his foreword to the first publication in Bengali of the working script of the film, "where I can assert boldly: there is a gap or a void between the physicality of reality and the artist's redemption of it, of which he may or may not be aware. The artist too often tries to cover up the void with his technique and all those efforts we characterize as artistry.... In *In Search of Famine*, we make a confession of our incapacities. We speak of the crisis in the arts when we hesitate to confront reality or fail to catch it in its true bearings." [Quoted in translation in the introduction to a translated and recreated version of the script of *In Search of Famine* by Samik Bandyopadhyay, Seagull Books, Calcutta, 1983.]

Essentially a film of confrontations at different levels, *Akaler Sandhaney* confronts urban with rural culture, a tragic past with a potentially tragic present, cinematic illusion with the reality it claims to recreate, and artistic commitment with the artist's latent instincts for exploitation in the guise of creativity. A film about the making of a film, it also structurally reinforces the multiple levels of the reality it presents and the various perceptions of that reality. Moving as Sen's artistic self-analysis is, the film at the same time affirms that reality often defeats all artistic truth. While economists still wrangle over the likely true figures of the death toll of the Great Bengal Famine forty-five years ago, rural India annually repeats a phenomenon where the same face of hunger reappears again and again.

AMAR AKBAR ANTHONY
colour, 184 minutes, Hindi, 1977

Production: MKD Films/ Story: Mrs J.M. Desai/ Direction: Manmohan Desai/ Screenplay: Prayag Raj/ Dialogue: Kader Khan/ Camera: Peter Pariera/ Music: Laxmikant Pyarelal/ Lyrics: Anand Bakshi/ Playback: Lata Mangeshkar, Mohamed Rafi, Kishore Kumar, Mahendra Kapoor, Shailendra Singh, Mukesh/ Art Direction: A. Rangraj/ Editing: Kamalakar/ Sound: Kuldeep Singh/ Action Composer: Ravi Khanna
Cast: Vinod Khanna, Amitabh Bachchan, Rishi Kapoor, Neetu Singh, Parveen Babi, Shabana Azmi, Nirupa Roy, Pran, Jeevan, Yusuf, Mukri, Nazir Hussain, Kamal Kapoor, Hercules, Shivraj, Protima Devi, Mul Chand, Bittoo, Ravi, Sabina, Tito, Helen, Nadira, Madhumati, Ranjeet

HAVING SERVED a sentence for manslaughter, Kishanlal returns to find his family starving, and his wife Bharati seriously ill. He confronts Robert, a Mafia don, who had actually caused the fatal accident, and promised to look after his family if Kishanlal took the blame. Ridiculed and beaten, Kishanlal steals one of Robert's cars with smuggled gold in it. Back home he finds his wife gone. She has left a note saying that his earnings should feed the children rather than cure her. Kishanlal takes his children and chased by Robert's men, leaves them in a park, promising to return soon. The eldest, Amar, running after Kishanlal, is knocked down by Robert's car and rescued by a police officer. The second child goes to find food for his baby brother. A Muslim tailor picks up the baby, thinking him abandoned. On his way home, he finds Bharati, blinded and stunned, pinned down by a tree uprooted in the storm the night before. He drops her home, where a policeman neighbour, who saw the children in the stolen car, and the subsequent accident that sent it up in flames, tells Bharati that her family has perished. The second boy, tired of looking for his brothers, falls asleep in front of a church, clutching his mother's note, and is found by the priest. Kishanlal returns to an empty park.

Twenty-two years later, Anthony, brought up by the priest, finds a woman lying bleeding on the road and rings the police station. The officer he talks to is Amar. In the hospital, the doctor, Salma, requests her suitor, the Muslim tailor's adopted son Akbar, to donate blood for an accident victim. On the hospital bed lies Bharati. Near her lie three young men—Amar, Akbar and Anthony, all giving their blood to save an unknown woman.

While arresting a gang of robbers, Amar meets Lakshmi. In the scuffle, the gang-leader Ranjeet escapes. When Lakshmi tells him that Ranjeet, her step-brother, forces her to work for him, Amar takes her under his wing. Meanwhile Kishanlal, now a rich smuggler, has enslaved Robert by kidnapping his daughter Jenny. Knowing she is due back from her studies abroad, Robert flees with a box of gold after shooting Amar's foster father in an encounter with the police. Kishanlal too escapes. Robert meets Anthony by accident, and pursuades him to give him shelter. The investigations of the shooting lead Amar to Anthony, who refuses to talk and is put in the lock-up. On the way to court, he is kidnapped by Kishanlal's men who are also looking for Robert. Anthony escapes and intrigued by everyone's interest in Robert, returns to Amar. When he learns about the injured officer, he takes Amar to Robert's hideout; but Robert has fled. At the airport, Robert waits for Jenny, but misled by Kishanlal, kidnaps the wrong girl. Soon Anthony sees Jenny, meets her in church and falls in love; but Zibisco, her bodyguard, has other ideas. While Kishanlal is away, he ties her up and phones Robert. He will hand Jenny over provided she is married to him. Returning home just then, Kishanlal rescues Jenny, but is chased by Robert. Akbar and Anthony notice Jenny as Kishan-lal's car overtakes them on the road, followed by Robert. While Anthony rescues Jenny, Akbar saves Kishanlal when his car has an accident. Foiled again, Robert refuses Zibisco his pay-off. Zibisco now produces Robert's twin, Albert, a scholar who has come from abroad to attend a conference. If Jenny is married to Zibisco, he will hold on to Albert; while Robert escapes in the guise of his brother from the police.

At the hospital, Kishanlal is given the bed Akbar has vacated that day, having recovered from the beating he had received from Salma's father's hirelings. Bharati, who keeps in touch with the men who saved her life, comes to visit Akbar and hears that the patient is in the operation theatre. Anxious to give Akbar her blessings, she bangs on the theatre door. Inside, Kishanlal lies anaesthetized, and Robert insists that Salma revives him, for he must know where Jenny is. Ranjeet who has joined Robert, opens the door to Bharati, and recognizing her, Robert kidnaps her as a hostage. But on the way they have an accident, and before the men recover, Bharati scrambles towards a temple where Akbar is heard singing. At the temple gate her pursuers are frightened off by a snake which allows the blind Bharati to pass. As she lies on the steps, two heavenly flames move from the eyes of the stone image, and give back her vision. In Akbar's home, his foster father recognizes Bharati as the woman he helped twenty-two years ago. Seeing a photograph of little Akbar, Bharati knows she has found her youngest son. The same day Akbar saves Salma and her father from a fire, and finally overcomes the old man's animosity. From Salma, Akbar learns of the incident in the hospital and how Robert revealed that Kishanlal was Bharati's husband. Overjoyed, Akbar takes Bharati to see him; but Kishanlal has left and Akbar seeks Amar's help to find his father. On a nostalgic visit to his old home, Kishanlal sees Amar searching for him. Old memories stir and Amar digs out a toy pistol he had buried near his home as a child. Kishanlal remembers the incident, and recognizes his eldest son. Amar discovers his relationship with Bharati and Akbar.

Leaving Akbar's home after ordering Jenny's wedding gown, Anthony and Jenny are seen by Zibisco. While Anthony goes to prepare for the wedding, Jenny hears the Father announce the happy event at church, recalling how he found Anthony as a child. Knowing how Kishanlal lost his children, Jenny is sure that Anthony is his son. She slips out to a call box at the back, and is about to reveal Anthony's name when Robert drags her away, stabbing to death the Father who has just come out of the church. Lakshmi, seeing Ranjeet near the getaway van, hides in the back of the van and is caught by Ranjeet in Robert's house. When Anthony finds the Father's body, a chain that he last saw round Kishanlal's neck drops from the dead fingers. Unaware that it was stolen by Robert at the hospital, Anthony goes to Kishanlal. Protesting his innocence, Kishanlal tells him about Robert and his daughter who is to marry Kishanlal's long lost son. Anthony greets his real father. Meanwhile, Zibisco goes to fetch the wedding gown. Suspecting mischief, Akbar, disguised as the tailor's older brother, takes the gown to Robert's house. There he sees Jenny and Lakshmi and overhears Robert phoning for a band and a priest. Pretending he needs his sewing machine, he sends Ranjeet home with a note in Persian script, alerting Amar and Anthony. Salma, claiming to be the old tailor's young bride, insists on carrying the sewing machine to him. Amar and Anthony knock out the priest and the one-man band, in whose clothes they join the fray. Having revealed their identities to the girls, the three men try to carry out a crazy scheme to outwit the crooks. But before they can get away, the real priest and one-man band appear in their underclothes. While the pacifist Akbar plays the band, Amar and Anthony tackle the hoodlums till the police arrive. Kishanlal, who has already surrendered to the police, is reunited with his family. His sons take their girls in a jeep and go singing into the sunset.

THE SUCCESS of Ramesh Sippy's *Sholay* in 1975, gave the formula film a new validity. Two years later, Desai stretched the formula to its furthest limits in *Amar Akbar Anthony*. Eschewing the grim, the violent and the emotional, Desai offered the zany, make-believe world, where all the elements that go into the formula film were exploited to the hilt within the carefully woven maze of an impossibly complicated story. After the censorship restrictions of the nineteen months of Emergency, four of Desai's films were released at one go, under the liberal patronage of the new government. Each a tremendous box-office success, they took a fresh step towards obliterating the demarcation between good and evil, right and wrong. Under the guise of laughter, the villain became the naughty prankster, the lovable rogue. New villains were created, but they were mostly inferior beings, no match for the protagonists. *Amar Akbar Anthony* not only typified Desai's novel approach to the Hindi film formula, it also provided everything the audience might want, in a single package. As a "multi-starrer," it presented three established young actresses with three major stars in the main roles. The villain, Robert, was played by an actor who had spent a lifetime playing the role of a sly fox, heartily despised by the audience, but never inspiring fear. Pran as Kishanlal, is a man pushed into crime, who recants and is united with his family. By the time *Amar Akbar Anthony* was made, Pran, the arch villain of the fifties, had already diluted his image to pass for a man more sinned against that sinning. The tortuous story accommodated everything and more: the separated brothers, the incredible coincidences, the love angle in triplicate, the fights and the chase, the songs and dances, disguises and miracles. There was something in it for everybody in the family; even a sop for the government: a spurious interpretation of the philosophy of national integration.

Sociologically, the last item is the most interesting in Desai's collection of trivia that was welcomed so heartily by the post-Emergency audience starving for a bit of fun. It was the correct mixture of acceptable moral righteousness. Religions in India, barely co-existing ever since Independence, can only allow so much and no more of "integration." Amar, Akbar and Anthony, though they take on different religions, do so only by accident. Each falls in love with a girl of his own religious community in a seemingly unconscious adherence to social norms. When they are finally together, it is under the all-absorbing banner of their Hindu birth. What happens to the separate faiths of Jenny and Salma, are left to the imagination of the public who are in any case too overwhelmed by the narrative maze to be able to think at all.

AMMA ARIYAN (Report to Mother)
b&w, 115 minutes, Malayalam, 1986

Production: Odessa Movies/ Direction, story and screenplay: John Abraham/ Camera: Venu/ Music: Sunitha/ Art Direction: Ramesh/ Editing: Beena/ Sound: Krishnanunni
Cast: Joy Mathew, Maji Venkitesh, Nilamboor Balan, Harinarayanan, Kunhulakshmi Amma, Iringal Narayani, Nazim

PURUSHAN bids his mother good bye, promising to write regularly. He is on his way to Delhi. In the thinly populated mountainous regions of north-eastern Kerala, the jeep in which he is travelling is stopped by the police who need it to carry a body found hanging from a tree. The dead man's face looks familiar to Purushan, and he finds he cannot rest till he knows who it was. He abandons his trip to Delhi, and decides to seek out his friends who may have the answer.

Purushan meets journalists and doctors and finally reaches a veteran communist, Balettan. Balettan thinks that the dead man was the musician who accompanied Satyajit, a guitarist. Satyajit immediately identifies the man as his friend Hari. Together, they decide to inform Hari's mother, who lives in Cochin, about his death. The journey from the northern highlands of the state to the southern sea port is a long one, and as they move from Calicut through Beypore, Crangannore, Trichur, Kottapuram, Vypin, and finally into Cochin, their band swells as they come across different people who have known Hari. Through their recollections, Hari's rather confused history unfolds. There are many contradictions in these recollections. If the dead man is Hari the *tabla* player to one, he is Tony the jazz drummer to another. His classmates remember Hari as an introvert, weak and indecisive. His worker-comrades can only recall the resolute Marxist, a dare-devil, who attacked police stations and forcibly took over food-laden trucks. But this motley group of young people, all friends of Hari, have one thing in common. They have all been touched by the same youthful idealism and faith in the common man's revolution.

As they wait for Hari's mother, they analyse their own past, and the emerging debate focuses on the romantic evasions and the tragic failures of the extremist movement. When Hari's mother finally faces the multitude of young men, she asks, "Suicide, wasn't it?"

IN THE FORM of an open letter from a son to his mother, *Amma Ariyan* discusses the confusions of a generation, the troubled youth of the seventies, in the context of a turbulent political and economic environment. Fact is intermingled with fiction, and actual coverage of historical events becomes an essential part of a dramatized experience, giving it the credibility of real history. As in all old cultures which have the power to overcome contradictions of faith, in Kerala too, radicalism has gone hand in hand with mother worship. The deity of the common folk is still Durga, the consort of Lord Shiva. The traditional matrilineal kinship influences Purushan's personal radicalism. His journey begins and ends with this same belief. For the director, John Abraham, a disciple of Ritwik Ghatak, the mother image is the most important cohesive force in Nature.

"The documentary technique distances the audience and invests the film with a Brechtian epic quality even as it helps to see places and events in a historical perspective," says critic T.M.P. Nedugadi. "The diversions into the turbulent events of the seventies in Kerala only add to the distancing techniques.... There is hardly a trick of the trade that Abraham does not use; the sound effects (the lub-dub on the way to the hospital mortuary, the irony of the cry of the new born babe while Purushan seeks the dead son); the ordinary symbolism (the little doll hung by its hair behind the windscreen of the car when the dialogue is about youngsters hanging themselves); music (the frenzy of the drums, the sanctity of the Edakkai, the sensuousness of the Hindustani song); understatement (police torturing the Marxists); and above all, the visuals which

capture the serenity that hides the seething discontent of sensitive youth."
[*Cinema in India,* January 1987.]

John Abraham, who has been called the "true maverick of current Indian cinema," died recently in a road accident, bringing to an abrupt halt a highly unorthodox life and career. *Amma Ariyan,* his last film, was financed in a novel manner. Abraham and his band of young enthusiasts, set up Odessa Movies to carry good cinema to the common people. Voluntary contributions from thousands of people, of two and ten rupees, and shares of Rs 100, formed the core of the production capital, and made the film the people's offering to the movement for good cinema.

AMRIT MANTHAN (The Churning of the Oceans)
b&w, 155 minutes, Hindi, 1934

Production: Prabhat Film Company/ Direction: V. Shantaram/ Story: N.H. Apte/ Camera: K. Dhaibar/ Music: Keshavrao Bhole/ Art Direction: S. Fattelal/ Sound: V. Damle
Cast: Nalini Tarkhad, Shanta Apte, Sureshbabu, Chandramohan, Kelkar, Kulkarni, Varde

KRANTIVARMA, king of Avanti, is a reformist who bans the killing of human beings and animals in the name of god. Rajguru, the orthodox royal priest, opposes the reforms and selects one of his followers, Yashodharma, a nobleman, to assassinate the king. At night, before doing the foul deed, Yashodharma leaves a note for his son and daughter, Madhavgupta and Sumitra. After the assassination, Yashodharma, denied protection by Rajguru, is condemned to death. Madhavgupta and Sumitra flee their home, but Madhavgupta is caught by Rajguru's men, and Yashodharma's note, implicating Rajguru in the assassination, falls into his hands. When Mohini, Krantivarma's daughter, succeeds to the throne, she is forced by Rajguru to order the sacrifice of Madhavgupta to the goddess. But during the ceremony, a sudden fierce storm destroys the temple, and Mohini escapes to the forest with Madhavgupta. But his sister Sumitra, maddened by shock, is picked up by Rajguru's men.

Mohini is discovered in the forest and Rajguru compels her to return; while Madhavgupta escapes and learns of his sister's imprisonment. Back in the palace, Mohini learns of Rajguru's role in her father's death from one of the trusted ministers, Viswas. When Rajguru catches Madhavgupta trying to free his sister, he once again prepares to sacrifice him. All Mohini's attempts to secretly save the young man fail. In desperation, Viswas tells the people of Avanti the truth about Rajguru. Cornered by the violent mob demanding justice outside the palace, and the by now irate courtiers inside, Rajguru attempts to escape, but is grievously hurt in the eye by Viswas. Hanging on to his monstrous pride, he drags himself to the royal temple and offers his own head to the goddess as a sacrifice. Mohini declares, this must be the last time that blood is shed in the name of religion in her land.

ONE OF THE last living pioneers of the Indian film industry, V. Shantaram began his career in a railroad repair and maintenance workshop when still in his teens. To supplement his meagre income, he also worked as an odd jobs man at the local tin-shed cinema, and was inevitably drawn to the new madness of the times—the moving image. By the time he was twenty-eight, he had already done a long stint of apprenticeship in Baburao Painter's Maharashtra Film Company in Kolhapur. Painter, so called because he was by profession a trained landscape painter, was also a mechanical genius whose interest in special effects and technical excellence was imbibed by those who worked with him. Together with Shantaram, two other pupils of Painter, V. Damle and S. Fattelal, set up the Prabhat Film Company which moved to Pune in 1933.

Although he had already made films in Marathi, Hindi and Tamil in the first five years of the new company, *Amrit Manthan,* made in both Marathi and Hindi in 1934, established Shantaram as a powerful director as well as a man with a social conscience. The first film to be produced in Prabhat's newly built sound-proof studio, *Amrit Manthan* demanded huge magnificent sets, and ornate costumes. Fattelal's genius for art direction was brought into play, and the palace intrigue became a spectacular drama. The publicity leaflet said, "Shanta Apte made 200,000 persons shed tears at Krishna Talkies." But the film is no tear-jerker. Instead, its fast pace, quick succession of dramatic action, large array of characters, all contribute to a tightly knit narrative that must have kept the audience at the edge of their seats. But the most spectacular element in the film is the characterization of Rajguru by Chandramohan who established himself not only as a tremendous actor but also the most feared villain of the times. Even the last, absurd act of beheading himself does not take away from the dignity and strength of the portrayal. Rajguru emerges not as an ordinary evil doer, but as a man to be respected and feared even as a fanatic. He is as difficult an enemy as Satan, once a favourite of God. The portrayal carries through the director's message with greater force—the powers of evil are not to be belittled. Unfortunately, unlike the mythical populace of Avanti, Shantaram's audience was merely entertained. And his message remains important even today, for history has been dominated by bloodshed in the name of religion long after *Amrit Manthan* was made.

The curious ambiguity of the film's name bears mention here. It refers to the churning of the oceans by the gods for the elixir of life. To avoid contaminating the earth, Lord Shiva swallowed all the poisonous substance that emerged during the churning, leaving only what was good for mankind.

ANDAZ (*Beau Monde*)
b&w, 142 minutes, Hindi, 1949

Production: Mehboob Productions Ltd/ Direction: Mehboob Khan/ Story: Shums Lucknavi/ Screenplay and dialogue: S. Ali Raza/ Lyrics: Majrooh Sultanpuri/ Songs: Mukesh, Mohammad Rafi, Lata Mangeshkar/ Music:

Naushad/ Camera: Faredoon A. Irani/ Art Direction: Keshav Mistry/ Editing:
Shamsudin Kadri/ Sound: Kaushik
Cast: Nargis, Dilip Kumar, Raj Kapoor, V.H. Desai, Cuckoo, Murad, Anwari
Bai, Amir Banu, Jamshedji, Abbas, Waskar, Abdul, Dyke

DILIP, the son of a wealthy expatriate, saves Neena, the beautiful daughter of a
rich industrialist, from certain death on the hillside when her horse goes out of
control. Neena befriends him out of a deep sense of gratitude, even though the
friendship is looked upon with disfavour by her father. Dilip falls in love with
Neena, and assumes from her easy friendship that she returns his feelings. He
does not pay attention to the hints to the contrary thrown out by Neena, and
her close friend Sheela, who is herself in love with Dilip. Inevitably he is
shocked and hurt by the return of Rajan from his studies abroad, the man
whom Neena is pledged to marry. Dilip, who has been managing the family
business after the sudden death of Neena's father, finds that he cannot walk
away from her on her wedding day without creating a scandal. But Neena,
who by now has finally learnt of Dilip's predicament, arranges to leave town
with her husband.
  Somehow she never manages to explain to Rajan the problem, and two years
pass on a hill-station, where Neena gives birth to a baby girl. Her sense of
guilt about Dilip, and her fear of confronting him again, keeps her from going
back. But Rajan, tired of his idle existence, finally prevails upon her, and they
are back in her home to celebrate the first birthday of their daughter. Dilip
decides that he must leave now, and secretes a letter in a toy that he brings as a
present for the little girl. The lights go off accidentally during the party, and
Neena, thinking that she is addressing Dilip, asks him to leave, for he is
destroying her happiness. When the lights come on again, she realizes that she
has actually spoken to Rajan, who misunderstands her completely, and starts
behaving with bitter cruelty towards her. When Dilip tries to tell him about his
wife's innocence, Rajan, in a rage, hits him with his tennis racquet.
  Neena's sense of gratitude and guilt towards Dilip confuses her further. Her
husband's rejection hurts her and she contemplates suicide. But a hand grasps
her wrist as she points the pistol towards herself. It is Dilip, grotesque in his
bandages, and out of his mind. In the scuffle that follows, Neena, in
desperation, shoots Dilip, who dies protesting wildly that she loves him, not
Rajan. In the courtroom, Rajan lets out a string of accusations against his
wife, which help to condemn her. She herself refuses to defend herself. Back
home, Rajan discovers the letter in the toy, and realizes that his wife is actually
innocent of all the crimes that he has heaped upon her head. But now she is a
murderer and there is no reprieve for her. Rajan goes to see her one last time
before she is sent for life-imprisonment. Neena has no word of reproach for
him. She is guilty, she says, for she has been spoilt and self-centered, and
because she has willingly adopted the false mode of conduct of her upper-class
society.

ANDAZ is supposed to be the only film which managed to bring together the
three great names of popular Indian cinema—Dilip Kumar, Nargis and Raj
Kapoor. The two men were already stars in their own rights, and the dramatic

conflict of the story must have been enhanced by their being portrayed as antagonists, for as actors, they made formidable opponents. *Andaz* has many points of interest. Nargis is delightful in the role of a high-society butterfly who still retains her innocence and old-worldly loyalties. Necessarily westernized, her clothes are straight out of *It Happened One Night,* or *The Philadelphia Story.* And she carries them remarkably well. Dilip Kumar retains his brooding look as the rejected lover, a character he has played with great success in a number of films. But Raj Kapoor gives an unusual and moving performance as the happy-go-lucky young husband who refuses to suspect his wife's attachment to a stranger, and who changes overnight once he allows the suspicion to take hold of him. His bitterness and cruelty find expression in hostile and destructive jocularity—brutal humour that can kill. But *Andaz* does not live up to its promise. One of the most interesting elements in the plot is the possibility that Neena does after all fall in love with Dilip, though she denies it as she is already pledged to Rajan. It is certainly a likely development, for Rajan has been away for many years. But Neena's upbringing, strictly moralistic in these matters, would bar her from even recognizing her own feelings towards another man. And the unfolding of the drama, the dialogue, the characterization of Neena, all point to such an emotional conflict. Yet, when it comes to the denouement, the director chooses to make it quite clear that for Neena, Rajan has been the only god and she herself a flower offered in worship, which once given, cannot be taken back: an old-fashioned attitude unsuitable for a modern young miss, however many times in the film she may repeat it. In fact, the rather drastic method of getting rid of Dilip from the story seems highly contrived, and so does Neena's uncomplaining surrender to punishment that she does not really deserve. But popular cinema has always worked under the cover of traditional morality, and the quite appealing complications of a love triangle must firmly be put in their place at the end.

APARAJITO (The Unvanquished)
b&w, 113 min, Bengali, 1956

Production: Epic Films (Private) Ltd/ Direction and screenplay: Satyajit Ray/ Story: Bibhutibhushan Bandyopadhyay/ Camera: Subrata Mitra/ Music: Ravi Shankar/ Art Direction: Bansi Chandragupta/ Editing: Dulal Dutta/ Sound: Durgadas Mitra
Cast: Karuna Bandyopadhyay, Kanu Bandyopadhyay, Smaran Kumar Ghosal, Pinaki Sengupta, Ramaniranjan Sengupta, Charuprakash Ghosh, Shanti Gupta, Ranibala, Sudipta Roy, Ajay Mitra, Subodh Ganguly

HARIHAR, Sarbojaya and ten-year-old Apu, live in the great temple city of Varanasi, on the banks of the Ganga. Harihar earns a meagre living as a *Kathak*, reciting and interpreting holy verses from the scriptures to the devotees who throng the river banks every day. They live in rented accommodations, on the ground floor of a house in one of the many winding lanes of the city. It is still a hard life, and Apu, with no opportunity to go to school, spends his days playing with the urchins of the area. During the autumn festivals, Harihar comes home one day ill with fever. He refuses to take it seriously, and goes back to the river bank next morning. Coming up the wide steps of the *ghat* after a dip in the holy river, his feet falter, and he collapses on the ground. That night, Sarbojaya sits looking after Harihar, but in the early hours of the morning she wakes Apu and asks him to go to the river and bring back some holy water to put in his father's mouth, for he is dying. Harihar's death leaves mother and son destitute. As a Brahmin widow, she takes a job as a cook in the household of a rich family, but seeing that her son is being used as an unpaid servant in the house, she decides to take the advice of an old uncle, and leaves for Mansapota, a prosperous village where the uncle works as a priest.

In Mansapota, Apu is initiated into priesthood and takes over the old man's work, but is unhappy, for he wants to go to school like the other boys in the village. His mother understands his ambitions, and Apu joins the big local school, but continues with his priestly duties for a livelihood. He does well in school, for he has a great urge to learn. Life has once more fallen into a peaceful routine when Apu, now sixteen, wins a scholarship at the school-leaving examination. He decides to join a college in Calcutta. It breaks his mother's heart, but she relents in the end. She waits for the day when Apu will get a good job in the city and take her away with him. She has not been feeling too well lately, and the loneliness in the village takes its toll. But Apu, now part of a new world, away from the gentle shadow of his mother, is unaware of the change in her. His visits get shorter as the months pass. The physical distance between mother and son is inevitably transformed into an emotional distance, unnoticed by the growing Apu. But it hurts Sarbojaya deeply. She waits silently for her son to come and visit her, as her illness accelerates. She dies alone, in the lonely village home, and Apu comes back to an empty house where no trace remains of the woman who had sheltered and nurtured him, and given him the life he wanted. Apu grieves for his mother, for the snapping of his last ties with the life he has left behind. Then he leaves the village for the last time, to pick up the threads of his new existence.

APARAJITO, the film, took shape from the latter part of the novel, *Pather Panchali*, and a section of its sequel, *Aparajito*. The original story, conceived by the novelist in epic dimensions, had many more characters and events woven into it. On the whole, the film, *Pather Panchali*, had retained the framework of the original narrative. In the second film, Ray took much greater liberties with the story, concentrating on the core of it, on the changing relationship between Sarbojaya and Apu, and on Apu's craving for a dubious freedom from a past that has been left behind by history. It probably shocked and disappointed his Bengali viewers who had expected a visual repetition of the much loved novel. When released, the film was considered a total failure, till it won the highest award at the Venice film festival. Not unnaturally, Indian critics rediscovered the film with great promptness. Watching *Aparajito* can still be a claustrophobic and painful experience. If his mother's death releases Apu from a primal bond that pulled him away from the forward flow of life, it does not remove the agony from a separation that is inevitable and even, perhaps, desirable. As an experience, it is not only universal, but shared by every generation. And there lies the pain. Yet Apu steps out of his prison of love with hope. Once again, Ray has used mostly unknown faces with great poignancy, and the intimate drama is further internalized by long stretches of silence. The mother's hurt remains unspoken, so does the son's rebellion. Visually the metropolitan anarchy of Calcutta is poised against the calm, still, ordered existence of the village, of a life style that is passing away. The silent Sarbojaya leans against the gnarled bark of an ancient tree, with the shadow of death on her patient, determined face, while far away against the horizon a train grinds past on its iron wheels, carrying civilization on its back. But Apu does not come home.

APUR SANSAR (The World of Apu)
b&w, 106 min, Bengali, 1959

Production: Satyajit Ray Productions/ Direction and screenplay: Satyajit Ray/ Story: Bibhutibhushan Bandyopadhyay/ Camera: Subrata Mitra/ Music: Ravi Shankar/ Art Direction: Bansi Chandragupta/ Editing: Dulal Dutta/ Sound: Durgadas Mitra
Cast: Soumitra Chattopadhyay, Sharmila Tagore, Alok Chakravarty, Swapan Mukhopadhyay, Dhiresh Majumdar, Shefalika (Putul), Abhijit Chattopadhyay

APU NOW lives in a rented room on the terrace of a crowded house in Calcutta, right next to a busy railway yard. Having passed his Intermediate examination, and unable to afford further studies, he finds himself part of a growing population of the unemployed in this great city. The landlord duns him periodically for unpaid rent. He sells a few books to catch up with his dues, till he finds a job. Looking for work is sometimes a hilarious experience, at others a pathetic one. But with no responsibilities in life, Apu does not really care. He wants to write a great novel, a magnum opus that will make him famous one day. His friend, Pulu, a young engineer, snatches Apu out of the peaceful confines of his existence, and takes him away to Khulna, in East Bengal, to attend a wedding in the family. On the day of the wedding, however, it is revealed that the bridegroom is mentally deranged. Before the auspicious hour can pass, and the girl left unmarried forever, Pulu insists that Apu must save the situation and take the bridegroom's place. Quite unprepared for the grave responsibilities of marriage, Apu finally relents out of a half-formed notion of saving the girl's life.
Apu's fears about how Aparna, the daughter of a landed family, will take to the life of a poor man's wife in a ramshackle room in Calcutta, are soon dispelled. A warm and precious feeling grows between the two young people, and Apu takes the clerical job that he has so far avoided, to run the household. After many years, he finds himself bound by love, and willingly so. The rented room is transformed into a home, and a stranger becomes an inseparable part of Apu's life. Aparna goes to her parents' home before the autumn festivals, to have her baby. The child is born after a long and difficult labour, and

in Calcutta, Apu receives the news of Aparna's death. The world shatters around Apu. He refuses to have anything to do with the child whom he holds responsible for his mother's death, and leaves Calcutta to lead the life of a wanderer in search of peace.

Pulu, coming back from abroad after a few years, is shocked to find the child growing wild and uncared for in his grandfather's home in Khulna. Aparna's mother having died soon after her, Apu's son, Kajal, is left to be brought up by the servants under the stern and bitter supervision of the lonely old man. Pulu goes in search of Apu, and finds him working temporarily in a colliery, far away from Bengal. He scolds Apu, and pleads with him to no avail. He leaves, saddened and horrified by Apu's unnatural revulsion for the child. But the encounter releases Apu from his self-created prison of grief. He goes in search of his son who refuses to accept him as his father. But Apu does not give up easily. With renewed interest and hope, he wins over the little boy, and carries him away towards a new beginning.

"THE APU TRILOGY was not conceived as a trilogy," wrote Ray in a recent piece on the films. "When we made *Pather Panchali*, we couldn't think beyond the film. The critical and box-office success of *Pather Panchali* triggered off *Aparajito*, which flopped and left me confused as to what I should do next. I made two contrasted films—*Parash Pathar* and *Jalsaghar* —by which time *Aparajito* had gone on to win the top prize at the Venice Film Festival. It was at the press conference in Venice that I was asked if I had a trilogy in mind. I found myself saying yes. At that time I didn't know if there was a third film in Bibhutibhushan's novel. I came back home, reread *Aparajito* and discovered *Apur Sansar* in it." Separated from the first two films by the intervening years and the experiences they brought to Ray as a filmmaker, *Apur Sansar* was made as an independent film to all intents and purposes. The new Apu, a young man with a poetic disposition, was played by a young Calcutta intellectual, Soumitra Chattopadhyay, who immediately became established as the most popular hero of the Bengali screen after the legendary Uttam Kumar. Through the years, in spite of his success in what is known as the "commercial" cinema, Chattopadhyay has retained his links with Ray, and appeared from time to time in major roles in his films, the last being in Ray's latest, *Ghare Baire* (The Home and the World). Sharmila Tagore, an unknown young teenager from an aristocratic background, who was chosen to play the role of Aparna, became the sex symbol of the sixties in the domain of Hindi cinema! She too has appeared in other Ray films, in perfectly sober roles, followed up with a sensational marriage to a greatly admired cricketer from an erstwhile royal family, and has recently made a comeback as a serious actress.

Apur Sansar has neither the documentary realism and epic dimensions of Ray's first film, nor the camouflaged intensity and personalized impact of his second. In many ways it is a far simpler story, presented with greater technical ease, with an archetypal Bengali romantic as its protagonist. The subtleties of silence, though present, are not its dominant features, and perhaps it lacks the greatness of the two previous films. It remains, nevertheless, an important contribution in the evolution of Ray as one of the finest craftsmen of the cinema. As a part of the trilogy, *Apur Sansar* is a continuation of a human document in three independent movements, covering the experiences of two generations of a family in the changing perspectives of history.

ARDH SATYA (Half Truth)
colour, 130 minutes, Hindi, 1983

Production: Neo Films/ Direction and Camera: Govind Nihalani/ Screenplay: Vijay Tendulkar/ Music: Ajit Verman/ Art Direction: C.S. Bhali/ Editing: Renu Saluja
Cast: Om Puri, Smita Patil, Amrish Puri, Naseeruddin Shah, Sadashiv Amrapurkar, Achyut Potdar, Shafi Inamdar

ANANT WELANKAR has recently joined the Bombay police force as a sub-inspector. It is not a job of his own choosing. His father, himself a policeman, a ruthless and brutal man who has always been a terror in his own home, insisted that his son follow his footsteps. Nevertheless, Welankar enters his new profession with a certain idealism and a naive sense of social duty, which leave him wide open to the frustrations inherent in the system within which he must operate.

When Welankar arrests three of Rama Shetty's men for attacking a constable, Shetty, the leader of the local Mafia, a gambler and a rising politician, merely rings up the powers that be, to get his three companions released. Welankar, whose sense of righteousness is his source of strength, is outraged by the event. Shetty becomes for him the archetype of all evil that he must confront as a policeman. A victim of his father's violence at home, Welankar falls a prey to his own violence when he savagely beats up a gang of youths arrested for molesting women. In a crowded bus a man makes a pass at Welankar's girl-friend, Jyotsna. Welankar vents on the man all his pent up rage against his father's treatment of his submissive mother. His ungovernable temper nearly costs him his job, to save which he must take another step to entrench himself within the corrupt system—help from a "Delhi connection" to overlook his excesses. His immediate superior, Haider, gives him realistic advice. There is no point in fighting a criminal like Shetty who has powerful political connections, and controls a large portion of the votes in the district. Haider also points out to Welankar the fate of Lobo, once a police inspector, now disgraced into alcoholism and vagrancy. But Welankar will not learn. When one of Shetty's men is doused with kerosene and set on fire, armed with his deathbed declaration, Welankar goes to arrest Shetty on a murder charge. Shetty makes a phone call and Welankar is ordered to lay off.

Unwilling to accept Haider's modes of compromise, Welankar takes to alcohol. Jyotsna is increasingly upset by his violence and drunkenness, and urges him to give up his job. Meanwhile Shetty stands for the local elections with the full support of the ruling party. On a routine encounter, Welankar traps a dacoit with great skill and courage, but the medal is awarded to a rival policeman. At the police station, the frustrated Welankar vents his fury on a petty thief accused of stealing a transistor. The man dies in custody. Welankar is suspended. Haider advises him to seek Shetty's support. But in Shetty's posh apartment, facing the criminal turned father of society, Welankar is consumed with shame and rage at his own cowardice. In a final act of protest and realizing that he has nothing left to lose, he kills Shetty and surrenders to the police.

"WHAT IS important is the individual's realization of his relationship with the system," says Govind Nihalani. "I catch the individual first as his crisis with the system is beginning, and I follow him till the point when he is forced to make a choice. The kind of choice he makes is what interests me." In an interview with Rajni Bakshi, Nihalani further elaborates that his effort is "to portray the dilemma of a person with a great sense of power and responsibility, who is faced with humiliating situations which demean him.... I believe that the individual cannot bring about change by himself—he can only initiate a process and others must come together to take action. The important thing is to react and not take things lying down."

In spite of its dubious stand on police morality, *Ardh Satya* won the approbation of critics and the public, and became the forerunner of other box-office successes with unconventional themes. That, probably, was the film's most significant contribution to Indian cinema. With Om Puri's powerful portrayal of Anant Welankar, the violence in the film could be effectively sublimated by its condemnation. Yet Welankar seems not so much a product of the corrupt system, as of the abnormal upbringing by his obviously peculiar father. There is no indication that the father was himself brutalized by the frustrations and injustices of his profession. There is no excuse but a touch of madness for the violence that the elder Welankar displays. How far, then, is Anant Welankar himself a victim of the system he fights against? Is his aggression a personal perversion or an expression of protest? And did our film viewers actually empathize with the impotence of Welankar's situation, or did they merely enjoy his orgy of violence? The confusion, which seems to arise out of the director's own ambiguous perspective of the problem, remains unresolved. But the purity of Welankar's rage manages to effectively silence most doubts.

ATITHI (The Runaway)
b&w, 112 minutes, Bengali, 1965

Production: New Theatres Pvt Ltd/ Story: Rabindranath Tagore/ Direction, screenplay and music: Tapan Sinha/ Camera: Dilip Ranjan Mukherjee/ Editing: Subodh Roy
Cast: Parthasarathi Mukherjee, Salil Dutta, Sunita Sinha, Samita Biswas, Soumen Mukherjee, Bankim Ghosh, Ajitesh Banerjee, Krishna Basu, Dipali Mukherjee, Swati Mukherjee, Benoy Lahiri, Manojit Lahiri

TARAPADA is a pleasant young lad, the apple of his mother's eye; but he is often attacked by a strange wanderlust that tears him away from the comforts of his happy home. That is when he finds himself in the company of wandering performers, musicians and acrobats who roam the land—the magic of their peripatetic lives draws Tarapada to them again and again. During one such flight, Tarapada comes across Motibabu, a rich landlord who is returning home by boat with his family from a pilgrimage. Tarapada wants a ride in the boat, and during the journey, endears himself to Motibabu and his wife. Tarapada himself becomes attached to the family, and is amused by Charu, the little daughter of the landlord, who envies him for all the affection her parents shower upon him.

When the journey is over, Motibabu takes Tarapada to his home. Motibabu and his wife Annapurna have grown so fond of the boy that they happily take on the task of educating him. For once Tarapada is caught by their bonds of love, and even Charu accepts him as a friend. To make sure that he never escapes again, Motibabu writes to Tarapada's mother, expressing his desire to marry Charu to the boy. Tarapada's mother is overjoyed—her little bird has found a gilded cage at last. She prepares for her journey to Motibabu's home to settle the marriage.

But two years of bondage has not killed the wanderlust in Tarapada. The call of the unknown is too strong for him. The shackles of love fall away again one day. When Tarapada's mother arrives, the boy has fled once more. Playing his flute with gay abandon, he rides a boat that will carry him to a life of excitement and adventure, and to a strange destination.

THE NAME of the film and the original story literally means "The Guest." *Atithi* is a charming story of another time, when the romance of the unknown had still not been destroyed by the stresses of an industrial society, when folk performers still had a livelihood, when generosity of the spirit could match the generosity of the purse. Today Tarapada would be a junkie, and Motibabu might just feel generous enough to give him a menial job in his home. And as for the travelling performers, they would either participate in ethnic cultural revivals abroad or starve at home. What Sinha did for Tagore's simple tale was to recreate that elusive freedom that the human spirit searches for even today. Only, the world has changed beyond recognition, and *Atithi's* open skies, rolling fields, sleepy streams, recall to life a vision that slumbers in a neglected corner of the human mind. One of the most attractive features of the film is its presentation of rural Bengal. The camera revels in the outdoors and freedom becomes a tangible reality. *Atithi* was not only a great success with the regional audience and critics, but also won a Certificate of Merit at the International Film Festival at Venice in 1966.

AURAT (Woman)
b&w, 154 minutes, Hindi, 1940

Production: National Studios/ Direction: Mehboob Khan/ Dialogue: Vajahat Mirza/ Lyrics: Dr Safdar 'Aah'/ Camera: Faredoon A. Irani/Music: Anil

Biswas/ Art Direction: V.H. Palnitkar/ Editing: Shamsudin Kadri/ Sound: Chandrakant Pandya
Cast: Surendra, Sardar Akhtar, Yakub, Aroon, Harish, Jyoti, Kanhaiyalal, Vatsala Kumtekar, Sunalini, Brijrani, Akbar Ghulam Ali, Kanu Pande, Waskar, Amirbanu

SHAMU, a young farmer, marries Radha, a girl from another village. The marriage has been arranged by his mother who has mortgaged all her land to pay for the spectacular wedding ceremony. The harvest is good that year, and the old woman is quite confident that her debt to Sukhilala, the village moneylender, will be paid soon. Six years pass. Radha now has two little sons, and a third baby is on the way. Sukhilala comes to complain that even his interest has not been paid. Shamu, who has been toiling on his land to feed his growing family, is in despair. A few months after his third son is born, he quietly leaves his home one night, never to return. Shamu's mother dies, and Radha, who now gives birth to her fourth child, is left to fend for herself. Sukhilala offers to keep her, but she proudly refuses and tills the land on her own.

Drought and famine ravage the land. Sukhilala refuses to help the villagers. Radha loses her two older children. Crazed with grief, and determined to save her two remaining children, Radha goes to give herself to Sukhilala. That night the storm breaks. Before she can be defiled by the moneylender's evil touch, a tree crashes in through the roof and pins the man down. Taking it as a warning from God, Sukhilala appeals for help, and addresses Radha as his sister. From that day he is a changed man.

Years pass, and Radha's two boys, Ramu and Birju, are young men. Ramu, the image of his father, looks after their land. The debt has been paid and Radha, now an old woman, is much respected in the village. Ramu marries Jumna, while Birju teases Tulsi, the daughter of Radha's friend Kamla. Spoilt by his mother, Birju soon becomes a problem for the family as well as the whole village. He lies and gambles, joins a gang of robbers, and finally becomes a murderer. His exploits lead the villagers to ostracize Radha. The final blow comes when Birju kidnaps Tulsi during her marriage ceremony. To save Tulsi from shame, Radha shoots the fleeing Birju, then dies of a broken heart in Ramu's arms.

AURAT was one of the most successful films of its time. Its popularity led its director to make a colour version of the film years later. *Mother India* as it was called, starred the darling of the fifties, Nargis, in the role of Radha, and established her as a serious actress of considerable talent. The new version, of which an American critic wrote: "with mother we go through mud, flood and blood," was perhaps an even greater success, especially since it led to a real life romance between Nargis and Sunil Dutt, who played Birju in the later film. *Aurat*, however, remains an archetype that has appeared again and again in popular Indian cinema. The saga of a rural family, completely distorted by a popular urban concept of entertainment for the masses, moves from song to song, establishing the mood, and destroying the narrative pace. The characters are set in the same heroic mould of the early mythological films. Primal relationships are threatened by the confrontation between good and evil, both undeniably larger than life. At the same time there is unwavering faith in the basic goodness of man. A timely intervention changes Sukhilala. If Birju is doomed within a cycle of evil, it is because he is fated to be so. But his genuine love for his mother is never in question, and he dies with a smile on his lips and tears in his eyes, in his mother's arms. The obsessive mother-son relationship, the fanatical familial loyalty, the glorification of a woman's continued suffering in the hands of her men, have not only been the selling points of many a popular film, but also firmly established themselves in the popular psyche. *Aurat*, indeed, is the story of the ultimate Indian woman on celluloid, an image that is still revered in reality, however dubious its value may be today.

AVAIYYAR
b&w, 174 minutes, Tamil, 1953

Production: Gemini Pictures Pvt. Ltd/ Direction, story and screenplay: K. Subbu/ Music: M.D. Parthasarathy and others/ Lyrics (other than Avaiyyar's own compositions): Papanasam Sivan and others/ Art Direction: A.K. Sekar, K.R. Sharma, M.S. Janakiram
Cast: K.B. Sundarambal, Kusala Kumari, G. Pattu Iyer

IN A DENSE forest, a baby is born to a low-caste young woman. The father, a Brahmin and an ascetic, insists on abandoning the baby in the forest. Soon the forest is shaken by a mighty storm, the rain starts a flood which gushes through the trees and bushes, carrying the basket with the baby into the river, and to another shore. Next morning, Banar, another Brahmin, finds the baby in the river when he goes for a morning dip. Banar and his wife are childless, and they bring up the little girl with loving care. Even as a child, Avaiyyar's devotion to Ganesha, the elephant-headed god, and her knowledge of religious verse, surprise everyone. As she grows into a pretty young woman, her prayers evoke visions that only she can see. But it is increasingly obvious to all that she is no ordinary girl. Her foster parents arrange her marriage, but Avaiyyar prays to Lord Vigneswara, the god who removes all obstacles, to free her from worldly bondage. When the bridegroom's party arrives, she is still praying, and in front of their eyes, she turns into an old woman by divine intervention.

Avaiyyar travels across the land, singing her message of faith and love, and wins over both the rich and the poor. Her poetry is simple and memorable, and with her miraculous powers tinged with an earthy commonsense, she solves the problems of the people. When there is drought in the land, her song brings the rains down on the parched earth. A shrewish wife is tamed, a domestic quarrel averted, a miser is reformed. When she walks up to a king's palace, her song dissolves the chains and bolts and the heavy doors open on their own accord. In her attempt to help two orphaned princesses—their father has been killed by a rejected suitor, and the prince they both love has been imprisoned—Avaiyyar prays for divine aid. The gods send an army of elephants who storm the fortress where the prince lies in bondage. The walls shake and collapse under their attack, and the prince is freed. But the enemy now comes with a large army. Avaiyyar goes to meet them alone, and, as she stands on a cliff, facing them, the earth cleaves apart forming a deep gorge which the warriors cannot cross.

Almost at the end of her journey through life, she meets Lord Krishna, in the shape of a little cowherd, and pleases him with her songs. When it is time for her to leave the earth, she climbs the stairs to heaven, watched by the divinities who wait to greet her on Kailash, the abode of Lord Shiva.

AVAIYYAR was a great saint-poetess of Tamil Nadu, whose simple faith, liberal approach to religion, and broad humanism, put her in the forefront of the Bhakti movement. Her historical authenticity has been clouded over with the many miracles that legend attributes to her. But, the clarity and directness of her faith, her simple and unambiguous attitude towards religion and its role in society and politics, as revealed in her songs, ring true. The little old woman who went around solving problems in a most down-to-earth manner made no distinction between kings and their subjects. Her understanding and compassion extended to them all, equally. Even today, many a Tamil child is initiated into his language and culture through Avaiyyar's verses. Made five years after *Chandralekha*, *Avaiyyar* was Vasan's attempt to create a new image for Gemini Pictures which had come to be known for spectacular fairy-tales, rather than films with any serious content. Kothamangalam Subbu, who directed the film, was himself a poet and one of the trusted lieutenants of Vasan. The role of Avaiyyar was played by the famous stage singer, K.B. Sundarambal, whose glorious voice still moves the viewer much more than the simplistic presentation of the miracles she performs on the screen. Though the film lacks the glittering pageantry of *Chandralekha*, it has its share of the spectacular, the hallmark of Gemini. The herd of divine elephants storming the castle to free the captive prince, the earth cracking open at Avaiyyar's feet, are no less impressive visually than some of the sequences in the previous film.

AWARA (The Vagabond)
b&w, 170 minutes, Hindi, 1951

Production: R.K. Films/ Direction: Raj Kapoor/ Story: K.A. Abbas, V.P. Sathe/ Screenplay and dialogue: K.A. Abbas/ Camera: Radhu Karmakar/ Lyrics: Hasrat Jaipuri, Shailendra/ Playback: Lata Mangeshkar, Mukesh, Mohammad Rafi, Manna Dey, Shamsad/ Art Direction: M.R. Achrekar/ Editing: G.G. Mayekar/ Sound: Allauddin
Cast: Prithviraj Kapoor, Nargis, Raj Kapoor, K.N. Singh, Shashiraj, Cuckoo, B.M. Vyas, Leela Misra, Zubeida, Leela Chitnis, Honey O'Brien, Om Prakash, Rajoo, Mansaram, Rajan, Manek Kapoor, Prayag, Ravi, Vinni, Bali, Shinde, D. Basheshernath

TENSION prevails in the courtroom as Rita, a young woman lawyer, examines Judge Raghunath on the witness stand. On trial is Raj, a vagabond, who has been accused of attempting to kill the judge. Rita methodically traces the judge's past.

Raghunath's wife was kidnapped by Jagga, who had turned to crime after being convicted by the judge for an offence he did not commit, all because Raghunath found it easy to accept that a criminal's son could only be a criminal, and Jagga's father was a well-known offender. On discovering that the judge's wife was pregnant, Jagga hatched a diabolical scheme and sent her home, unmolested, after four days. Not surprisingly, with social opinion against her, the judge too started suspecting his wife of infidelity, especially since he had not known of the baby before; and one rainy night, Jagga found the woman and her new-born baby in the street.

Though she kept his father's name hidden from the child, Raj's mother always said that he must grow up to be a judge like his father. But the circumstamces in which they survived made it impossible for Raj to even complete schooling. With no money at home and his mother ill, Raj started working as a shoe black till he was rusticated for coming late to school. His dearest friend in school was Rita, the daughter of a friend of Raghunath. Raj had even met the judge in Rita's home, and been berated by him for not being able to tell his father's name. Years later, as a confirmed criminal, Raj comes across Rita again, now a young lawyer and the ward of the judge, and the childhood friendship transforms into love.

Raghunath, who does not know of Raj's antecedents, is suspicious of the young man. Raj himself is acutely aware of the difference in their status. He tries to make a joke of his mysterious profession, but Rita will believe no ill of him. On her twenty-first birthday, she invites Raj to her home. In search of a suitable gift, Raj steals a costly necklace from the very box that Raghunath is carrying home for his ward. At the party, the judge not only recognizes Raj as the person who had knocked down the box on the street outside the jewellers, but is shocked to discover the box empty, and his chosen necklace hugging Rita's slender throat as a gift from Raj. Raj leaves the party before he is apprehended. Disturbed by the course of events, Rita starts probing into Raj's life. She puts the pieces of the puzzle together and comes up with the truth, but has no real evidence that she can use to convince Raghunath that Raj is his son. Meanwhile, in an awkward confrontation between the judge and Raj, the younger man in a moment of anger, threatens to kill Raghunath.

In the courtroom Rita accuses Raghunath of being responsible for Raj becoming a criminal. For had he not blindly suspected his innocent wife, Raj would have had more opportunities in life. Raghunath still refuses to believe that a common vagabond can be his son. Raj, who is at last aware of the truth about his origins, refuses to defend himself for he is deeply hurt by Raghunath's rejection. But he does make a plea for all those children who grow up in the same environment that has turned him towards crime. Criminal instincts are not inherited, he says, but grow in the gutters of a great city. Raghunath is disturbed by Raj's appeal, and thinking it all over, finally accepts that Raj is his son. He goes to see Raj in his cell, and admits that it is he who is really guilty—at least in the eyes of God. Raj, who must now spend three years of rigorous imprisonment, tells Rita that on his release he will strive to make good in life, to be a judge after all, like his father.

THE PHENOMENAL success of *Awara* spread beyond the boundaries of India. In the Middle East, where Hindi films are now an established feature, Nargis and Raj Kapoor became popular pin-ups in the bazaars of the Arab world. In the Soviet Union the film was dubbed into several languages as part of a massive distribution set up, and prints were even flown out to two Soviet expeditions near the North Pole. The songs from the film, translated into different tongues, were sung in the streets of the many countries where the film was shown. *Awara* revolves round a fundamental dichotomy, between environment and heredity. But the essential seriousness of the theme is glossed over by a complex emotional tangle, and a series of incredible coincidences.

The strength of the film, however, continues to lie in the acting prowess of the three main characters. Nargis and Raj Kapoor, already a popular romantic pair, could create a sexually charged atmosphere without taking recourse to the obvious means adopted by later films. Those were the days of stricter morals, and films being family entertainment only, a sedate one-piece bathing suit and a few chaste embraces were as far as they could go. Yet the electricity between the young lovers was palpable.

On the other end of the spectrum was the ageing Prithviraj Kapoor, Raj Kapoor's father in real life, and a handsome and respected actor of the stage and screen, in the role of Judge Raghunath whose embittered shadow darkens the young lives. The brooding possessiveness that he displays towards Rita, has a curious undercurrent of actual jealousy towards Raj, though the relationship is never overtly expressed in those terms.

Ever since the sound era began, songs have been an essential part of cinema in India, and the songs of *Awara* are still remembered with loving nostalgia. The film also has an incredibly spectacular dream sequence, in keeping with Raj Kapoor's later style, which portrays the vagabond's conflicting loyalties towards Jagga the criminal, and Rita, the image of truth and justice.

BAAZI (A Game of Chance)
b&w, 143 minutes, Hindi, 1951

Production: Navketan/ Direction: Guru Dutt/ Story: Guru Dutt, Balraj Sahni/ Screenplay and dialogue: Balraj Sahni/ Camera: V. Ratra/ Lyrics: Sahir Ludhianvi/ Art Direction: Jadhav/ Editing: Y.G. Chauhan
Cast: Geeta Bali, Dev Anand, Kalpana Kartik, Roopa Varma, K. Dhawan, Rashid Ahmed, Shree Nath, Abu Baker, K.N. Singh

MADAN, once a taxi driver, is now unemployed, making a living out of gambling, so that he may look after his sister. One day, he is taken by a stranger to meet the boss of the Star Club, who always sits with his face away from the light. The boss offers Madan a job. He has heard of Madan's skill as a gambler, and wants him to tempt new customers to the club where they will gamble for high stakes, and with Madan as an opponent, lose heavily. Madan refuses the offer, but has to return to the boss when his sister falls ill, and the pretty young doctor, Rajani, tells him that she has to be sent to a sanatorium. Refusing monetary help from Rajani, Madan joins the Star Club, and becomes affluent overnight. Rajani, who is the daughter of a successful businessman, finds out the source of Madan's income and, being in love with him, tries to reform him.

Ramesh, a young police officer, who has been wooing Rajani with the consent of his father, is disturbed by Rajani's interest in a gambler, especially since he himself has been trying to pin down the mysterious boss of the Star Club where Madan works. Rajani's father contrives to meet Madan and Rajani together, and makes his disapproval evident to both of them. At the Star Club, Madan, summoned by the boss, tells him that he knows his identity. After all, he was a taxi driver once, and can recognize voices very easily. The boss comes out in the light and is revealed to be Rajani's father! The boss now insists that Madan stays away from his daughter and keeps his mouth shut. Madan agrees, partly because he is acutely aware of their unequal social status, and partly because the job at the Star Club has helped to save his sister's life.

Madan avoids Rajani who pursues him, and they are seen together by a henchman of the boss, who decides to have Madan killed. He forces Rina, the dancer in the club who loves Madan, to take him to a strange hotel room where someone shoots at them in the dark, and Rina is accidentally killed. Madan is arrested for her murder. At the police station, Madan promises to tell Ramesh all he knows providing he meets Rajani once. But her father warns Madan through a decoy, that he must keep his mouth shut, or his sister will be killed. Madan is condemned to death. Ramesh is convinced that Madan is innocent, and feels suspicious of Rajani's father. But Madan will not talk. In desperation, Ramesh raids Rajani's father's desk and comes up with proof of his guilt. But there is still not enough evidence for the court, and Ramesh has to trick the older man into a confession to save Madan's life.

GURU DUTT'S apprenticeship in film making began in the famous Prabhat Studios in Pune. *Baazi* was his first film as a director, and his first big break. Produced by Navketan, then a new concern run by the already established actor Dev Anand who was once Dutt's colleague at Prabhat, the film was a huge success. With a different audience emerging from the lower middle and the working classes in the city, Dutt created a new image of the popular hero. Instead of the traditional characterizations of the sophisticated romantic, the poet, the dreamer, the warrior or the saint, *Baazi* focused on the social outcaste, the loner, the underdog, the urban tough with a soft and true heart hidden below a rough exterior.

Watching the film today one is amazed by the fast pace of the highly complicated story and the finesse with which the plot unfolds. Heavily reminiscent of the Hollywood productions of the times, it portrays a fictitious underworld which is yet convincing in its shadowed interiors where doors open into secret chambers, and men hide their faces in the dark. A sense of threat and of despair hang over Madan throughout the film. Trapped by his circumstances, he moves towards a tragic end in so convincing a manner, that the hurried solution to his predicament in the very last reel, obviously a peace offering to the audience, comes as a surprise. In some of his later films, Dutt was to develop this theme of the tragic hero trapped in time, with far greater passion—films that have made him into the cult figure that he is today, more than twenty years after his death.

BARSAAT (Rain)
b&w, 171 minutes, Hindi, 1949

Production: R.K. Films/ Direction: Raj Kapoor/ Story, screenplay and dialogue: Ramanand Sagar/ Camera: Jal Mistry/ Music: Shankar Jaikishen/ Lyrics: Hasrat Jaipuri, Shailendra/ Art Direction: S.N. Desai/ Editing: G.G. Mayekar/ Sound: Allauddin
Cast: Nargis, Raj Kapoor, Prem Nath, K.N. Singh, Cuckoo, Nimmi, B.M Vyas, Ratan Gaurang, Vishwa Mehra, Dolly Baldeo, Pushpa, Prakash Arora, Master Sandow, Susheela Devi

EVEN THOUGH Pran and Gopal are the best of friends, they are very different by nature. On a holiday in the hills, the casual, easy-going Gopal woos Neela, a poor peasant girl. He leaves her without a backward glance, blithely promising to return with the rains. Neela waits for him in hope. But when, on a similar holiday in Kashmir with Gopal, Pran meets Reshma, the daughter of a poor villager who looks after visiting tourists in a remote bungalow, it is the real thing for Pran. With her father away from home, Reshma must row across a stream to look after the guests in the bungalow. She listens to Pran playing a soulful tune from another land on his violin, and is drawn to him by his innate loneliness.

When her father comes back, he forbids her from crossing the stream again. The poor have nothing but their pride. That too will go if Reshma is used and discarded by a rich man. But at night the violin plays and Reshma steals to the stream. Her father has broken the boat and she ties a thick rope to a pole and wades into the water. In a fit of rage the old man hacks off the rope, and Reshma is swept away.

Pran returns to the city with a broken heart. Gopal returns to the clubs and drinks and dances, uncaring of Neela who waits for him in the hills. The unconscious Reshma is found by a fisherman downstream, a village simpleton who is physically powerful and unaware of his own strength. He nurses Reshma back to health with animal devotion. Thinking that the gods have sent him a beautiful bride, he prepares for the wedding. Reshma is a prisoner in his hut. But one day he takes her to the city to buy clothes and bangles for the wedding. Meanwhile Gopal drags the unwilling Pran to the club where the violinist plays Pran's favourite tune. Unable to bear it, he leaves. As their car comes out of the gate, Reshma rushes in, for she too has heard the tune. But the violin player is not Pran and the fisherman drags her back to her prison.

Watching the sorrowing Pran, Gopal remembers Neela and is confused by this new emotion. He takes Pran off on a holiday, determined to prove that love can be bought and sold. He pushes Pran into a hut in the hills, but Pran discovers the sorrow behind the girl's smile, and cannot take advantage of her. Continuing their journey, they drive past the fisherman's hut where the wedding is about to take place. Hearing the village musicians play a merry tune, Pran remembers Reshma, and loses control of the car. The wedding stops before it has begun, and the fisherman carries the badly wounded Pran into the hut. When he realizes that Reshma is in love with the stranger he has taken in, the fisherman is wild with rage and tries to kill the wounded, unconscious Pran. But a jeep load of policemen make a timely appearance and a massacre is averted.

At the hospital in the city, waiting outside Pran's room, Reshma tells Gopal that true love can never die. Gopal promises that he too will turn a believer if his friend's life is saved. Miraculously Pran survives. In great joy, Gopal takes Pran and Reshma to the hills where Neela waits. From a ledge high up in the hills, Neela watches as Gopal escorts Reshma up the steps of the tourist bungalow, and all hope dies in her. Unaware of their innocent friendship, Neela takes her own life in despair.By the time Gopal goes in search of her, she is dead. He carries her inert form to the funeral pyre with a heavy heart. The fire leaps over Neela's body as the rain clouds gather in the sky.

ENTERING THE popular film industry as a clapper boy in the Bombay Talkies studio, Raj Kapoor became producer, director and actor for his first film, *Aag,* in 1948. The film portrayed an intensely romantic relationship within the framework of a brooding melodrama that seemed ideal for the black and white medium; and though it did not have a great impact, it paved the way for Raj Kapoor's second film, *Barsaat,* which dealt with the same passions dressed in a different narrative, and was a phenomenal success. Raj Kapoor has never really looked back. There have been occasional failures, but none of them could take away from the power and respect he has commanded in the industry for the last forty years. *Barsaat* also established Raj Kapoor and Nargis as the most successful romantic pair the Indian screen had known for a long while.

When Raj Kapoor moved on to other heroines, the complexion of romance changed from the ethereal to the physical. The times had changed as well, and Raj Kapoor had his ear to the ground. The image that Nargis best projected, the exalted, spiritual bond that yet had a promise of great passion, had to give way to the buxom belles of later years and flashing glimpses of bare breasts. "Love Sublime," says the publicity leaflet of *Satyam Shivam Sundaram,* made in 1978, but the visual sensuality in the film is overpowering. Surprisingly though, throughout his career, he has made the same statement over and over again in his films—that true love never dies, that it rises out of sacrificial fires rejuvenated. The naive and sentimental lover has ruled Kapoor's imagination for four decades, and most of that time his audience as well.

Incidentally, the man who wrote the story, screenplay and dialogue for *Barsaat,* Ramanand Sagar, is today himself an established producer and director. Recently he suddenly shot into prominence once again with his blockbuster on television—a costume drama of the Hindu epic *Ramayana.* In spite of its technical incompetence, simplistic presentation and questionable merits, the programme with its bagful of miracles and an array of divinities, provides every Sunday a visual feast for the pious Hindu audience of India.

BHAVNI BHAVAI (A Folk Tale)
colour, 135 minutes, Gujarati, 1980

Production: Sanchar Film Cooperative Society Limited/ Direction and screenplay: Ketan Mehta/ Camera: Krishnakant 'Pummy'/ Music: Gaurang Vyas/ Art Direction: Mira Lakhia, Archana Shah/ Editing: Ramesh Asher
Cast: Naseeruddin Shah, Smita Patil, Mohan Gokhale, Om Puri, Dina Pathak, Suhasini Mulay, Benjamin Gillani, Nimesh Desai, Gopi Desai

A GROUP OF untouchables whose homes have been burnt down the previous night, are migrating with their families. When they stop for the night, an old man gathers the children around him and tells them a tale of long ago, when the untouchables had to tie a broom behind them to erase their offensive footprints, hang a clay spittoon round their neck so that their spit did not soil the earth, wear a third sleeve as a symbol of submission and only unwoven yarn as a headdress.

There was a king in the land, with two wives, but no children. The people were poor and oppressed under his rule. Finally, when the elder queen gave birth to a boy, the younger queen conspired with the astrologer to get rid of the child on the pretext that he was destined to cause the death of his father. But the soldiers who were to kill him, set him afloat in a box, and he was found by an untouchable called Malo who brought him up as his own son and called him Jivo. One day, Malo was discovered trying to fetch water for the child from the clean, upper-caste well in the village. Though he managed to escape, the villagers took their revenge by burning down the dwellings of the untouchables. Meanwhile, the king ordered a well to be dug to propitiate the gods, so that he might get another son. Malo and the other untouchables started digging the well.

The years passed, and they went on digging, but no water came in the well. Little Jivo grew up to be a handsome lad, lazy and carefree, spoilt by his doting foster parents. The younger queen discovered his identity and once again conspired to kill him. The king was told that to get water in the well, a human sacrifice was necessary, and that Jivo was the gods' chosen sacrifice. Bewildered and scared, Jivo nevertheless demanded that he would let them catch him alive only if the untouchables were allowed to dress like normal human beings from now on. The king was forced to agree, and the helpless Jivo was brought for the sacrifice. But at the last minute, the conspiracy was revealed, Jivo was saved, and it all ended happily.

But there are few happy endings in real life, and one of the homeless young untouchables in the group offers a more disturbing conclusion: The conspiracy is not revealed in time, and Jivo is beheaded, but no water comes in the well. Maddened with rage, Malo jumps into the well, and curses the king with his dying breath. His blood releases a flood in the well that washes away the evil king and his courtiers.

KETAN MEHTA'S fascination with the Bhavai form, which contains elements from all the performing arts—music, drama, mime, dance—led to the making of his first film, *Bhavni Bhavai* , literally, the Bhavai of Life. Produced by a cooperative which Mehta formed with a few other graduates of the Film and Television Institute of India, the film won two national awards and eight state awards. It was selected for the festival at the Museum of Modern Art in New York, and received the Unesco Club Human Rights Award at the Nantes Festival in France.

The origins of the Bhavai can be traced back to Asait Thakore, a Brahmin from Gujarat, who was excommunicated for having shared a meal with a member of the lower caste. He later settled down among the lower caste peasants, and married members of his family into the community. The *targalas* , born of this union, finally became the traditional performers of the Bhavai, folk plays written by Asait as an offering to the Mother Goddess, Amba.

With his unhappy encounter with Hindu orthodoxy, Asait created a new dramatic tradition outside the closed precincts of the palace and the temple. Through the years, with popular interaction, the religious sentiments in the Bhavai plays lost their significance, to be replaced by a social and historical content which has become increasingly important. In later years Asait's authorship of all the three hundred odd Bhavai plays has been disputed, but it is more than probable that he was the first to gather the scattered plays together, and give them a cohesive character.

Using the same faces to enact the characters in the fairy tale as well as the real story, moving back and forth between reality and illusion, time past and time present, *Bhavni Bhavai* documents the historical continuity of social exploitation with a deep sense of outrage. The traditional dramatic form has been bent to suit the language of contemporary cinema, with the participatory character of a Bhavai performance transformed into Brechtian distancing. Verse and song, speed, rhythm and colour, noisily build towards an angry climax. The film ends with the dispassionate voice of an anonymous newsreader, listing out the statistics of violence and exploitation, but for the viewer, the reality remains Malo's last curse: Today the deluge will come!

BHUMIKA   (The Role)
colour, 142 minutes, Hindi, 1977

Production: Blaze Film Enterprises/ Direction: Shyam Benegal/ Screenplay: Girish Karnad, Satyadev Dubey, Shyam Benegal/ Camera: Govind Nihalani/ Music: Vanraj Bhatia/ Art Direction: Shama Zaidi/ Editing: Bhanudas
Cast: Smita Patil, Anant Nag, Amrish Puri, Naseeruddin Shah, Sulabha Deshpande, Kulbhushan Kharbanda, B.V. Karanth, Amol Palekar

USHA'S grandmother is a noted singer who was a courtesan in her youth. One of Usha's few pleasures is to learn music from the old woman. Otherwise her life is confined within the strange and unhappy surroundings of a courtesan's family in the Maharashtra of the thirties. Her mother, herself an illegitimate offspring, is married to an alcoholic, and finds her dubious fulfilment in a relationship with Keshav, a family friend and benefactor, who takes more than a casual interest in the spirited child. When Usha's father dies, Keshav steps into the vacuum. He brings the family to Bombay in the hope that little Usha, with her musical talent, will get a break in the singing, dancing, talking pictures that have recently taken Bombay by storm.

Usha grows with the nascent industry. The first man she is drawn to is her co-star, the dashing, handsome, self-centered Rajan. To find stability, and in defiance of her mother, Usha marries Keshav and decides to quit acting. But the entire family depends on her earnings, and Keshav insists that she continues working. With her grandmother dead, and pressured by her weak, grasping, jealous husband and her resentful mother, Usha finds life at home stifling in spite of her little daughter. She becomes more and more vulnerable, and with her undefined needs and frustrations as a woman, runs to Rajan who has no intention of committing himself.

A rising young director, Sunil Verma, now becomes part of the unreal glamour of her life. Usha gets pregnant; her husband, accusing her of adultery, forces her to abort. Sunil and Usha enter into a melodramatic suicide pact in which they both dupe each other. When Usha wakes up next morning, Sunil has vanished.

Usha leaves her husband and becomes the mistress of a wealthy, middle-aged man whose immense authority seems to her a firm basis on which to build her life. But Kale's feudal estate, where she is totally accepted and given the respect of his family, including that of Kale's neglected paralysed wife, becomes a prison for Usha's restless spirit. True to tradition, she cannot be seen outside the house. Usha writes secretly to her husband who comes with the police to rescue her. Back in Bombay, her daughter, now married and settled, offers her a home. Keshav requests her to give him another chance. Rajan telephones, insisting on picking up the threads of their past relationship. But Usha decides to face her future alone.

BENEGAL made *Bhumika* when he was already established as an important director, known for his unusual themes and his repertory of serious acting talents. During the ten years after *Bhumika,* his popularity among serious film viewers and his place in the parallel cinema reached a peak before taking a downward swing with the entry of new and younger film makers in the field. But *Bhumika* was a result of a happy combination of talents. Benegal wrote his script with the help of two men who dominated the Kannada and Hindi stage as playwrights, actors, and directors. His music director was a versatile talent, with experience in Indian as well as western musical scores for the theatre as well as film. For *Bhumika,* he delved into the popular Nautanki tradition of Maharashtra, participatory and folk based urban musicals which were very popular in the thirties and forties. With his art director, Benegal recreated the atmosphere of the new sound studios of those days with great verisimilitude.

Bhumika was also one the early films of Naseerudding Shah, now accepted as a major actor on the Hindi screen. But it was Smita Patil, whose portrayal of Usha from bewildered youth to maturity and wisdom will be long remembered as one of the landmarks of Indian cinema. Among the serious film makers who admired and utilized her talent were Satyajit Ray, G. Aravindan and Ketan Mehta and Kumar Shahani. A great favourite among the directors of the parallel cinema, Smita who recently died tragically at the height of her career, had also become a star of the popular Hindi screen where, however, she always seemed a misfit.

The role Smita plays in *Bhumika,* is based on the real-life story of Hansa Wadkar, a star of the Marathi folk theatre and cinema of the forties. If her biography provided the basic material for Usha's chequered career, it also gave Benegal a glimpse into the predicament of a woman straining against the boundaries of a convention ridden society with her store of talent and a restless spirit, a woman who needed security as much as she needed her freedom.

BHUVAN SHOME
b&w, 96 minutes, Hindi, 1969

Production: Mrinal Sen Productions/ Direction and Screenplay: Mrinal Sen/ Story: Bonophul/ Camera: K.K. Mahajan/ Music: Vijay Raghava Rao/ Editing: Gangadhar Naskar
Cast: Suhasini Mulay, Utpal Dutt, Sadhu Meher, Shekhar Chatterjee

BHUVAN SHOME is a true representative of the bureaucratic traditions of the Raj. A senior officer in the railways in the late forties, and raised in colonial mores, he is strict, self-righteous and completely lacking in the human failing of laughter. A stern disciplinarian, he sacked his own son for "gross negligence of duty" when he was found guilty of a minor misdemeanor. But being a dedicated civil servant is a tiresome job, and bored with his routine, Shome decides to take a duck-shooting holiday. He plans to go to a remote shoreline of Gujarat where there would be opportunities for bird watching as well. As if to atone for his weakness in seeking a holiday, he issues orders at the last minute to sack Jadav Patel, a young ticket collector, for accepting a bribe.

For the middle-aged, lonely widower, his sudden entry into a carefree new world is fraught with discomfort. Accustomed to the dreary confines of his office, Shome treads warily in his new environment. He bears the hazards of a speedy bullock-cart drive with fortitude, listens perforce to the homely philosophy of its driver, makes an undignified dash for a tree faced by a marauding buffalo, and meets Gauri—casual, graceful, vivacious—a cheeky young village belle who worms her way into his heart. He soon finds out that by some absurd coincidence, she is the wife of Jadav Patel, the heinous acceptor of bribes. But her youthful exuberance, her novel approach to weighty moral issues, her mischievous smile, all combine to become the first humanizing influence in Shome's life.

When he returns, Bhuvan Shome has changed beyond repair. Alone in his office room, he suddenly indulges in most uncharacteristic boisterousness. Though the slowly settling snowstorm of boring official documents that Shome has flung around his desk and the sense of liberation he has achieved from his first irrational act remains hidden behind the four walls of his room, Jadav Patel's inexplicable reprieve becomes a nine day's wonder in the railways.

HARBINGER OF the "new Indian cinema,"*Bhuvan Shome* was one of the first low-budget films, made by a director outside the mainstream, that destroyed the myth that the Indian audience asks for nothing but fairy tales. With a boring middle-aged bureaucrat as its hero, who has absolutely no romantic inclinations towards the heart-warming young heroine of the film, *Bhuvan Shome* was greeted by the masses with encouraging enthusiasm.

For Mrinal Sen it was no flash in the pan. This was his ninth feature film. He had already established himself as a serious director, with seven films in Bengali and one in Oriya before he took on the challenge of the Hindi screen. Four years before *Bhuvan Shome*, Sen had made *Akash Kusum* in Bengali, where his Walter Mitty like hero entangles himself in a series of lies till all his dreams crash and he walks away a sadder and wiser young man. *Akash Kusum* marked a definite change in Sen's style, from the straightforward narrative to a whimsical, playful story-telling, released from the constraints of time and space, where the narrative illusion is deliberately broken by a seemingly irrational editing pattern.

In *Bhuvan Shome* the style gains maturity, adding to the nuances of the protagonist's rueful awareness of the humour and pathos of his predicament. Writing about the riotous last sequence, Sen says: "It is difficult to find any earthly logic to support the bureaucrat's action in this concluding sequence unless you grant Mr. Shome a certain touch of insanity. As you examine the sequence, you will see that the same can be said about the editing pattern, all erratic and illogical.

"But all this has been very much planned, all done with utmost care and precision. And this is what I believe Jaques Tati meant by that delightful expression 'inspired nonsense.'

"I, as the maker of the film, indulge in such nonsense as much as the protagonist does....I wish someone were there to watch and see how, twenty years ago, I also had a mad kick of an experience not much dissimilar to my protagonist's....I wonder if Utpal Dutt who invented his action all by himself also re-enacted one of his private experiences."

Utpal Dutt, Bhuvan Shome in the film, is a well-known stage director and playwright, with his own repertory which has had a long and successful career on the Bengali stage, presenting Bengali classics, original plays and adaptations from modern western drama. Suhasini Mulay, young Gauri in the film, did not become a star in spite of her obvious beauty and personality, but after training in Canada, went on to make her own documentaries on controversial contemporary themes. She is occasionally seen in films by other directors of the new Indian cinema movement.

BOBBY
colour, 168 minutes, Hindi, 1973

Production: R.K. Films/ Direction and editing: Raj Kapoor/ Story: K.A. Abbas/ Screenplay: K.A. Abbas, V.P. Sathe/ Dialogue: Jainendra Jain/ Camera: Radhu Karmakar/ Music: Laxmikant Pyarelal/ Art Direction: Rangraj/ Sound: Allauddin
Cast: Rishi Kapoor, Dimple Kapadia, Pran, Premnath, Sonia Sahni, Durga Khote, Farida Jalal, Aruna Irani, Prem Chopra, Pinchoo Kapoor, Piloo Wadia, Jagdish Raj, Shashi Kiran

RAJ NATH, the neglected son of a millionaire father, returns home to Bombay after completing his studies in a boarding school. At his eighteenth birthday party, which is really a collection of his father's business contacts, he has a brief glimpse of a very young girl. He soon discovers that the girl is Bobby, the sixteen-year-old granddaughter of Mrs Braganza, his old governess who now lives with her widower son, a wealthy fisherman, in a fishing village near the sea. Raj's friendship with Bobby soon grows into a deeper relationship which they both recognize as something precious in spite of their youth and lack of experience. But Raj's father is extremely suspicious of this youthful romance. Hoping to nip it off in the bud, Nath asks Raj to invite the Braganzas to his home. Bobby's father who hides a warm heart under a simple, rough exterior, is shocked when, after sending the children out of the room, Nath accuses him of trapping his innocent son for the sake of his inheritance. Next day, Nath goes to Braganza's home and insults him further by offering him money in exchange for his son's freedom. Furious, Braganza tells Raj to keep away from his daughter.

Unaware of the developments between Braganza and his father, Raj is bewildered by this sudden rejection. He confronts his father at home and learns that as a minor, his marriage with Bobby can be disputed in court. Realizing that in a little over two years Bobby will be nineteen and he twenty-one, Raj is willing to wait, but soon finds out that his father has arranged a marriage between him and the mentally disturbed daughter of a very rich businessman. In a panic, he takes his motorbike and runs away to Goa where Bobby has been sent with her grandmother to their family home.

Mrs Braganza is shocked and distressed to learn that Raj has actually run away from home. She knows that her son will be furious if he finds Raj with

Bobby. She also loves Raj and fears his parents enough to know the consequences of giving him shelter. It is a hard choice, but she manages to lock Bobby and Raj into separate rooms, and sends off a wire to Bombay. In the night, while Mrs Braganza dozes off, Raj gets out by breaking a window and climbs into Bobby's room. Together they escape on the motorbike, till finding the police after them, they let the bike take a fatal toss from a hill road; but the police are not taken in by the ruse.

Meanwhile, refusing to believe that Raj is with Bobby in his Goa home, and promising to murder his daughter if that is the case, Braganza goes with Nath and the police to Goa. When they discover both the children have fled, Braganza turns on Nath with the accusation that it is his son who has kidnapped Bobby, not the other way round. While Nath accompanies the police, Braganza goes searching for them independently, and finds them in the hands of a group of ruffians who have seen Nath's advertisement in the papers and want the reward. He charges at them like a bull and is about to win the battle when one of the ruffians gets hold of Raj and holds a knife at his throat. Braganza now takes a beating, while he desperately pleads for the life of the boy in exchange for his own.

Coming upon them with the police, Nath overhears Braganza's words. But by the time the ruffians have been finally subdued, the children have vanished again, and the two fathers have no time for a reconciliation. Raj and Bobby, who believe that once their fathers get to them they will be separated again, leap into a narrow creek and are swept away by the current. Nath and Braganza dive into the rough waters and while Braganza rescues Raj, Nath grabs hold of Bobby and crawls to safety on another rock. Braganza shouts, "Your son is safe!" "And my daughter is safe too!" shouts back Nath holding Bobby close, "*My* daughter!"

CRITIC ELLIOT STEIN once described *Bobby* as "a charming commercial film, a quality confection, a tasty all-India bonbon." With its breezy narrative style, the freshness and innocence of its two young protagonists, its variety of bathing suits, its rambunctious humour and the vivacity of its musical score, Bobby was a runaway success, to be imitated a number of times but never to be paralleled.

The rough, tough fisherman's role is played by Premnath, the dissolute Pran of *Barsaat*. Raj Kapoor's son Rishi had appeared earlier in the role of the hero as a chubby adolescent in his father's magnum opus, *Mera Naam Joker* in 1970. Three years later, in *Bobby*, he is a handsome young lad who has not yet lost his innocence, but already possesses a great deal of the Kapoor charm. Though he followed *Bobby* up with a number of fairly successful films, Rishi Kapoor's acting talents have never been fully exploited. Today he is no longer a major star, his most recent big banner film being Ramesh Sippy's *Sagar*, an elaborate and costly production, where though he wins the heroine in the end, his role is less interesting than that of his screen rival who steals the show.

Sagar brought together Dimple Kapadia and Rishi Kapoor after almost one and a half decades in the hope of reviving and cashing in on the *Bobby* magic. But it was nowhere near as successful in the box-office. Dimple Kapadia, a Kapoor find whose buxom unworldliness had charmed a whole generation of

Indian youth, disappeared from the screen soon after, eloping with the reigning superstar, Rajesh Khanna, while she was still a minor. Subsequently, after two daughters and a divorce, and years spent away from the studio floors, she has fairly recently begun trying to revive her career.

CHAKRA (The Vicious Circle)
colour, 140 minutes, Hindi, 1980

Production: Neo Films/ Direction and Screenplay: Rabindra Dharmaraj/ Story: Jaywant Dalvi/ Camera: Barun Mukherjee/ Music: Hridaynath Mangeshkar/ Art Direction: Bansi Chandragupta/ Editing: Bhanudas
Cast: Smita Patil, Naseeruddin Shah, Kulbhushan Kharbanda, Ranjit Choudhuri, Anjali Paigankar, Savita Bajaj

AMMA AND her son Benwa live in a slum in the teeming city of Bombay. They fled here after Amma's husband had killed the village moneylender for trying to rape her. But bad luck dogged them, and her husband was shot dead by the guards, while stealing tin sheets from the railway yard to build a shack for his family. Now Benwa grows up in the shadow of one of Amma's lovers, Looka, pimp, illicit distiller, all-purpose crook. He has quite a way with the slum dwellers, and Benwa follows him around, watching in awe as he preens and whores, gets drunk and tells tall tales.

Amma who started her life in Bombay as a labourer in a road building site, wants her son to lead a clean life, and Benwa tries his hand at the job of a shoe-black. But he cannot retain it in the face of local rivalry. Meanwhile Looka is externed from Bombay, Amma settles down with another lover, Anna, a truck driver, and gets pregnant by him. Benwa marries a girl Looka had found for him.

Then Looka reappears again, striken with syphilis, a shadow of his former self. In search of drugs to alleviate the pain, Looka kills a chemist and hides in Amma's hut. When the police track him down, Looka and Benwa are severely beaten and arrested. Amma has a miscarriage and is too ill to look after Benwa's young bride who is left alone and helpless. Anna comes back next morning and finds his home in ruins. In the meanwhile the municipal authorities decide that the slum is an ugly spot on the face of the city and a source of constant trouble.The site is condemned and the bulldozers arrive to raze the shacks to the ground.

CHAKRA was the only feature film made by its director, who died at the age of 33 in 1981, soon after his film had received critical acclaim during its showing at the International Film Festival in Delhi. Dharmaraj came to film making with varied experience in media and equally varied experience of life. He belonged to the generation of the sixties, to the band of "flower children" who emerged out of cultural exposure to the west at a time when most of India was still locked within its own spatial confines. After his sojourn in war-devastated Vietnam, his short span in Delhi as newsreader for the national radio, and a stay in a magical old penthouse in Bombay where the wall clock had stopped at ten minutes to three, Dharmaraj wandered back to his roots in the south of India. He joined the Primitive Pentecostal Church, abandoned his tinted glasses with their thick lenses, and saw the world in the light of faith. It did not last, for he soon returned to the big bad city of Bombay, this time to become a highly successful advertising film maker, helped by a course he had taken years earlier in advanced film and video techniques at the University of California.

Dharmaraj's greatest talent was for tasting life, and *Chakra* is a bitter-sweet chunk of Indian existence that he shares with his reluctant audience. The film got Smita Patil, as Amma, the National award for the best actress of the year, and was viewed by the international audience in Cannes and Locarno. The responses were predictably mixed. Many critics found in the relentless squalor of the slums and the naturalistic treatment of its doomed inhabitants an unbearable expression of middle-class guilt, an intellectual exercise in experiencing the wretched and the damned first hand. Others, like Jay Scott of *Globe & Mail*, Toronto, responded with enthusiasm: "Reports of Indian poverty, like nuclear survival scenarios or pictures of Auschwitz, have become part of the informational content of our lives—insane aspects of contemporary existence we accept with equanimity to remain sane.

"*Chakra* humanizes those reports by giving the statistics flesh; humanizes woebegone photographs of starving Indian children by giving them personalities; and humanizes a culture we may have thought is more alien than it actually is by illustrating that hope, love, pain and grief are identical, regardless of region or religion.

"It does this with a sense of humour that is nothing short of astounding— *Chakra*...is also, for long periods of time, a satiric comedy dealing with rebellious and lazy teenagers (adolescent angst and arrogance are no strangers to this strangest of all subcontinents) and with their rebellious and lazy elders.

"Those who see the poor as inherently noble will find *Chakra* tough going: Dharmaraj insists that the single thing that separates his subjects from the rest of humanity is the fact that their living conditions are inhuman. In all other ways, the people caught in this vicious cycle are not inherently anything different."

CHANDIDAS
b&w, 118 min, Bengali, 1932

Production: New Theatres/ Direction and screenplay: Debaki Bose/ Camera: Nitin Bose/ Music: Raichand Boral/ Sound: Mukul Bose
Cast: Durgadas Banerjee, Krishna Chandra Dey, Amar Mullick, Manoranjan Bhattacharya, Dhirendranath Banerjee, Chani Datta, Umashashi, Sunila

CHANDIDAS was a Vaishnavite poet saint of the sixteenth century. Born in a Brahmin family, he belonged to a society ridden with religious bigotry and strong Brahminical authoritarianism. Though he was the disciple of a Brahmin priest who believed in harsh and ascetic principles, Chandidas's love for poetry inevitably came in the way of his religious devotion. He was also a bit of a romantic, and spent hours idling near the river, where Rami, the washerman's daughter came to wash clothes. Rami, the daughter of a low-caste, was also a young widow, and barred on both counts from any social intercourse with a man like Chandidas. But she was a cheeky young thing all the same, and had a divine voice. Chandidas would sit listening to her songs for hours. Rami was aware of the young Brahmin's interest in her, and was herself a great admirer of his poetry. Inevitably, they were drawn to each other.

In the closed-in community of the village, their romance could not remain a secret. Also, the local rich landowner, Bijoynarayan, himself a connoisseur of women, had his eyes on Rami. But Rami despised him for his double standards. Bijoynarayan, being an upper-caste and rich man, would not share a meal with the low-castes, nor would he contaminate his body with their touch. But when it came to women, his greed would overcome all social taboos. Rami's rejection and her outspoken condemnation of his behaviour roused Bijoynarayan's ire. He now made it his mission to persecute both Rami and her community, and Chandidas's romance became a major scandal. Though the strength of Rami's personality sustained Chandidas for a while against the attacks of the Brahmins, he was still in awe of the temple priest, whose overpowering hold on the young man finally led to his denouncing Rami in public and agreeing to perform a religious ceremony in the temple to repent for his past sins.

Rami, refusing to believe that Chandidas would actually disown her, battled with Bijoynarayan's hirelings to reach the temple on time. Distraught and bleeding with wounds inflicted upon her by the landowner's men, she confronted Chandidas in the presence of his religious mentor. Chandidas, believing in a more just and loving god in place of the harsh divinity offered by the priest of the temple, renounced his religious bindings, dissociated himself from the orthodox Brahminical order, and left the village with Rami.

B.N. SIRCAR, the founder of New Theatres, was the pioneering spirit behind the newly emerging cinema movement in the Bengal of the thirties, and known for his special ability to put the right pieces together. Debaki Bose was one of his recruits. A nationalist, steeped in the Vaishnava tradition and its music, he was chosen, even as a relative newcomer in the field, to direct the story of the legendary Vaishnavite singer-poet from Bengal—Chandidas. The film ran for a record sixty-four weeks, and not only established Bose as a front-ranking director, but also sent the distributors flocking to New Theatres for the next few years.

Its enormous popularity in Bengal led to the making of a Hindi version two years later, directed by Nitin Bose, the cameraman of the first *Chandidas*. With his musical leanings, Bose made the film into a lyric, devotional drama, with a large number of songs in it based on the works of Chandidas. His novel approach to background music led to a new understanding of its use in Indian cinema. No longer was it a mere filler between dialogue and events;

instead, it took over the mood of the moment, intensifying what was being said.

But looking at it today, one tends to feel impatient with its slow pace, and the stilted, unreal style of acting, with every word enunciated with unnecessary clarity, even though the cast contained some of the most famous stage and screen performers of the time. That, however, does not undermine the historical importance of the film, nor does it reduce the significance of its progressive stand in a country where even today caste wars are not unusual and untouchability is a major social evil.

CHANDRALEKHA
b&w, 207 minutes, Tamil, 1948

Production: Gemini Pictures Pvt. Ltd/ Direction: S.S. Vasan/ Story, screenplay and dialogue: Gemini's Story Department, K.J. Mahadevan, Subbu, Sangu, Kittu, Naina/ Camera: Kamal Ghosh/ Music: S. Rajeswara Rao/ Lyrics: Papanasam Sivan, Kothamangalam Subbu/ Dance: Jaya Shankar, Mrs Rainbird, Natanam Nataraj, Niranjala Devi/ Fencing: Stunt Somu/ Art Direction: A.K. Sekar/ Editing: Chandru/ Sound: C.E. Biggs
Cast: T.R. Rajkumari, M.K. Radha, Ranjan, Sundari Bai, N.S. Krishnan, T.A. Mathuram, L. Narayana Rao, V.N. Janaki, T.E. Krishnamachariar, Subbaiah Pillai, N. Seetharaman, Pottai Krishnamoorthy

IN A FICTITIOUS kingdom, at an unknown point in history, lives a king with two sons, Virsingh and Sasank. Going past a village on his horse one day, Virsingh encounters a village maiden, Chandralekha, and promptly falls in love. Back in the palace the king decides to abdicate in favour of Virsingh, which enrages Sasank who, with his band of toughs, takes to looting and plundering. In the chaos that follows, Chandralekha's father is hurt and dies. Left to her own devices, Chandralekha joins a band of travelling musicians. Sasank's men raid their caravan, and Sasank demands that Chandralekha must dance for him. She does, but only at the crack of a whip.

A plucky girl, she finally eludes her guard and manages to escape. But meanwhile, Sasank mounts a surprise attack on his brother and takes him prisoner. The fleeing Chandralekha sees Sasank's troops galloping past, with Virsingh as their captive. She follows them and hides when they take the prince into a cave and block the mouth with a huge boulder. Chandralekha finds a circus troupe moving down a road nearby. She manages to win them over to her side, and with the help of their elephants, removes the boulder and frees Virsingh. The two fugitives now join the circus to hide from Sasank's men.

Sasank takes over the palace and throws his parents in the dungeon. He crowns himself king, watched by a sullen crowd who applaud only when the soldiers nudge them. He then sends his spy to search out the beautiful dancing girl. The man spots her in the circus, and Chandralekha is saved only at the nick of time by Virsingh. They escape once more and join a band of gypsys.

But while Virsingh goes looking for assistance, Chandralekha is discovered by Sasank's men. In the palace, Sasank tries to woo Chandralekha who pretends to faint everytime he comes near her. Finally one of her friends from the circus come to Sasank in the guise of a gypsy healer, and claims that she can heal Chandralekha. Behind locked doors a quick conference takes place between the two girls. Sasank is pleased to find Chandralekha miraculously cured and even ready to accept him as a bridegroom. In return he gladly agrees to her request for a Drum Dance to celebrate the royal wedding.

Huge drums are arranged in rows in front of the palace. Chandralekha joins the dancers, and Sasank is charmed by her performance. Then the drums open and from within them swarms of soldiers appear and attack Sasank's men. The women rush into the palace and overpowering the guard manning the bridge over the moat, lower the bridge and Virsingh and his men troop in. Sasank manages to drag Chandralekha away and locks her in a room in the palace.But when he comes out of the room, his brother is waiting for him. Now Virshingh and Sasank match their swords against each other. After a long, arduous battle, Sasank is overpowered and imprisoned. Virsingh releases his parents and takes over as the new king. Chandralekha becomes his queen and the people of the kingdom share enthusiastically in their happiness.

NEARLY THREE and a half hours of spectacle and romance: the audience certainly got their money's worth from *Chandralekha*. Song and dance, romance and buxom belles, horsemanship and trapeze work, fierce battles and dazzling swordplay—all part of the package prepared with so much care by the man called S.S. Vasan, the man behind the highly successful Gemini Studios in Madras. Building his own film company literally on the charred remains of a lesser venture, Vasan got through the war years with a variety of films, biding his time for a more ambitious effort. *Chandralekha* was planned on a mammoth scale, with massive sets, glittering costumes, and even an extraordinary promotion campaign. The investment was huge for the times. The film was made in two versions, Hindi and Tamil, and proved to be the first South Indian film to penetrate the Northern market successfully in over a decade. For all its unreal story, and incredible spectacle, *Chandralekha* has some surprisingly well simulated battle scenes, along with a demonstration of excellent swordsmanship by the two princely brothers. In fact, the last confrontation of the brothers, with their swords locked in battle and the swaying chandelier above, brings *Prisoner of Zenda* unmistakably to mind. Many of the "action" sequences were visually well-conceived, and appear to be rather ill-matched with the triviality of the romantic or the comic sequences. The drum dance was, of course, the *raison d'etre*, and was executed to perfection. The sets, the choreography, the costumes must have provided a gigantic management challenge, but no less than that of filming and editing the sequence. The dramatic crescendo of the soldiers rushing out of the drums, the women letting the bridge down over the moat, and the evil prince Sasank leaping over the drums to hold the beautiful Chandralekha hostage, all become one sweeping, noisy, tumultuous experience leading up to the magnificent confrontation between the brothers, where time stands still and silence reigns while the swords cross.

CHARULATA
b&w, 103 minutes, Bengali, 1964

Production: R.D. Bansal/ Direction, screenplay and music: Satyajit Ray/ Story: Rabindranath Tagore/ Camera: Subrata Mitra/ Art Direction: Bansi Chandragupta/ Editing: Dulal Dutta
Cast: Soumitra Chattopadhyay, Madhavi Mukherjee, Sailen Mukherjee, Geetali Roy, Shyamal Ghosal

IT IS 1879, a time when the Bengal Renaissance is reaching its peak, and liberal philosphies of the West are breaking into the stronghold of feudal orthodoxy. Charulata, the childless wife of a wealthy young Bengali intellectual, lives in seclusion in her husband's spacious and ornate home, while winds of change are blowing the cobwebs away outside. Her husband, Bhupati, is himself inspired by the gospels of Mill and Bentham, and spends his inherited wealth in the pursuit of freedom and equality through a liberal political weekly in English that he edits, called*The Sentinel*. But he has no time for Charu, who has little to do in the home which is run like a well-oiled machine by a fleet of old retainers. She embroiders, reads Bengali novels, and peers out of the closed shutters of her window at the strange world outside. Bhupati, who senses her boredom, invites Charu's elder brother Umapada and wife Manda to live with them in Calcutta.

Umapada keeps busy managing the running of the magazine and the printing press, and Manda with her foolish chatter is no company for the sensitive and intelligent Charu. At this point arrives Amal, Bhupati's young cousin with literary ambitions. With Bhupati's encouragement, a close friendship grows between Amal and Charu, based on their common interest in contemporary Bengali literature, a friendship that slowly moves towards rivalry, for Amal the mentor finds his pupil soon racing ahead of him. For Charu the intellectual sparring hides a deeper attachment and a need which she is herself not fully aware of, and one which her society, only too slowly emerging from its chains, will not sanction.

Meanwhile Umapada, who is a petty crook, embezzles and escapes with funds put at his disposal for running the press. It shatters the upright Bhupati who confesses his hurt to Amal, admitting that now Amal is the only man he can trust. Amal, aware of the nuances of his relationship with Charu, feels decidedly guilty in relation to Bhupati. He also begins to feel discomfited by Charu's intellectual superiority which he himself has helped to nurture. Taking the easy way out, he leaves unannounced, and it is Charu who now feels betrayed. Though she hides her disappointment, she gives in to her grief when news comes of Amal's decision to marry and go away to England. Accidentally coming into the room, Bhupati realizes the truth about Charu's feelings and is bewildered by it. He rushes out of the house and roams aimlessly in his carriage in an effort to understand the implications of his new knowledge. When he returns, they both make a hesitant effort to reach out to each other. But their extended hands remain frozen in a tentative gesture of compromise that can only confirm their inner separation.

CHARULATA remains a triumph of Ray's craftsmanship and genius and one of the most important achievements among all his work. Apart from the film's visual beauty, structural perfection and conceptual purity, *Charulata* has also a great number of incidental points of interest. For an Indian audience, the ambiguity of Charu's relationship with Amal is easily comprehensible. In the traditional Indian home, where the younger brother of the husband is often closer by age and accessibility to the wife (an Indian family makes no distinction between a cousin and a brother), the relationship between the two has always been an ambiguous one, an easy friendship tinged with the possibility of an uneasy and illicit emotion which lends piquancy to it. In some parts of the country there has also been the tradition of marrying off the elder brother's widow to the younger brother. The complexities of such a situation were exploited in a well-known novel by Rajinder Singh Bedi, *Ek Chadar Maili si,* which has been recently made into a not too interesting film. Tagore's own story has a reflection of his personal traumatic relationship with an older brother's wife, who committed suicide at an early age. With her the youthful Tagore had shared the same interests that bring Amal and Charu together.

Tagore ends his short story at a point when Bhupati is about to go away for a while, leaving Charu behind. Charu, who at first pleads with him to take her on the journey, accepts her final isolation. When Bhupati takes pity on her and agrees to take her with him, she refuses to go. In the film (and this is not a comparison between two art forms, but an interesting juxtaposition of two perceptions), Ray's Charu and Bhupati do make an attempt to come together. But their extended hands are frozen in time before they can meet.

The exquisite interiors created by Bansi Chandragupta were among the best of his work, as was the subtle use of lights and the sensitivity of Subrata Mitra's camera (this was unfortunately one of his last films with Ray before the master decided to virtually take over this function as well). The costumes, the faces, the detailed structuring of the film, jointly created an all-time classic, a superbly colourful piece of monochrome cinema. *Charulata* has the quality of a miniature painting, where minute details are revealed by a stroke of the finest brush, and the unspoken is made visual by a mere suggestion.

Says Chidananda Dasgupta (filmmaker, critic, and pioneer of the Indian film society movement) of the characters who enact the drama of *Charulata*: "Their lack of conscious knowledge of what is happening inside them gives them a certain nobility of innocence; it is in their awakening that their tragedy lies. Amal, the younger man, is the first to realize the truth; for Charu it is an imperceptible movement from the unconscious to the conscious in which it is difficult to mark out the stages; for the husband, it is a sudden, stark, unbelievable revelation of truth. All three wake up, as it were, into the twentieth century, the age of self-consciousness. The rhythm of the unfolding is so gentle and true, that there is no sense of shock even for the conservative Indian, although Ray's film is as daring for the wider audience as Tagore's story was for the intelligentsia of its day." [*Film Quarterly,* 1965.]

CHEMEEN (The Wrath of the Sea)
colour, 140 minutes, Malayalam, 1965

Production: Kanmani Films/ Direction: Ramu Kariat/ Camera: Marcus Bartley, U. Rajagopal/ Music: Salil Chowdhury/ Editing: Hrishikesh Mukherjee, K.D. George
Cast: Sathyan, Sheela, Madhu, Kottarakkara Sreedharan Nair, S.P. Pillai, Adoor Bhavani

THE SEA dominates the lives of the fisherfolk of Kerala. Drawing their sustenance from it, they love and fear its mysterious depths, where lives the goddess of the sea, Katalamma, the all-seeing arbiter of their destinies. Her bounty goes to the good; for the evil she unleashes her ferocious wrath to destroy them. Chembankunju, a fisherman, lives with his wife and his two daughters in one of the many coastal villages of Kerala. With no capital and a surfeit of ambition, he arranges to buy a boat and a net with the help of Pareekutty, a young Muslim trader, in return for which he promises to sell to the younger man the fish hauled by the boat. The family prospers, but the old man gets more and more greedy. Money becomes the sole object in his life. Meanwhile, Chembankunju's elder daughter Karuthamma is attracted to Pareekutty's innocence and honesty. Dreamy-eyed and a bit of a loner, he is different from any other young man in the village. But he is a Muslim, and she knows she can never marry him. Yet the tenderness that flows between them cannot be denied. Kruthamma's mother warns her of the need to preserve the traditions of their community. Violation of her codes will only draw the wrath of the goddess on them.

As more and more money collects in his box, Chembankunju stops selling his haul to Pareekutty, driving him gradually to bankruptcy. Unhappy at home, Karuthamma accepts the inevitable, and agrees to marry Palani, an orphan boy from another village along the shore. Her selfish father wants her to stay and look after him while her mother is ill, but determined to be a good wife, she leaves with Palani. Her mother dies, and Chembankunju loses no time in marrying again, this time a widow with a son. Neglected by her father and ill-treated by her stepmother, Karuthamma's younger sister finds solace from the other villagers whom Chembankunju has alienated with his greed and miserly habits. Discovering that his second wife has given money from his box to her son, he beats her and drives her out. He also throws out his younger daughter, and as his fortune takes a downward plunge, slowly slips into madness.

On another shore, Karuthamma tries to build a happy home. The people in her husband's village come to know of her friendship with Pareekutty, and decide to ostracize them. Palani, who loves his wife and has faith in her, builds a hut at a remote spot on the shore and takes to fishing alone. Karuthamma gives birth to a baby. Pareekutty, penniless, heartbroken and alone, pines for Karuthamma. One night, when Palani takes his fishing boat out to sea, a storm is brewing and a shark circles the waters. But the shore is calm, and when Karuthamma comes out of her hut, she sees, as if in a dream, Pareekutty waiting for her in the moonlight. She goes into his arms. On the rough sea, the shark plays with Palani till he is drawn into a whirlpool. In the morning, on the calm shore lie the bodies of Karuthamma and Pareekurtty. The unforgiving sea has claimed the sinners.

RAMU KARIAT, who died young, managed to express in *Chemeen* an essentially local reality in terms that were universal enough to be appreciated by a diverse audience. Though totally different from anything that the South Indian cinema had produced till then, the film was a great success at the box-office. Supported by critical acclaim, the film was also the recipient of the highest National Award for the year, the only film from the South to receive such recognition till Rama Reddy's *Samskara* five years later. For the first time, a South Indian film presented a story with none of the popular contrivance of a tortuous plot and not even a happy ending. Most of the faces looked real, a great deal of the film was shot outdoors, and the visual mobility and freedom of the medium were exploited as they had never been done before. It was a totally new experience. The colour, the sharp editing, the simple pathos of the theme, the sweep of its emotional drama, and most of all the majestic presence of the sea made the film a unique cinematic effort.

The name *Chemeen* literally means "shrimps," as sea-food constitutes a major part of the livelihood of the fisher folk in the Keralan coastline.

CHIDAMBARAM
colour/ 103 minutes/ Malayalam/ 1985

Production: Suryakanthi Film Makers/ Direction and screenplay: G. Aravindan/ Story: C.U. Sreeraman/ Camera: Shaji/ Music: Devarajan/ Sound: Harikumar
Cast: Gopi, Smita Patil, Sreenivas, Mohan Das

SHANKARAN, a mild-mannered loner, works as the office superintendent in a vast government farm in the hilly and picturesque border areas between Kerala and Tamil Nadu. Unlike his colleague Jacob, Shankaran has no social pride and finds it easy to be friendly with the workers. Muniyandi, the man who looks after the cattle, joins him for a drink the evening before he goes for his wedding in the village. Being a god-fearing man, Muniyandi says a quick prayer before he takes a swig of Shankaran's rum, and bursts into song, much to the embarrassment of Shankaran. As an amateur photographer, Shankaran goes to Muniyandi's wedding, stopping on the way to immortalize on film the village potter's work. Back at his office, he watches Muniyandi another day when he brings home his bride, Shivkami, from the brown, barren land of Tamil Nadu to the green, undulating meadows of the farm.

Slowly Shivkami takes her first hesitant steps in this new, lovely world. Muniyandi offers her timid devotion, and Shankaran gentle concern. She stops being afraid of this silent man, no longer shies away from his camera, and goes to him when an address has to be written on a letter she writes home. Jacob arranges for Shivkami to work on the farm, but Muniyandi, suspicious of his motives, politely refuses the offer. Enraged, Jacob orders him to take over night duty in the cattle shed. Muniyandi is alert to every sound in the night. When a motorcycle rushes past, he runs all the way home to check if Jacob is with Shivkami. But the man who swiftly vanishes into the darkness near his quarters is not Jacob. It is Shankaran, Muniyandi's friend. Early next morning, curious faces pressed against the high windows of the cattle shed find Muniyandi's portly body swaying gently from the wooden beam. Shankaran runs away from Muniyandi's voiceless accusation till he falls exhausted on the cushioned floor of the forest.

Guilt changes his life. He wanders in the city alone, goes listlessly from one liquor den to another. His friends find him a job in a printing press, where he sits in a daze over the proofs. Muniyandi's swinging body and the creaking beam are his constant companions. The doctor he visits keeps talking about religion and the peace of mind it offers. But the devil within will not be subdued, and Shankaran goes wandering again. Coming out of the Chidambaram temple, he stops to find his shoes and pay the woman who sits looking after them. She lifts her face, and Shankaran sees Shivkami. Old, worn out, with a horrible gash on her face, where Muniyandi had lashed out at her before killing himself. Shankaran has reached his journey's end.

CRITIC SADANAND MENON writes: "Aravindan returns with mesmeric regularity to the theme of the antagonism between human beings and nature as being the prime generator of the alienation in post-industrial societies. And he says that for any resolution of this human predicament there must be a synthesis of the objective and subjective dimensions of radical consciousness. Restructuring the relations of production is not all; the landscape of human imagination itself has to be explored afresh and restructured." [*Express Magazine,* 12 April 1987.]

Nature, with its warm, bounteous colours, its soft, generous contours, is indeed a living force in the first half of Aravindan's *Chidambaram.* Shaji's extraordinary camera piles detail upon detail to build an image of the eternally beautiful earth where Shivkami (literally, the one who desires Shiva) wanders alone, discovering each leaf, each flower, the soft feel of the grass under her feet. It is a primeval landscape, shattered by tractors and machinery, and sustained by the gentle lowing of the cattle, the twitter of birds. The adversity remains, and culminates in Shankaran's betrayal. Muniyandi hanging from the creaking wooden beam pursues Shankaran through the verdant forest. He too is of the serenity of nature which Shankaran's disturbed spirit has shaken out of place. In his wanderings, Shankaran looks for a destination for his guilt. He finds it in the ravaged face at the temple. Is it really Shivkami? Has Shankaran (his name is just another name for Shiva) completed his destined cycle of suffering after all? Aravindan, the master of silence, moves his camera away from the earthly to the cosmic, to the rising tiers of the temple which stands where Shiva was transformed from the primordial phallus to the Nataraja, the divine dancer who liberates the human soul from its earthly shell. His camera rises to the open sky, freeing his protagonists from the temporal cycle of guilt and retribution.

CHOMANA DUDI (Choma's Drum)
b&w, 141 minutes, Kannada, 1975

Production: Praja Films/ Direction and music: B.V. Karanth/ Story and screenplay: Dr Shivarama Karanth/ Camera: S. Ramachandra/ Editing: P. Bhaktavatsalam
Cast: M.V. Vasudeva Rao, Padma Kumta, Jayarajan, Sunder Rajan, Honniah, Nagaraja, Venkatesh, Govind Bhat, Mahalakshmi

CHOMA AND his family are Harijan bonded-labourers toiling all their lives for the interest piled upon a paltry sum of twenty rupees borrowed years ago from the landlord. Being an "untouchable," Choma is by tradition forbidden to till his own land, and that is the one thing he desires most. He has reared a pair of bullocks found straying in the forest long ago; vast fields lie untended in front of him; yet the landlord will not rent him a piece of land. The Christian missionaries wean away Harijans with the lure of land. But Choma will not give up his traditional faith. His inarticulate fury at his fate is given a voice only through his little drum.

Two of Choma's sons toil in a distant coffee estate to pay off the family debt. He loses one to cholera; the other son marries a Christian girl and becomes a Christian himself. Now it is his daughter Belli's turn to work in the plantation. She is seduced by Manvela, the estate-owner's writer, and later raped by the owner himself, and Choma's debt is written off. Choma, who knows nothing of Belli's situation, is happy to see her back home, and once again begs his master in vain to rent him a piece of land. A few days later, his youngest son is drowned in the river, watched by Brahmins who will not touch the boy, let alone rescue him. Choma drowns his sorrow by playing on his drum. Finding Belli one day making love to Manvela, Choma is shattered. He beats her and pushes her out of the hut. In defiance against his fate, he ploughs a piece of land with his bullocks, then chases them away into the forest. Returning home late, he shuts himself in and plays on his drum for a last time. Choma dies defeated, but his angry drum plays on.

A SIMPLE STORY of a Harijan family of a half-century ago, *Chomana Dudi* tells a familiar tale with remarkable passion and anger. A leading stage director, actor, music scholar and composer, B.V. Karanth was thrust into the cinema almost by accident. When a famous author insisted on Karanth as a director before selling the film rights of his story, Karanth persuaded dramatist, actor and director, Girish Karnad, to come to his aid. *Vamsha Vriksha,* made in 1971, was the result of their joint effort, which Karanth followed with his independent venture, *Chomana Dudi.* The film not only won the National Award for the best feature film of the year, it also gave actor Vasudeva Rao a lifetime's opportunity to display his tremendous talents. Shot on actual locations, with documentary realism, Choma's story represents a curious transposition. Choma, the man, with his inarticulate anger, his voiceless passion, is essentially primordial, at one with earth's diurnal course. Not so his drum, a symbol of the invincible human spirit. It plays on in the darkness, speaking wordlessly of human anguish and thwarted desire, of centuries of human deprivation and anger. Choma returns to the primeval night, but his drum is transformed into the human voice of rebellion.

DAMUL (Bonded until Death)
colour, 125 minutes, Hindi, 1984

Production: Prakash Jha Productions/ Direction and screenplay: Prakash Jha/ Story: Shaiwal/ Camera: Rajen Kothari/ Music: Raghunath Seth/ Art Direction: Gautam Sen, Prabhat Jha/ Editing: Apurwa Yagnik/ Sound: A.M. Padmanabhan
Cast: Manohar Singh, Sreela Mazumdar, Annu Kapur, Deepti Naval

BACHCHA SINGH, a local politician in a remote Bihar village, manipulates the untouchable community, the Harijans, into setting up their own candidate in the coming elections against Madho, the village chief with whom he is involved in a power struggle. Madho, a rich landlord who heads the powerful Brahmin camp, sends a Harijan labourer, Punai, to Bilaspur to collect crude local firearms to intimidate the Harijans. But Madho's brother, Radho, discovers that Punai has betrayed them, and arranges to murder him. Madho wins the election by keeping the Harijans away by force. When Punai's body is discovered, to ensure his son Sanjeevana's silence, Madho makes him sign a promissory note for a fictitious loan taken by Punai. Madho also implicates Sanjeevana in a theft in the village, forcing him to ask the landlord for shelter. He is given shelter, but on condition that he steals cattle for Madho. With the loan to repay and the police after him, Sanjeevana has no alternative but to agree; and for every head of cattle fifty rupees are written off his loan.
   A series of events follow. Illness brings back Mahatmaeen from a self-imposed exile. A still young but faded Brahmin widow, she too has been in the clutches of Madho who now unofficially looks after her land. Uneasy about her return, Madho tries to threaten her into submission before she can cause any trouble in the village. Meanwhile Harijan labourers working at the canal site for Radho gather angrily as his manager manhandles a pregnant woman worker. Bachcha Singh quietly incites the labourers to leave for Punjab where there are better jobs and better pay. Madho's men steal the oxen of Nageena, Sanjeevana's brother-in-law. At the village *panchayat,* Madho as the headman decides that to release the oxen supposedly lost through his own carelessness, Nageena must pay a large penalty. As he does not have the full amount, Madho generously makes up the difference. Now Nageena too becomes his bonded slave, stealing cattle to pay him back.
   The situation in the village deteriorates. Mahatmaeen threatens to take back her land when she is offered a paltry bag of rice by Madho. Bachcha Singh promises to loan money to Radho's Harijan labour force for the train fare to Punjab. Nageena is killed trying to steal cattle. When Sanjeevana brings his body to Madho, he refuses help and tells his manager to dispose of the corpse. Harijans going to Punjab are intercepted by Radho's men and shot at and their homes ransacked. Bachcha Singh advises the Harijans not to touch the corpses

till the police come. Furious, Madho sends his brother into hiding and concentrates on buying off Bachcha Singh. When the police arrive, the Harijans misled by Bachcha Singh give conflicting evidence and the carnage is blamed on bandits. The visiting Minister views it all as a conspiracy of the opposition parties. Outraged by the turn of events, Mahatmaeen decides to give evidence against the Brahmins. Sanjeevana gets a message that she wants to see him. When he arrives at her lonely home, he finds her dead—raped and murdered by Madho's men. The same men now appear in the empty house and pin the murder on Sanjeevana.

Sanjeevana is sentenced to death on the basis of evidence given by Madho's men. Sanjeevana's wife Rajuli, a silent witness to the continuing cycle of oppression, returns from the court to her empty home. In the gathering darkness her helplessness is transformed into passionate protest. And at Madho's home, the sharp blade of Rajuli's knife descends in a final act of retribution.

DAMUL describes the system of *panha* exercised in the Ganges belt of Bihar state, which literally means "shelter and protection;" but is actually a manipulative process by which poor farmers and labourers become bonded slaves of rich landlords. The mechanism is simple and diabolical. When a labourer dies, his son is made to sign a paper promising to pay the debts of his father. When the illiterate labourer puts the imprint of his thumb on the paper, he is unaware that not only may the loan be fictitious, but also that the interest claimed far exceeds the original amount. To strengthen his hold, the landlord then involves the labourer in some petty crime which is a plant. The trap closes in when the labourer is given shelter from the police in exchange of his free services in some criminal act on behalf of the landlord. The business of stealing cattle is itself a well-organized racket. The stolen cattle are deposited with an agent who then tells the owner to come and get the animals released as they have strayed (through the owner's carelessness) into somebody else's land and perhaps spoiled the crops. The sum of money to be paid is fixed arbitrarily. When the owner cannot produce the money, the cattle are sold in the open market. If he disputes the sum, influential men of the locality sit in the *panchayat* (the local self-governing body) to arbitrate on the matter. As these men are most often the ones who have instigated the theft, the verdict is invariably unjust.

Damul is a faithful, almost documentary representation of an amazingly tortuous process of exploitation that carries on today in one of the most corrupt states of the Indian republic. Though Jha's penchant for a circumambulatory camera tends to overstate the metaphor of a vicious circle, the faces of the oppressors and the oppressed in their indisputable credibility establish a powerful rapport with his audience. A fairly new director, with three feature films to his credit so far, Jha began his career as a documentary and short filmmaker. *Damul*, his second film, received the National Award for the best feature film of the year.

DEEWAR (Wall)
colour/ 174 minutes/ Hindi/1975

Production: Trimurti Films Pvt. Ltd./ Direction: Yash Chopra/ Story, screen-play and dialogue: Salim Javed/ Camera: Kay Gee/ Music: R.D. Burman/ Playback: Asha Bhonsle, Kishore Kumar, Manna Dey, Bhupinder/ Lyrics: Sahir/ Editing: T.R. Mangeshkar/ Sound: M.A. Shaikh/ Fights: Shetty Cast: Amitabh Bachchan, Shashi Kapoor, Neetu Singh, Parveen Babi, Nirupa Roy, Manmohan Krishna, Madan Puri, Iftikhar, Satyen Kappu, A.K. Hangal, Sapru, Satyadev Dubey, Aruna Irani, Jagdish Raj

SUB-INSPECTOR Ravi is being awarded a police medal for bravery. He requests his mother to come and receive the award, for it is she who has given him courage when he most needed it. On the stage Ravi and his mother, Sumitra, face each other sorrowfully, remembering their past.

Sumitra's husband, Anand, a labour leader of great charisma, discovers during a major strike that his employers are holding his family to ransom. Helpless, he betrays the workers, survives their assault, but unable to face their scorn, vanishes from the hospital where he was convalescing. Her hostile surroundings force Sumitra to leave for the city where she toils at a con-struction site while Vijay works as a shoe-black to send his little brother Ravi to school. A proud and rebellious child, Vijay hates the humiliations that pov-erty brings and finds it impossible to forgive his father's cowardice. When his mother takes them to the temple to pray, Vijay sits outside, waiting, fighting his silent battle with an unjust god.

Years pass. Vijay now works as a porter in the dockyard. Old Rahim, a fellow porter, tells Vijay that his metal identification tag carries an auspicious number. He should keep it with him always. One day, tired of paying protection money to a gang of hoodlums at the dockyard, Vijay protests vio-lently when they manhandle a new recruit. Unlike his father, he faces the consequences and emerges bloodied but victorious. The leader of a rival gang befriends Vijay, who becomes a highly successful smuggler, and has ample chance to try out his lucky amulet—the porter's tag. He pretends to be a businessman at home, and obsessively tries to make up for their past depriv-ations with his new-found riches. In the underworld of gambling dens and risky adventures, Vijay meets Aneeta, a nightclub dancer. Their individual loneliness and their struggle to succeed in an alien environment bring them closer together.

Ravi joins the police force where his first assignment leads him to suspect that Vijay is an established smuggler. He accepts the case unwillingly and finally confronts his brother, who protests that the police must first penalize those who have victimized and humiliated them when they were poor. For Ravi that is no justification for what Vijay has become. He takes a heartbroken Sumitra and leaves Vijay's opulent home. Vijay is shattered, for has he not sold his soul to give them a better life? Increasingly isolated by rivalries within his organization and the relentless pursuit of his brother, Vijay still decides to risk visiting his ailing mother in hospital. Ravi, who now has a warrant in Vijay's name, is torn between Sumitra's secret longing for her fugitive son, his own love for his brother and his commitment as a protector of the law. Aneeta tries to hold back Vijay who decides on a last gamble before facing the police. He goes to the temple and faces god instead. "Do not punish her for my sins," he says in anger and pain, "do not punish her because I love her. I want my mother's life back!"

Sumitra gets a new lease of life. At the temple the priest tells her of Vijay's battle with god. Vijay hears of his mother's recovery; he also learns that Aneeta is carrying his child. Moved by visions of an elusive happiness he plans to marry Aneeta and surrender to the police. He calls his mother to come and meet him at the temple and give her blessings. Aneeta goes back to her flat to change, and is brutally killed by members of a rival gang. Vijay comes in search of her, finds a cigar on the floor and knows the identity of the killer. In a rage he guns down the members of the gang, then goes looking for Samant, their leader and Aneeta's murderer. When Ravi learns of the massacre, Sumitra, facing the inevitable, hands him the gun, then leaves for her vigil at the temple. Vijay kills Samant and is chased by Ravi who begs him to give himself up. Jumping across a gate, Vijay loses his amulet. Before he can retrieve it, Ravi closes in and shoots. Wounded and dying, Vijay still makes his way to the temple, and rings the holy bell. Sumitra holds her dying son close and blesses him.

Back at the police reception, Ravi escorts his mother off the stage.

A LONG AND complicated story that established Amitabh Bachchan as the "angry young man" of the Hindi screen. It also established in the popular mind the image of the anti-hero, valiantly fighting destiny, a man whose inner distortions damn him even in the eyes of god, but for whom the audience has nothing but sympathy. It is a curious but not unfamiliar paradox—a creation of god's will, that god himself wills to destruction. For god plays a major role in this drama, testing the patience and faith of its protagonists through their travails. Extremely well-acted by Bachchan who reached the height of stardom at the time, the film is remarkable for its tightly knit script, and the strength of its dialogue which was remembered and repeated by fans for years to come. Bachchan's Vijay is explosive in his suppressed rage, his rebellion against the uncontrollable flow of events in his life, his intense loneliness and his obsessive rivalry with god. One can think of more sophisticated European parallels. But in the land of the eternal happy endings, *Deewar* was one of the first popular films to present as a hero a man hounded and damned by fate, a hero who, for once, just cannot win. It started a trend and Bachchan made his millions on more of not quite the same, for in spite of its tortuous plot, *Deewar* had a finesse that was not to be repeated.

Unfortunately, the peculiar demands of the box-office have led to the creation of a new monster who can claim his lineage from Bachchan's portrayal. The social outcaste turned criminal of the silver screen is today a trigger-happy avenging angel, whose solution for every injustice may very well be a series of mass murders, fully condoned by the audience, and at least partially by the Indian board of film censors. Considering the social pressures that turn the screen heroes and heroines to crime, even the screen judges feel uncomfortable about sentencing them to anything more than a few months behind the bars.

The audience comes out of the hall convinced that a bloody solution is a speedy solution. If the urban crime rate shows a steady increase, it is probably a healthy sign. Meanwhile Amitabh Bachchan joined the ruling party, became a Member of Parliament, then survived a political scandal by withdrawing from politics temporarily and going back to his film career.

DEVATHA (Divinity)
b&w, 186 minutes, Telugu, 1941

Production: Vauhini Pictures/ Direction: B.N. Reddi/ Story, screenplay and camera: K. Ramnoth/ Music: V. Nagaiah/ Dialogue and lyrics: Samudrala Raghavacharya/ Art Direction and sound: A.K. Sekhar/ Editing: Narayanan
Cast: V. Nagaiah, Lingamurthy, Bezawada Rajarathnam, Ch. Narayana Rao, T. Suryakumari, Master Aswathama, Subba Rao

VENU, AN ambitious young man, returns to his village after finishing his legal studies abroad. In his home, his mother and his sister Seetha welcome him back joyfully, watched by Lakshmi, a young girl who helps in the house, but has become a part of the family. Venu finds Lakshmi a charming girl, and cannot help feeling attracted towards her in spite of the difference in their status. Meanwhile, an affluent family friend hopes that Venu will marry his smart and fashionable daughter, Vimala. But in a moment of weakness, Lakshmi allows Venu to seduce her, and soon becomes pregnant with his child. When Venu realizes the consequences of his rash act, his immediate response is to offer Lakshmi money as consolation. Deeply shocked, Lakshmi leaves Venu's home. Venu's strong sense of guilt makes him avoid any discussion about his proposed marriage to Vimala. Fortunately for him, Vimala, who is a young woman with a mind of her own, decides to elope with a bogus poet called Sukumar. Venu decides to confess his guilt to his mother. Surprisingly, she understands his predicament and agrees to accept Lakshmi as her daughter-in-law. Venu leaves home to find Lakshmi.
   With a young brother and a baby to feed, Lakshmi goes to the city to earn a living once again, and is lured into a brothel. She escapes after assaulting the woman who runs the brothel, and lands in jail. Hunger forces Lakshmi's little brother to beg in the streets of the city, where he is discovered by Venu's mother and Seetha, who have come to join Venu in his search. They finally find Lakshmi in prison and arrange to free her. Venu begs Lakshmi to forgive him, so that a new life may begin for them all.

THE THEME of *Devatha* was obviously far ahead of its times. Pre-marital sex, unwed motherhood, and the flouting of strictly maintained barriers of class, all made it a daring venture. Surprisingly, it turned out to be a big box-office success. In an era of theatrical sets, immobile camera and narrative dialogues in South Indian cinema, *Devatha* made unusual use of the freedom of the form. Ramnoth, who held the camera and also wrote the story and the screenplay, himself had reservations about how the audience would respond to such an unconventional story. Yet, not only was the film a success, its songs, highly popular at the time, are still heard in remote parts of Andhra Pradesh.

"*Devatha* serves as an excellent source material for any social historian making a study of Madras city in the early 40s," writes Randor Guy in his monograph on B.N. Reddy [National Film Archive of India, 1985]. "Tram cars clanging their way through the city—once the finest mode of transportation in Madras, with their cheap fares, dark drivers and conductors in khaki uniforms with tufts of hair peeping out of their soft caps and bright caste-marks on their faces. Madras Central Station with no nameboard, 'inter-class' compartments in trains owned by companies with familiar acronyms like 'M&SM' (Madras and South Marhatta Railways Ltd), incorporated in England,...all these visuals delight the viewer today."

Bommireddi Narasimha Reddi came to Madras city as a child from Cuddapah district in the old province of Madras, now in Andhra Pradesh. Though trained as an auditor, he took to the theatre and acted in many Telugu plays before investing in a film production company. But the administrative role he played there was not enough for his creative spirit and soon he promoted his own company, Vauhini Pictures Limited, and directed his first film, *Vande Mataram*, in 1939. The friendships that had sprung out of the first venture, were carried over to the second, and Reddi's success as a serious filmmaker within the popular genre was supported by a strong team of artistes, writers and technicians. The themes he chose—whether it was unemployment, dowry, or widow remarriage—were all of vital social significance. However, Reddi veered off from genuine social themes once his association with K. Ramnoth, writer and cameraman, broke off; and his later films mostly deal with family dramas and traditional romances. When the winds of change brought the Bomaby "formula" into Telugu cinema, Reddi retired from filmmaking, though by that time he was much revered as a pioneer in the industry, and had received national recognition.

DEVDAS
b&w, 141 minutes, Hindi, 1935

Production: The New Theatres Limited/ Direction and screenplay: P.C. Barua/ Story: Saratchandra Chatterjee/ Camera: Bimal Roy/ Music: Timir Baran/ Editing: Subodh Mitter
Cast: K.L. Saigal, Jamuna, Rajkumari, A.H. Shore, Raju, Nemo, Biswanath Bhaduri, Krishna Chandra Dey

DEVDAS, son of a rich landowner, and Parvati, the daughter of a middle-class neighbour, have been childhood playmates. As they grow up, their casual friendship changes to something deeper almost imperceptibly. When Devdas is sent away to Calcutta to continue his education, the parting is painful for both of them. A simple, unsophisticated boy, Devdas is laughed at by his fellow students in Calcutta till one of his new friends, the dissolute Chunilal, takes him under his wing and smartens him up with the right clothes. While Devdas is learning to be a man of the world, Parvati pines away for him at home. Parvati's mother decides to approach Devdas's family and make arrangements for their marriage. But the rich landowner thinks it beneath his dignity to accept such a lowly proposal, and Parvati's father, insulted and angry, prepares to have his daughter married within the week.

Devdas comes home, and discovers that Parvati's marriage has been arranged with Rai Saheb, a wealthy widower with grown-up children. Devdas is confused by this sudden development, and when Parvati comes to his room late in the night, he is in a terrible quandary, fearing that someone might have seen her coming there. Parvati, who knows she has little to lose, is unafraid. She has come to ask whether Devdas will save her from her predicament by marrying her. Devdas aware of his parents' attitude, hesitates, and Parvati, realizing that she has failed, allows him to escort her back home. Next morning Devdas goes back to Calcutta with his old retainer Dharamdas, who has looked after him ever since his tumultuous childhood. He writes to Parvati explaining that he cannot defy custom and tradition and disobey his parents' wishes; that he has never loved her the way she has loved him; that she must find happiness in her life now by forgetting him. But the moment the letter is on its way, Devdas is distraught and seeking oblivion, goes with Chunilal to the home of a dancing girl, Chandramukhi. He does not find oblivion there, and is only disgusted by the atmosphere of the place. In desperation, he leaves for home.

Parvati's wedding day is drawing close. Devdas finds a moment with her alone when she goes to fetch water at the pond. But it is too late. Parvati, with her hurt pride and her broken heart will not forgive him. Nor can she any longer stem the flow of events that are overtaking her life. Suddenly angered by her coldness, Devdas lashes out at her with his fishing rod. Parvati leaves, carrying on her forehead the mark of his now desperate love. In Calcutta, Devdas turns to drink and Chandramukhi's silent adoration, but can find no peace any more. Parvati immerses herself in her role of a Hindu wife, and wins the affection and respect of her new family. But she too has lost her peace forever. Both Chandramukhi and Parvati try to hold back Devdas from the ruinous course he is set upon. When Parvati pleads with him to stop drinking, he only promises to come to her once before he dies. Chandra-mukhi, who has given up her profession out of her love for Devdas and left the city, returns to look after him. For months no one can tell where he is, till one day she finds him lying drunk on the roadside. But Devdas refuses her ministrations and goes on an aimless journey with Dharamdas as his sole, faithful companion.

One day Parvati hears of a stranger who has died in the night outside their home. Slowly the pieces of information fall into place, and she realizes it was Devdas, come to see her for a last time. Behind the high, surrounding walls of her home, rushing to the massive gates in full view of her shocked family, Parvati already knows that only a handful of ashes remain of the man she had loved.

DEVDAS continues to be a legend in contemporary India. Written in the early years of the century by a well-known Bengali novelist, the story created enough storms in Bengal. Its doomed young protagonist, with his implied criticism of arranged marriages, his rebellious addiction to the forbidden charms of alcohol, his curious but not immoral relationship with a golden-hearted prostitute, became the hero of Bengali youth. At the same time, the elders reacted with outrage and accused the author of corrupting youthful morals. The intense romanticism of the story captured the imagination of generations of Indians, for it was read in translation all over the country. Prince Pramathesh Chandra Barua, son of the Raja of Gauripur and a Devdas-like character himself, made his Bengali and Hindi versions of the film under the New Theatres banner. In the Bengali version Barua played the role of Devdas, but for the Hindi one, he chose Kundan Lal Saigal as his hero. The film was a phenomenal success and nothing that he made later on in his career ever matched up to its popularity. Saigal, a typewriter salesman, had been picked up for his singing voice by B.N. Sircar, the dynamic founder of the New Theatres. With negligible acting talent, and a total lack of physical charm, Saigal still became a rage, his singing style and his gentle, musical voice enthralling the audience even today. A Telugu version of the film was made in 1953, with popular hero Akkineni Nageswara Rao in the lead. In 1956, Bimal Roy, the cameraman for Barua's *Devdas*, directed another Hindi version which was equally spectacular, with the charismatic actor from the Hindi screen, Dilip Kumar in the main role; Suchitra Sen, the most popular actress from Bengal as Parvati; and Vaijayantimala, a South Indian actress and dancer who had become a star in Bombay as Chandramukhi.

Watching Barua's film today would be a curious experience. Devdas is undoubtedly spineless, cowardly, indecisive, and unable to take the responsibility for his actions. Parvati, though a proud and bold woman, accepts her lot not just out of hurt, but because she is essentially submissive to the norms laid down by her society. Chandramukhi is the final absurdity, and the imaginary character of the lovable but doomed prostitute rising above her sordid surroundings has remained a tragic fixture in Indian literature and cinema ever since. Saigal is positively wooden in his role, and Jamuna as Parvati presents a face totally devoid of expression. Yet the dramatic intensity of the film is as mysterious as it is overpowering. A generation has wept over it willingly, and Saigal's songs are still heard all over the country. As a last word, it must be said, however, that it is Dilip Kumar's portrayal of Devdas as the ultimate romantic, in Bimal Roy's version more than forty years later, which will probably remain memorable much longer.

DHARTI KE LAL (Children of the Earth)
b&w, 125 minutes, Hindi, 1946

Production: K.A. Abbas for IPTA Pictures/ Direction, dialogue and screenplay: K.A. Abbas/ Story: Based on Bijon Bhattacharya's Bengali plays *Nabanna* and *Jabanbandi,* and Krishen Chander's Hindi story *Annadata/* Camera: Jamnadas Kapadia/ Music: Ravi Shankar/ Lyrics: Ali Sardar Jafri, Prem Dhawan, Nemichand Jain, Wamiq/ Editing: D. Vishrambhai

Cast: Shambhu Mitra, Usha Dutta, Damyanti Sahni, Balraj Sahni, Anwar Mirza, Tripti Bhaduri, Hamid Dutt, Pratap Ojha, Rashid Ahmed, Randhir, Zohra Sehgal, Mahendranath, Snehprabha, David, K.N. Singh

IN A VILLAGE in Bengal in the early forties, lives old Samaddar, the head of a family of farmers. The household consists of Samaddar, his wife, the elder son Niranjan and his childless wife Binodini, and the younger son Ramu who is soon to marry Radhika. The family look forward to the harvest so that they may have a proper feast at Ramu's wedding. The harvest is good, but the big landlord and the grain dealer from the city refuse to pay a fair price for it. The price of rice has gone up in the city, with the British drawing on reserves of grain for the war effort. But old Samaddar is unable to comprehend why he should be paid a pittance for his year's toil while the landlord and the grain dealer are obviously out to make a fast buck. For Ramu, life with his newly wedded wife starts on an ominous note of impending poverty. There is not even a grain to offer to the gods when his child is born. Natural calamities follow and famine takes over the land.

Selling off their land, the villagers leave one by one in the hope of a better life in the city. Old Samaddar's family still hang on to their land while starvation casts its grim shadow over them. Ramu quarrels with his brother and leaves for Calcutta. Finally the rest of the family too decide to go to the city along with a caravan of hungry peasants. But the city is the death of all hopes for them, for it has no place for the starving people who throng there from the countrysides of Bengal. Samaddar's family becomes a part of the growing population of pavement dwellers, homeless, jobless, and hungry. Radhika is forced to sell her body to keep her child alive, unaware that somewhere in the city's dark alleyways, is her husband Ramu starving and unable to find employment. The absolute destitution of his family breaks old Samaddar's heart. He dies, exhorting them with his last breath to go back to the land. With nothing left to hope for in the city, the family go back to their village with the other peasants.

In the village, only a few still have their land, yet they too lack the means to start afresh. But their sufferings have given the peasants a new sense of solidarity. This fight for survival will be fought together. They decide to work as a collective and with immense determination, sow and reap a new harvest and a new way of life. Celebrating their success, the villagers do not see the two silent figures standing in the shade, watching them with longing. They are Ramu and Radhika, two human beings who have been sucked into the terrible vortex of the city. Severed from their roots they cannot any longer return to the honest simplicity of rural life. But they are together at last, even as they leave behind the new hopes and the new world they cannot share.

KHWAJA AHMAD ABBAS produced *Dharti ke Lal* on behalf of the left-wing cultural organization, the Indian People's Theatre Association (IPTA), of which he was a founder member. This was one of the first feature films to be made by a non-commercial group and Abbas and his associate producer, writer-journalist V.P. Sathe, had to finance the film with personal loans. One of IPTA's greatest contributions was the socially conscious theatre, and most of the actors and actresses in the film came from that background. The presentation is definitely amateurish cinematically, with a large dose of theatre in the performance. It is not surprising, though, that with Abbas's own strong propagandist slant and the artistes' orientation in the same area, the film ends on an idyllic picture of collective farming introduced by Soviet Russia with such success. Historically, *Dharti ke Lal* retains its importance as one of the earliest examples of documentary realism in its depiction of the Great Bengal Famine of 1943. Made only three years later, the film displays an unusual clarity of perception over an event that was to have economic repercussions for years to come. Forty years later, filmmaker Mrinal Sen, in his *In Search of Famine*, investigates the ethics of artistic exploitation of a real tragedy, and in the process reveals the immense impact the event has had on the imagination of an entire generation of intellectuals.

Journalist and author, Abbas was lured into writing for the cinema by the taunts of a producer whose film he had criticized in his column. Following the success of *Naya Sansar* which won him awards for the best story and the best screenplay from the Bengal Film Journalists' Association, three of Abbas's stories were bought by other producers. But when the films were released, he did not recognize in them very much of his own work. And so the next challenge was thrown at him, and *Dharti ke Lal* became his first directorial venture. In the following years, Abbas created a production company of his own and named it *Naya Sansar* after his first film story. Abbas's intense involvement with his visions of a "new society," as *Naya Sansar* would be translated, has often worked against his artistic maturity as a filmmaker. Writes critic Kobita Sarkar [in "A Theme in Time," *Indian Cinema Today,* Sterling Publishers, New Delhi 1975], "Abbas' films which make passionate appeals to the sympathy of the audience might be more lasting in their effects if they were more objectively conceived. One is rarely able to get away from his political commitments." But she concludes her critical piece thus: "Abbas' efforts to direct the Indian film towards some form of honest social realism, remain the most memorable in the Indian cinema," a tribute which this intrepid little man received over and over again in his lifetime.

DIAMOND QUEEN
b&w, 155 minutes, Hindi, 1940

Production: Wadia Movietone/ Direction: Homi Wadia/ Script: Jamshed Wadia/ Dialogue and lyrics: Munshi Sham/ Camera: R.P. Master/ Music: Madhulal D. Master/ Art Direction: Pestonji D. Mistry/ Editing: S.R. Gaekwar/ Sound: K.M. Contracter
Cast: Fearless Nadia, Radharani, Nazira, Fatma, John Cawas, Sardar Mansur, Sayani, Dalpat, Kunjru, Chhotu, Baman Sharaf, Mitthu Miya, Mino the Mystic, Jijibhai, Chandkumar, M.K. Hassan, Bismillah, and the Fighting Squad of Wadia Movietone, along with Rolls Royce's Daughter and Punjab's Son.

IN AN UNKNOWN terrain two men have successfully ended their search for gold. One of them has his wife and young son with him in the log hut where they are celebrating their opulent future. The other man, Kedarnath, however, has other ideas. To be sole owner of all the gold, he tries to destroy the family and sets fire to the hut. Only the boy escapes, and grows up as an outlaw, Diler Daku, with revenge in his heart.

Diamond Town gets a visitor: a stupid looking young man called Krishna Kumar, who has been sent by Prince Ranjit Singh, the ruler of the country, to look into the complaints of mismanagement against the governor of Diamond Town, Sheth Kedarnath, the very same man who had betrayed and killed Diler's father. The same day sees the return of Madhurika, the prodigal daughter of Jamnadas, the owner of Diamond Hotel. In the hotel, a young dancer is insulted by Kedarnath's henchmen. Madhurika wades in with her fists, and though she does not do too badly, she is outnumbered. Help arrives unexpectedly in the shape of Diler, and as they rout the enemy, the two forge a binding relationship between them. Though Diler is promptly thrown out by Jamnadas once he knows that the young man is an outlaw, Madhurika insists on fostering the friendship in the hope of reforming him. Meanwhile Kedarnath is worried about Madhurika's prowess, and tries to do away with her. But his plans are thwarted by Diler, with the help of other friends, especially Punjab's Son, the miracle horse, and Rolls Royce's Daughter, the miracle car!

Diler and Madhurika meet and he agrees that to expose the corruption in the State, he must first surrender to the law. Sevakram, a respected social worker, goes to Kedarnath to plead for Diler's pardon. But in Kedarnath's palatial home, he overhears a conversation about Kedarnath embezzling the funds of the State. Kedarnath promptly locks up Sevakram, burns his home with the body of one of his errant henchmen, and puts the blame for the "murder" on Jamnadas who had threatened to kill Sevakram for pleading on Diler's behalf. This was because Madhurika had announced her intention to marry Diler, but Kedarnath now wants her for himself. The charred body of the henchman is taken to be Sevakram's, and Krishna Kumar comes to sympathize with the grieving daughter, Radha, with whom he has fallen in love. Sevakram, in the meanwhile, manages to send a note to Madhurika, while his jailors lie drunk in the next room.

Prince Ranjit Singh is to come to Diamond Town and a reception is organized for him in the town hall. To everyone's surprise, the foolish but good-hearted Krishna Kumar turns out to be the real prince and not such a fool after all! He orders the release of Jamnaprasad and Diler. Kedarnath, who has never bothered to take this young man seriously, is now worried about how much he has learnt during his stay in the town. Diler tells the prince and the people gathered there, how Kedarnath had actually made him into an outlaw. The people too start telling the prince their complaints against Kedarnath. While the town hall is still in an uproar, Madhurika is racing back in Rolls Royce's Daughter, after rescuing Sevakram. In the medley that follows when Sevakram appears in the town hall, Kedarnath quietly slips out and rushes away on the prince's horse-drawn carriage, with Madhurika hanging on to its back. Diler now leaps onto Punjab's Son to follow them. Madhurika and Kedarnath battle in the speeding carriage which breaks apart under the strain just as Diler comes by. Madhurika jumps onto his horse. The broken carriage goes hurtling down a slope with Kedarnath in it. So it all ends happily for Diamond Town. Kedarnath is killed in the accident. Madhurika marries the reformed Diler and the prince marries Sevakram's daughter Radha. As they all stand laughing in front of the camera, Punjab's Son comes in, drawing Rolls Royce's Daughter, which carries the banner: The End!

AN ACTION-PACKED fairy tale with a happy ending, *Diamond Queen* is still a treat to watch. Whatever the morals of the story, and there are many that are insidiously introduced, the film's unflagging pace, and a clever blend of humour and excitement would keep an audience of all ages glued to their seats. J.B.H. Wadia, who set up Wadia Movietone, had an M.A. in English and a law degree, but chose to take up stunt films as his career. His brother, Homi, who directed *Diamond Queen* and other films in the same genre, claimed to have been inspired by *Zorro*! Stunt films from America were indeed highly popular in India during the twenties.

Fearless Nadia, the star of *Diamond Queen*, had first acted in *Hunterwali* (The Lady with the Whip), a Wadia box-office triumph of 1935. Nadia was an Australian of Welsh-Greek extraction who had started in life as a steno-typist, joined a circus, and then become a dancer in a touring dance group. She was a large woman, at least by Indian standards, and possessed a great deal of physical strength and courage, which she displayed in her films where she did all her own stunts. The image that she projected as a woman was far ahead of her times, for it was the man who had to keep pace with her in her films.

John Cawas, who was Diler in *Diamond Queen*, was cast against her in many of her later films, and with his quiet strength, proved to be worthy of her as a hero, though the films invariably centred around Nadia. The fact that Nadia's "westernized" behaviour, or her extreme independence, was never questioned by the audience of the thirties was perhaps because they never really believed in her. An avenging Amazon has certainly never been part of the Indian psyche, but it did not stop them from cheering her on as she pulverized the villains on the screen. The avenging woman, though no longer of Amazonian proportions, is back now in popular Indian cinema. But she is an infinitely weaker character, usually doomed to a heroic but tragic end, being socially unacceptable. Nor would the actress playing the role ever dream of doing her stunts herself.

DO BIGHA ZAMEEN (Two Acres of Land)
b&w, 142 minutes, Hindi, 1953

Production: Bimal Roy Productions/ Direction: Bimal Roy/ Story and music: Salil Chowdhury/ screenplay: Hrishikesh Mukherjee/ Camera: Kamal Bose/ Lyrics: Shailendra/ Art Direction: Gonesh Basak
Cast: Balraj Sahni, Nirupa Roy

IN A SMALL village in West Bengal in the early fifties, where the drought ravages the land every year, Shambhu, a small farmer, waits for the rains to come. He is luckier than most in the village, for he actually owns two acres of land, while the rest must till the land of an absentee landlord. When the rains finally come after month's of burning heat, Shambhu looks towards the future with hope. If only there is a good crop, he will earn enough to recover his wife's jewelry from the pawnbroker. But unknown to Shambhu, the big landlord in the village plans to sell a large plot to a city contractor to build a factory and Shambhu's two acres are cutting into the land. When Shambhu refuses to sell to the landlord, he threatens to forcibly occupy the land unless Shambhu pays up an old loan at once. He inflates the figures and the poor illiterate farmer must go to the court to save his land. He manages a stay order for three months, then does what thousands of farmers still do, goes to the city to earn the extra money.

But Calcutta is a cruel city. Shambhu and his son Kanhaiya are bewildered by the extremes of wealth and poverty. Yet with great determination they settle down to their struggle. They must somehow keep their land. Shambhu takes to pulling a rickshaw, and Kanhaiya becomes a shoe black. Each day they feverishly count their meagre earnings and almost despair, for they are still far from their target. They face many a hardship, and in desperation, Kanhaiya takes to thieving. Horrified, Shambhu disowns his son.

In the village, Shambhu's wife, unable to cope with her worries, decides to go to the city in search of her husband and son. But where will she find them among the teeming millions of Calcutta? Escaping from an unscrupulous character, she is hit by a car and badly injured. Shambhu finds her accidentally, and takes her to a hospital. Kanhaiya, believing that it is he who has brought so much bad luck to the family, tears up the money he had stolen, and is reconciled to his father. But the cycle of suffering is not broken. The family return to the village only to find an ugly factory rearing its head on Shambhu's land. Shambhu is not allowed to take even a handful of earth from the land he has tended for so many years.

WITH THE spate of Bengali names in the credits of this film, it is not surprising that the story turns out to be a typical product of the Bengal of the fifties. Dramatized, fictionalized, fitted into a simplistic framework, it yet depicts the precise predicament of the Bengali marginal farmers who every year joined the exodus from the villages to the great city of Calcutta in the hope of survival. They still come today, if no longer with the same amount of ignorance, wonder and hope, at least with the same desperation. However, written by a popular Bengali writer, singer, composer with a leftist background, it was an unusual entrant in the Bombay film industry with its routine escapist fare of romance and fantasy. Yet *Do Bigha Zameen* with its simplicity and under-statement became one of the classics of Indian cinema. And dominating the screen is Balraj Sahni (like the author of the story a product of the leftist cultural movement of the forties) as Shambhu, totally convincing in spite of his Gary Cooper profile as the last innocent in a complex and cruel world. Made under the influence of the Italian neorealists two years before Satyajit

Ray's first film was released, *Do Bigha Zameen* brought Bimal Roy a rich crop of awards from Canne, Karlovy Vary and Venice.

For the Western audience it was one of the first glimpses of the real India, unglamourized and starkly truthful. Wrote the film critic of *Manchester Guardian* [18 August 1956]: "Here again is a specimen of neo-realism (directed by Bimal Roy), the more noteworthy because it is the very first of its kind to reach us from India. India is a new country—in the political if in no other sense—and it is very odd that, at this early movement of India's independence, any Indian director should make so savagely pessimistic a film." More than pessimism, the film seems to provide a warning even today; for the Indian peasant has found himself eternally dispossessed in the combat between the forces of industrialization and the feudal domination of centuries. Thirty-five years after the film was made, the majority of the peasantry still find themselves among the exploited and the deprived in a country which proudly claims self-sufficiency in foodgrains along with phenomenal progress in technology.

DR KOTNIS KI AMAR KAHANI (The Journey of Dr Kotnis)
b&w, 124 minutes, Hindi, 1946

Production: Rajkamal Kala Mandir/ Direction: V. Shantaram/ Story: K.A. Abbas/ Sceenplay: K.A. Abbas, V.P. Sathe/ Camera: V. Avadhoot/ Music: Vasant Desai/ Lyrics: Dewan Sharar/ Art Direction: Bal Gajbar
Cast: V. Shantaram, Jayashree, Dewan Sharar

A DECADE before the independence of India, Dr Dwarkanath Kotnis, a young doctor from Maharashtra, has a bright future at home. His father has built him a hospital where he can start his practice at once. But Kotnis is an idealist, inspired by the fierce nationalism of his times. When a medical team of five Indian doctors prepare to go to war-torn China on a humanitarian mission, Kotnis is one of them. Once in China, as the members of the team get down to work, they are joined, among others by a young Chinese boy, a fugitive from the Sino-Japanese war that is ravaging the Chinese countryside in the north.

The boy turns out to be Ching Lan, a woman in disguise, and as the small team struggles to keep abreast of the rising list of the wounded and the dead, Kotnis and Ching Lan fall in love. Their marriage is a partnership that can only be strengthened by the uncertainties of the times. Following heavy war casualties, the Chinese are soon on the retreat. The Indian team moves with them as they take shelter in the mountains. But then a mysterious illness starts afflicting the patients. Desperate to find a cure for the disease that is taking precious lives, Kotnis infects himself with the germs. He succeeds in finding a cure, but by that time it is too late for him.

Kotnis and Ching Lan are separated in the course of the war, when Ching Lan is already pregnant. When they meet again, she has a baby son, and they both know he is dying. But disregarding his own health, Kotnis rouses himself one last time to perform a serious operation on a leader of the Chinese movement. Ching Lan shares with Kotnis their last moments of happiness. When he dies, she remembers Kotnis's words about his home, and goes to India with her son.

THE IMMORTAL TALE of Dr Kotnis, as the Hindi title of the film reads, is certainly not one of Shantaram's best films. Though great pains were taken to recreate China of the thirties, the credibility of the sets, the faces and the extraordinary events was not established. The film's importance lies more in the circumstances that led to its making.

When World War II began, the initial perception of many nationalist Indians was that if Britain suffered in the war, it would only further the nationalist cause in her colonies. The leftists following the Soviet line, therefore, agreed to abstain from what they saw as an imperialist war. It was only when Hitler invaded Soviet Russia, and confusion reigned that the leftists urged cooperation with the British war effort. The Indian National Congress, while maintaining a policy of noninvolvement, displayed their anti-Fascist sentiments by sending a medical mission to China at the height of the Sino-Japanese war. Dr Dwarkanath Kotnis was part of this mission, and was briefly married to a Chinese nurse before his death while on duty in China. Though Kotnis's widow did visit India later on, the film's ending was entirely imaginary.

K.A. Abbas, an erudite and progressive journalist from Bombay, had written a short book on Dr Kotnis, *And One Did Not Come Back*. With a reputation for being a successful script-writer, Abbas now offered the book to Shantaram to make a film of it. "Because the story was anti-Japanese," wrote Eric Barnouw and S. Krishnaswamy, "the British promptly approved *The Journey of Dr Kotnis* as a war-effort project. Because it dealt with a Nehru-sponsored mission of mercy, the Congress promptly applauded. Because the Chinese force depicted in the film was the famous Communist Eighth Route Army of Mao Tse-tung—which eventually established Communist China—the Communist Party likewise applauded." [*Indian Film*, Orient Longman, 1963.] There was even hope of American distribution. With the foreign market in mind (a market the film never really reached, though it did well enough at home), Shantaram also filmed an English version, where he insisted on making the clothing of the Indian characters more ethnic to please a Western audience.

DUNIYA NA MANE (The Unexpected)
b&w,166 minutes, Hindi,1937

Production: Prabhat Film Company/ Direction: V. Shantaram/ Story and screenplay: N.H. Apte/ Camera: V. Avdhoot/ Music: Keshavrao Bhole/ Lyrics: Shantaram Athavale/ Art Direction: S. Fattelal/ Sound: V. Damle
Cast: Shanta Apte, Shakuntala Paranjape, Vasantee, Vimla Vashishtha, Keshavrao Date, Raja Nene

NIRMALA, a lively young girl, has been brought up by her uncle and aunt, who are so eager to be rid of her that they accept a bribe from an old lawyer, Vakilsaheb, and agree to give her away to him as a bride. Trapped into a shameful and unequal match, Nirmala keeps away from her husband in her new home. But there is also a grown-up son who is not above casting a roving eye on his young stepmother; and the shrewish aunt whose orthodox ideas do not make Nirmala's life any easier. However, she finds a friend in Susheela, the educated, reformist daughter of Vakilsaheb by a previous marriage.

Nirmala takes a spirited stand against the aunt's bullying and refuses to consummate the marriage. Meanwhile her aged husband is taunted and teased for marrying an unwilling teenager. All his efforts to win her over by force or by reason end in defeat, for Nirmala argues her position, and claims that she will not submit to the injustice of her situation. Talking to Vakilsaheb's widowed daughter, Nirmala says that her suffering will bring its reward, for the world will then not allow other women to suffer as she must. Susheela supports Nirmala's point of view, and even Vakilsaheb is forced to understand the indignity and unfairness of his demands.

Realizing the futility of the relationship, Vakilsaheb decides to free Nirmala from this unequal marriage. But in tradition-bound Hindu society only a widow can wipe off the vermilion from her forehead, the holy mark of marriage. Vakilsaheb leaves home one day, never to return. His clothes are found floating in the river and it is presumed that he has committed suicide. In a note he leaves behind, the old man tells Nirmala that she is free at last. But now that she is a widow, will Nirmala ever be free again?

DUNIYA NA MANE, which literally means "the world will not accept...," also had a Marathi version called *Kunku* —the mark of vermilion on the forehead of a married woman. It was one of the earliest attempts to make a genuine feminist statement on the Indian screen. Traditionally, in mythological, historical and fictionalized history films, women's characters have varied from the supremely sacrificing and submissive to the strong and domineering. Shantaram's own earlier films have portrayed women as central and forceful characters. But *Duniya na Mane* presented a contemporary woman in a predicament that is not unknown even today. By giving Nirmala the unusual ability to stand up for her own rights within an orthodox Hindu home, Shantaram brought to his audience a new perception of a woman's position in Indian society. Widowhood too remains a dubious freedom for Nirmala. For the legal acceptance of widow remarriage means nothing in a society where even today, women immolate themselves on the funeral pyre of their husbands to the sound of drums, watched by admiring policemen along with the entire community, and Sati temples are visited by pious Ministers and Members of Parliament. The law cannot change obsolete social norms and religious revivalism without the help of a vigilant social leadership. And *Duniya na Mane* carries a warning that remains pertinent even today.

The message is made more convincing by the film's subtle characterization. The old bridegroom is not just a villain, nor simply a figure of fun. If he has acted without questioning the customs of his society, he is also able to comprehend the tragic consequences of that act. Nirmala is confused and disturbed by her husband's final generosity. Her own rebellion has been against her unfair predicament, but its immediate target has been this essentially humane, perhaps a foolish old man, trapped like her within a social bind that is beyond both their control.

DUVIDHA (In Two Minds)
colour, 82 min, Hindi, 1973

Production, direction and screenplay: Mani Kaul/ Story: Vijaydan Detha/ Camera: Navroze Contractor/ Music: Ramzan Khan, Hammu Khan
Cast: Ravi Menon, Raisa Padamsee, Hardan, Shambudan, and the villagers of Barunda

A WEDDING PARTY on its way home, stops to rest under a banyan tree on which lives a ghost. The bride lifts her veil and the ghost falls in love with her. Soon after they arrive, the groom has to go away on a business trip for five long years. He passes under the same banyan tree, and the ghost, surprised and curious, takes on the guise of a man to find out his destination. Once he knows the situation, he takes the form of the young man, and goes to the village home. To explain his return to the business-minded father, he invents the story of a saint who has promised him five gold coins if he stays at home. But to the bride he tells the truth. The young woman accepts her ghostly lover and they live together for three years.
  When she is pregnant at last, her real husband, surprised by the news, hurries home. The father and the villagers are confronted with two identical sons. The father would prefer to disown the real son for obvious moral reasons, as well as the gold coins. But the villagers, keen to embarrass him, for he is a rich man, demand justice. A controversy rages while the young woman writhes in long and painful labour. Finally a girl is born, but the woman refuses to comment on the strange happenings.
  The two men are led away by the villagers who have decided to take them to court. On the way the real husband asks the ghost who he is. He is the spirit, says the ghost, that lives under the skin of every woman, and thus has the right to love them all. Before they reach the court, however, the villagers meet a wise shepherd who tricks the ghost into a bag which is thrown into a deep well. The real husband returns home in triumph. His wife silently picks up her homely tasks again with tragic submission, for it is the ghost whom she loves.

VIJAYDAN DETHA'S stories, based though they are on the folk traditions of Rajasthan, are inimitably his own. His special capacity to arrive at the commonplace by means of the impossible and the incredible often baffles his readers. But this is where the duality of his conclusions lie, as it does in *Duvidha*. Mani Kaul's screen rendering is faithful to the spirit of Vijaydan Detha's work, and to its atmosphere of mysterious passions held captive in time. Navroze Contractor's camera reinforces the timelessness, imbuing it with immense visual beauty.

Duvidha is Mani Kaul's third feature film, and not surprisingly, has never been released in the theatres for public viewing. Kaul's uncompromisingly cerebral style of film making is totally unsuitable for the box-office; which is a pity, since that does not diminish its significance or merit. *Duvidha* seems to carry different layers of experience, and an interpretation of the film, or even an appreciation of its many-tiered visualization would not be in place here. But one of the most expressive expositions of the film is to be found in a critique by Kumud Mehta, in the magazine *Enact*. " It seemed to me," she writes, " that the story condensed a valid experience and an awareness of a major impulse governing human activity. The experience it contained had to be conveyed through and to a modern mental state. And I think Mani Kaul managed to do so because he steered clear of the 'romantic' and the 'erotic' which has come to be associated with folk tradition. The film's appeal to the moderns lies in the subtle manner in which it lays its finger on the irrational and its place even in our present-day sensibility. Who is the ghost? The spirit lurking under the skin of every woman, the ghost explains. The ghost—is he yet another aspect of the husband himself? The husband, not as householder but male? The partner during the sex act, he who becomes an alien and distant personality during the day?

"The responses the film evoked were not dissimilar to that roused by Indian miniature paintings. This is not to suggest that the colour scheme or the compositions are in any way close to miniature paintings. But the cool, remote, somewhat sad and still atmosphere of these paintings is also mirrored in the film.

"The clash of two worlds, one which belongs to the blood's warm coursing and the other which claims our submission to family and society, could have been raised to a point of protest and agony. But the contradiction is allowed to exist: the shepherd traps the ghost, even so he is neither triumphant nor happy. His lean face is quiet and pensive. When we choose to negate the irrational, we do so at our peril. But the shepherd, mature and far-seeing, perhaps thinks that one cannot survive without taming it. The contradiction is allowed to exist, and suvive with its own form of ambiguity and mystery. The clash of these worlds is contained, almost resolved in a harmony of colours whose jewel-like clarity swamps, even overpowers any sense of immediacy."

EK DIN PRATIDIN (And Quiet Rolls the Day)
colour, 95 minutes, Bengali, 1979

Production: Mrinal Sen Productions/ Direction and screenplay: Mrinal Sen/ Story: Amalendu Chakraborty/ Camera: K.K. Mahajan/ Music: B.V. Karanth/ Art Direction: Suresh Chandra/ Editing: Gangadhar Naskar/ Sound: Durgadas Mitra, Himadri Bhattacharya
Cast: Gita Sen, Mamata Shankar, Satya Banerjee, Sreela Majumdar, Tapan Das, Tupur Ghosh, Kaushik Sen, Nalini Banerjee, Arun Mukherjee, Umanath Bhattacharya, Biplab Chatterjee, Gautam Chakravarty, Sunil Gupta Kaviraj

AN OLD, aristocratic structure, the house built by Baboo Nabin Chandra Mullick in Calcutta in 1857, the year of the Sepoy Mutiny, has been reduced to a beehive of small rented units. The owner, Dwarik Mullick, last of a noble line, only retains the aristocratic temper but none of its wealth and glory. Eleven families live in the sixteen rooms, sharing the water and electricity that is fiercely husbanded by the landlord; for the prices have gone up but the law does not allow him to raise the rents proportionately. On the ground floor lives Hrishikesh Sen Gupta, with his wife and five children in three rooms that he had rented twenty-three years ago. Now his retirement pension merely pays for the rent and a few extras. The household is run entirely on his eldest daughter Chinu's earnings. Chinu also pays for the education of the three younger children, Minu, Jhunu and Poltu, and provides her unemployed brother, Topu, with pocket-money. On this ordinary evening, two extraordinary things happen. First Poltu hurts himself badly while playing, and then, Chinu does not come home.

Late in the evening, Minu goes to ring her office from the dispensary but the office is closed. Hrishikesh waits aimlessly at the tram stop. Slowly the whole house gets to know. The rooms buzz with speculations. Could it be an accident? Calcutta is full of them. Women fall under the wheels of overcrowded buses, get raped and murdered, bought and sold everyday. She was a good girl though. She could not have run away with a man, or could she? A young neighbour Shyamal wonders what he can do to help. His wife Ratna says, "They haven't asked for your help, have they?" "That's because they are ashamed," says Shyamal. "Perhaps we too would behave the same way if it happened to us."

Later still, when Topu returns, and Chinu is still not home, Topu decides to go to the police station. "Look in at the morgue too," the police tell him. But Chinu is not there either—among the nameless, battered, burnt, bruised bodies in steel drawers. The police come to the house: there is a girl answering to Chinu's description fighting for her life in the hospital. She is in early pregnancy, and has attempted suicide. Shyamal takes Hrishikesh to the hospital. They find other families there too, for the description fits so many missing young girls in the city; they are all ordinary, like Chinu. When the girl dies at last, a nurse comes and in a most matter-of-fact manner arranges for the families to file past the body. She is not Chinu.

The neighbours return to their rooms one by one, leaving the family to face each other. Overwrought, Minu suddenly accuses all of them of living off Chinu, of never considering her needs. Now that Chinu is gone, it will be Minu's turn to look after them. She too will stifle within these crumbling walls, crushed by the burden of daily survival, till she too will escape—like Chinu. The bitterness accelerates, and in great anger and frustration, Minu's mother points at her silent husband. "Look at him!" she says. "All his life he has remained silent, and left me to face the music!" The bewildered, helpless Hrishikesh leaves the room and sits in the dark courtyard. A car stops outside and Chinu enters, apologetic, knowing that the family must be worrying. No one wants to hear her apologies. They just want her to go inside at once, away from the prying eyes of the neighbours. Hurt by their silence, she asks the tearful Minu, "Didn't you want me to come home? Don't you think I too might have something to say? But no one has asked or even scolded me. Do you distrust me so much?" Outside in the courtyard, Dwarik Mullick comes downstairs to tell Hrishikesh that they must look for another house. This is a respectable residence, not for the likes of them. Tapu, incensed, makes a scene, the neighbours join in, and Shyamal rushes to separate them and reestablish doubtful peace.

Morning comes. The courtyard once again fills with people bathing, washing clothes and dishes, chipping coal. Chinu's mother sits in front of a smoking coal oven, just as she does everyday, staring out through the prison bars of their window, as clouds of smoke swirl around her tired face.

MRINAL SEN'S nineteenth film in twenty-three years, *Ek Din Pratidin* (literally, "a day like any other") marked a decided shift in the director's style and approach to cinema. But then, unlike Satyajit Ray or Ritwik Ghatak, Sen has never conformed to a single artistic pattern. He has experimented, developed, matured, and changed constantly, drawing obvious enjoyment from each new adventure in craft and communication. His films therefore present a body of work distinguished by the uneven nature of their success with critics and audience alike. Till *Ek Din Pratidin*, however, Sen's involvement with the immense possibilities of the cinematic medium had often overtaken and sometimes interfered with his desire to convey an idea. With *Ek Din Pratidin* he has reached a plateau, a confident merging of ideas and expression. For the first time, the maverick camera is under control, so is the restless editing that had set the temper of many of his earlier works. The concentration is on the little cameos of life that surround the larger drama of the missing girl. In the petty trivialities of existence—Jhunu reminds her mother their clock is five minutes slow, Topu picks up a handy grinding stone to hammer in a nail in his shoes—B.V. Karanth's music contributes its own wry comment. A steady humming accompanies the busy activities of the morning in this human beehive. The little drum to which monkeys dance plays a quick tattoo when Dwarik Mullick descends the stairs to rebuke the family. Sen's emphasis is on subtlety, on the unspoken ambiguities that rule existence. The focus is on the silent compromises behind the facade of obsolescent respectability of an impoverished, disintegrating urban middle-class, faceless in its commonality. And central to them all are the emerging complex perceptions of this class, towards its women.

ELIPPATHAYAM (The Rat Trap)
colour, 121 minutes, Malayalam, 1981

Production: General Pictures/ Direction, story, screenplay and dialogue: Adoor Gopalakrishnan/ Camera: Ravi Varma/ Music: M.B. Srinivasan/ Art Direction: Sivan/ Editing: M. Mani/ Sound: Devadas
Cast: Karamana, Sarada, Jalaja, Rajam K. Nair, Prakash, Soman, John Samuel, Balan K. Nair, Joycee

UNNI IS the last male descendant of an erstwhile rich, landowning family in Kerala. He lives in a sprawling house that nestles among orchards of tapioca, coconut, banana and cashewnut, its ancient rafters bearing evidence of a craftsmanship of another time. It is a beautiful old structure, built to encompass the two worlds of the traditional family, the inner world of the woman and the outer world of the man. It is a house that has seen unbroken cycles of birth and death for many generations. But now, only the shadows remain, and in the shadows, Unni and his sisters, Rajamma and Sreedevi. Through the years the world has been changing outside Unni's home. Unable to cope with the transformations around him, Unni avoids confrontation with the changing reality by hiding behind his false pride and self-centred silence. He also refuses to take any responsibility for his inheritance, and the yields from the property have to be looked after by an old retainer whose familiarity Unni scorns.

Rajamma, the second sister, is past the marriageable age. In any case, whenever a proposal for her marriage is brought to Unni, he reacts with hostility. Unni knows he needs her to slave for him and pander to his many whims in silent submission. When Unni spots a marauding cow among the coconut saplings, he calls out for Rajamma to drive it away. When the assertive elder sister Janamma arrives with her wayward son to demand her share of the property, Rajamma not only patiently submits to her innumerable demands for attention, but also attempts to keep peace between the warring parties. The youngest sister, Sreedevi, a student in the local college, is totally immersed in herself. Spoilt and rebellious, she is already poised for flight.

Sreedevi, who has been exposed to the world outside, escapes Rajamma's fate by defiantly running away with a man. Unni, who is actually incapable of taking a stand, reacts to the event by hiding like a rat in his own home. He does not even try to look for Sreedevi. Rajamma watches with helplessness and despair Unni's growing paranoia, and finally collapses under her mental and physical strain. Finding her unconscious, helpful villagers carry her away under the guilt-ridden eyes of her brother, never to return. Alone in the house of shadows, Unni locks all doors and refuses to have anything to do with the outside world. As the lamps go out and the shadows darken, he sits like a trapped rat, waiting for his doom. In the darkness of the night the door crashes in, and strange hands drag Unni to the pond near the house where Sreedevi used to drown the rats she caught in her carved wooden trap. Standing in the water, near the steps of the pond, Unni cringes like a rat, as if begging his unknown assailants for mercy in his final act of compromise.

"I SUPPOSE all my films have some elements of autobiography in them," says Adoor Gopalakrishnan. "But...*Elippathayam* is probably the closest to me. I have almost reproduced my own family in it; the house that you see in the film is almost a recreation of my ancestral home where I grew up. In some ways the character is also me...." Perhaps there is a bit of Unni in all of us. But the autobiographical element is only one of many in *Elippathayam*. In an interview in *Accha* [May-June 1983], Gopalakrishnan also says, "The whole film has reference to Malayalee society in Kerala: our emergence into modern times."

For the viewer, *Elippathayam* provides multiple levels of experience, the most forceful of them all being that of the self-imprisonment of Unni and Rajamma. While Unni protects himself from a reality that is moving away from the comfortable status quo of the past with alarming rapidity, Rajamma, already a prisoner of Unni's apathy, allows herself to become an unpaid slave in her brother's home. Both refuse to break away from their own prisons and prefer the safety of their shadow world to the complex reality outside. But is it only a fear of the changing order, or a more deep-rooted cowardice, a more fundamental human failing, which destroys them both? Every turning away from a point of crisis, every hesitation in taking a stand, every withdrawal from progression and change, would be another step towards the rat trap for all of us.

Elippathayam received the National Award for the best regional film, and the British Film Institute award for the most original and imaginative film to be shown at the National Film Theatre in London during 1982.

GARAM HAVA (Hot Winds)
colour, 136 minutes, Urdu, 1975

Production: M.S. Sathyu, Abu Siwani, Ishan Arya/ Direction: M.S. Sathyu/ Story: Kaifi Azmi (based on an unpublished short story by Ismat Chughtai)/ Screenplay: Kaifi Azmi, Shama Zaidi/ Camera: Ishan Arya/ Music: Ustad Bahadur Khan/ Editing: S. Chakraborty
Cast: Balraj Sahni, Shaukat Azmi, Dinanath Zutshi, Badar Begum, Gita, Abu Siwani, Farouque Shaikh, Jamal Hashmi, Yunus Parvez, Jalal Agha

SALIM MIRZA, a middle-aged Muslim shoe manufacturer, has lived in Agra for generations. During independence from British rule, when the partition of India becomes a reality, along with a vast majority of Muslims in the subcontinent, Mirza too is faced with the dilemma of either leaving his home-land, or staying to face the carnage that is about to ravage the new republic. Mirza's elder brother, Halim, a shrewd politician, has no compunctions about opting for Pakistan. But Salim Mirza refuses to escape. This is his land. He will stay and look after his family business. The parting is made more painful for Salim Mirza's daughter, Amina, who is engaged to Halim's son Kazim. The border between the two countries is sealed and Kazim cannot return to claim his bride. When he finally manages to cross the border illegally, before the hurried preparations for the wedding can be completed, the police come and take Kazim away.

The complexities of the partition encroach upon Salim Mirza's life from every direction. The ancestral home which was in his brother's name, is now declared evacuee property, and allocated under the new laws to a Sindhi businessman refugee. Salim Mirza's old mother, terrified of losing her life-time's shelter, has to be carried out of the house to their rented accom-modation. Mirza's business is no longer profitable. People are scared to loan money to a Muslim, who might any day escape to Pakistan without repaying the loan. There are new entrepreneurs in the leather trade, refugees from across the border. Mirza cannot compete with new, more aggressive methods of business. His younger son, Sikandar, has a degree, but marked as a renegade race there are few jobs available for Muslims. As if to reinforce the suspicion and hostility, Shamshad, another cousin of Amina's, woos her and betrays her by running away with his father to Pakistan to avoid family debts. Seized with infinite despair, Amina commits suicide. Salim Mirza surrenders to the inevitable and prepares to leave the country. But on their way to the railway station, they find themselves in the middle of a procession—a mass protest that cuts across all barriers to unify the dispossessed of the nation. It is an affirmation of hope for Salim Mirza. The journey is forgotten. The gentle, isolated middle-class businessman joins the procession with his son, to share his solitary hopes, despair and anger with the multitude with whom he also shares his country.

SATHYU'S FIRST feature film seems to have been a lucky accident, for none of his later efforts have so far achieved the same level of cinematic impact. Though *Garam Hava* was never a commercial success, it received critical acclaim for its masterly handling of a still controversial theme. It also brought together a team of unusually talented Hindu and Muslim performers under the leadership of Balraj Sahni (Salim Mirza in the film), a Punjabi Hindu and the gentle giant of Hindi cinema in the fifties and the sixties. Sahni came from a leftist background, and had his groundings in the Indian Peoples Theatre Association, with which he retained strong links till his death, even though by that time the organization had reduced to a small local movement. Sathyu, himself born in an orthodox Brahmin family, comes from a theatre background and is still associated with the movement. His Muslim wife is a leading scriptwriter who has worked with directors like Benegal and Ray.

Till *Garam Hava,* and even after it, films with Muslim themes have stayed primarily in the realm of the "Muslim social," or second-grade religious cinema. As such, the film remains a landmark for its sensitive portrayal of an essentially human problem emanating from forces of history and politics beyond the individual's control. It also poses the Muslim dilemma, and the limited role offered by the new Indian republic to the largest "minority community" within its folds, with no attempt at romanticizing the very real trauma of the partition. The family drama, symbolizing the predicament of thousands of Muslim families in the new India, is played out against the backdrop of human and political betrayals, and the violently divided birth of two nations from an indivisible tradition and people.

"What I really wanted to expose in *Garam Hava* was the games politicians play," says Sathyu. "Actually there are no human considerations at all. I am not talking only about India, but even in Vietnam, Biafra, Germany...it is all the same. How many of us in India really wanted the partition?" [Quoted in *The New Generation: 1960-1980*, Directorate of Film Festivals, 1981.] Though the producers had anticipated a hostile reception of the film, it went on to win a National award for serving the cause of national integration.

GEJJE POOJE (The Mock Marriage)
b&w, 162 minutes, Kannada, 1969

Production: Chitra Jyothi/ Direction and screenplay: S.R. Puttana Kanagal/
Camera: S.V. Shrikanth/ Music: Vijaya Bhaskar
Cast: Kalpana, Gangadhar, Leelavathi, Arati

APARNA, an orphan girl, is brought up by Sangavva, a prostitute. In a weak
moment, she sexually submits to a young man who soon disappears from her
life, leaving her pregnant. In a prostitute's home it is no calamity, and
Sangavva is overjoyed when Aparna gives birth to a girl child. According to
the norms of her own restricted community, Sangavva dreams of performing
gejje pooje for little Chandra when she grows up—a mock marriage with a
wealthy man that will bind her to concubinage. Meanwhile she forces Aparna
to live with a rich man, Puttana Shetty. She moves with Chandra to Mysore,
where their immediate neighbours are an orthodox family, who are won over
by Chandra's charm, irrespective of the social barriers between them.
  Years pass. When the neighbour's daughter Lalitha's marriage is fixed,
Chandra realizes for the first time her own precarious social position, and
determines to break out of it by marrying and leading a respectable life.
Lalitha's brother Somu has grown to love young Chandra and promises to
marry her. Chandra refuses Sangavva's suggestion of a dubious alliance with
a rich man. But she receives a shock when after Puttana Shetty's death her
mother gives her a violin as a memento of her real father. Her past is suddenly
given a mysterious yet tangible identity.
  One day Somu's father brings home an old friend, Chandrasekhar, who
appears moved and disturbed by the strains of a violin being played in the
Shetty home. When he discovers Aparna, the truth is revealed, and he lovingly
embraces his daughter Chandra. Somu, who is an accidental witness to the
embrace, misunderstands its significance. Meanwhile Aparna extracts a promise from Chandra that she will not reveal the identity of her father, for he is
accepted in society as a respectable, married man. Accused by Somu, Chandra
cannot defend herself. By the time her mother realizes and tells her to disclose
the truth to Somu, it is already too late. Somu's parents have fixed his marriage with Chandrasekhar's legitimate daughter. Now Chandrasekhar pleads
with Chandra to keep their relationship a secret. For Chandra it is as if life has
turned full circle, and brought her back to the depths from where she had
sprung. She asks Sangavva to arrange for the mock marriage with the very
man she had earlier refused.

PUTTANA KANAGAL'S popularity, though restricted by language mostly to his
own region, was based on the originality of his themes as well as their
"different" presentation. Though his films never fell into the area of artistic or
intellectual cinema, he managed to break away successfully from the common
romantic storyline and its accepted melodramatic exposition, and yet retain the
interest and admiration of his audience. Known as a pathfinder in the motley
overgrowth of popular Kannada cinema, Kanagal also had a special talent for
discovering fresh faces for his central roles, artistes who became stars once

they had acted in his films. In many of his films, the thematic focus is on women characters who find themselves invariably in situations where they are helpless against social injustice. Within the framework of the popular cinema, which must always abide by the commonly accepted codes of behavious, Kanagal yet found an opportunity to express his unorthodox views.

Gejje Pooje is based on a well-known novel by M.K. Indira, and won the National Award for the best Kannada film of the year and the best screenplay.

GHATASHRADDHA (The Ritual)
b&w, 144 minutes, Kannada, 1977

Production: Suvarnagiri Films/ Direction and Screenplay: Girish Kasaravalli/ Story: U.R. Ananthamurthy/ Camera: S. Ramachandra/ Music: B.V. Karanth/ Art Direction: K.V. Subarna/ Editing: Umesh Kulkarni
Cast: Ajit Kumar, Meena, Ramaswamy Iyengar, Shanta, Jagannath, Suresh

YAMUNA is a young widow living with her father Udupa in an orthodox Brahmin village in Karnataka. An elderly widower and a Vedic scholar, Udupa runs a traditional school in his home, where little Nani is brought as a boarder. Youngest among the scholars and mercilessly teased by the older boys, Nani turns to Yamuna for sympathy and affection and follows her around with a fierce sense of loyalty. Nani's principal tormentor in the school is Sastri, an adolescent orphan, who frequently plays truant, bullies the other boys, and defiantly smokes, gambles and steals.

Yamuna is seduced by the teacher of the local government school and finds herself pregnant. There is gossip in the village while she tries a variety of quack medicines brought by her lover to induce an abortion. But nothing works. Sastri and the boys spy on Yamuna when she goes to meet the school teacher in the forest. Nani, who does not understand any of this, feels protective towards Yamuna who is gradually becoming ostracized by the villagers. Ganesha, the other resident pupil in Udupa's school is taken away by his father. Driven to despair by the wagging tongues in the village, Yamuna tries to commit suicide by putting her arm into a snake's hole. But Nani, helped by an untouchable labourer, braves the dark forest at night and drags her away in time.

Nani goes with Yamuna to an untouchable's home, where his wife prepares for an abortion. Drunken villagers gather outside, dancing the night away to the beat of drums. Nani is terrified by the noise of merriment merging with Yamuna's cries of agony. In the darkness of the night, the school teacher quietly leaves the village. The Brahmins who are looking for the fugitives, find Nani and Yamuna in the forest. Nani is wrenched away from the girl who is in pain and now has no hope for redemption. The self-righteous rage of the Brahmin community finds expression in Udupa's performing the ritual of *ghatasraddha* where, as part of the funeral rites for his living daughter, an earthen pot, the symbol of fertility, is broken in a final negation of life. Widowed in her childhood, Yamuna had lived in her father's home like an unmarried girl, a rare indulgence extended by the orthodox community. Now, her head shorn of all hair in strict Brahmin tradition, wrapped in a white sari, she is left outside the Brahmin village, an outcaste for life. Her frail white figure, huddled under a tree, is watched by the bewildered Nani as he is hauled away from the village by his father. Freed of his responsibilities and once again accepted in the community that has discarded his errant offspring, Udupa thinks of starting another family. There is already an eligible candidate, a Brahmin's daughter, sixteen years old.

A STUDENT OF the Film and Television Institute of India, Girish Kasaravalli made *Ghatashraddha,* his first film, at the age of twenty-six, from a script which was rejected by the Institute resulting in his diploma being withheld. But his diploma film, *Avashesh,* went on to win the Best Student Film award that year. A brief story by one of the most significant contemporary Kannada writers, *Ghatashraddha* unfolds on the screen as a saga of imperilled innocence within the rigid and outmoded framework of an orthodox religion. Set in the 1920s, the story still carries conviction, for religious bigotry continues to be a major impediment to economic, social or political regeneration in the country. Religion permeates life in India, and Kasaravalli, born in a Brahmin family, faced loud protest from the Brahmin community for making what was considered an anti-Brahmin film.

Critical acclaim and a National Award did much to establish the film as a major event. In spite of that, it has suffered the fate of most serious films in India: few people outside the film society circuit have had an opportunity to view it. Subsequently, Kasaravalli made two more films, once again using women as his protagonists, and exploring contemporary social morality in the context of obsolete traditions. Dissatisfaction with his later films which did not have the same critical impact as *Ghatashraddha,* and the problems of finding a financier for another "off the mainstream" effort, kept Kasaravalli away from film making for six years. But in 1987, the National Award for the best film of the year went once again to Kasaravalli for his latest film, *Tabarana Kathe,* made with finances from the National Film Development Corporation.

In *Ghatashraddha* Kasaravalli, using a new and inexperienced cast, displays a quality of rare conviction and immense artistic self-confidence. His reconstruction of another age and its mores which find their echoes in contemporary India, are shattering in their harsh reality. Conceived with great care, the film cannot be visualized in any medium other than the sombre black and white that it uses. The shadowed interiors enclose and protect the old way of life. The forest in the night holds on to its secrets. The flickering firelight, the drum beat of the drunken villagers and Yamuna's cry of pain rend the darkness, giving it a new dimension. Once publicly disgraced, Yamuna in her white garb is exposed to the harsh light of day. The play of contrasts carries on in another plain. The shrill outpourings of the village gossip Godavaramma conflict with the stark silence of Yamuna; the beleaguered innocence of Nani is opposed by the wilful delinquency of Sastri. *Ghatashraddha* is a connoisseur's film, to be enjoyed at leisure, as layer upon layer of precious details reveal themselves— each a significant contribution to a total artistic experience.

GUDDI (Darling Child)
colour, 122 minutes, Hindi, 1971

Production: Rupam Chitra/ Direction: Hrishikeh Mukherjee/ Story, dialogue and lyrics: Gulzar/ Screenplay: Hrishikesh Mukherjee, Gulzar, D.N. Mukherjee/ Camera: Jayant Pathare/ Music: Vasant Desai/ Playback: Vani Jairam/ Art Direction: Ajit Banerjee/ Editing: Das Dhaimade/ Sound: George D'Cruz
Cast: Dharmendra, Sumita Sanyal, Jaya Bhaduri, Utpal Dutta, Vijay Sharma, Samit, Hangal, Asrani, Arti, Keshto Mukherjee

KUSUM is a lively adolescent whose world revolves round filmstars, and the fantasy of the screen is more real to her than her daily life. Motherless, she has been brought up by an indulgent father and a loving brother and sister-in-law. While the men in the household refuse to be concerned, her sister-in-law worries about Kusum. She cannot be kept in minis forever; they must put her in a *sari* and find her a husband soon. Kusum's sister-in-law and her brother Navin have grown up as wards of an eccentric uncle, Professor Gupta, who lives in Bombay. Now Navin comes to Kusum's town to be interviewed for a job. A frequent visitor to her home, he settles down to a game of chess with Kusum's father till his sister appears and he shouts "Statue!" She freezes till Navin takes pity on her and says "Over!" and is rewarded with suitable sisterly chastisement. It is a game the whole family play with whoops of childish delight. Kusum is enormously pleased to find Navin at home, and insists that he takes her to the cinema. Navin has always known her as a lovable little girl, and is quite taken aback when goaded by his sister, Kusum appears in a *sari* for the date. Once they leave, Kusum's sister-in-law announces that she will speak to her uncle about marrying Kusum to her brother. Her husband and father-in-law heartily approve. Meanwhile Kusum is sorely disappointed when instead of seeing a film, they spend the day visiting ancient monuments. "I know why you have brought me here," says Kusum. "You hate films and love these broken pieces of stone." Navin tries to explain that he wanted to be alone with her, but it has no effect on young Kusum who cannot see any romance in real life.

Kusum's friend Tara's elder brother is determined to be a filmstar and hangs about film crews that occasionally come to their town. He manages to smuggle in Tara's friends with him one day, and they rush around taking autographs. Kusum, however, waits for an opportunity to be alone for a minute with her most favourite star, Dharmendra. A few commonplace words, an autograph on a film programme saying "with love," and Kusum runs home with her eyes full of dreams. At school the teacher talks about Meera Bai, who five hundred years ago left a kingdom to be a wandering devotee of Lord Krishna. She sang of human love for a god, love that can never find fruition on earth: just Kusum's cup of tea. When, after her annual examinations, her sister-in-law takes her to her uncle's home in Bombay, and Navin expresses his willingness to marry her, Kusum turns into a latter day Meera Bai. She loves another, she says, looking tragic. He is married and even has children, so her love must remain a secret. Worried at first, Navin is irritated to learn that the target of her emotions is no other than matinee idol Dharmendra. "Kusum is just behaving in an immature manner," says Navin's uncle, Professor Gupta. "Don't worry, I'll fix her." But Navin is not convinced.

Through an author friend, Professor Gupta meets Dharmendra, who agrees to help him. So Kusum visits the studios where stars come and go, surprising her with their day-to-day personalities, so often the opposite of the stereotyped roles they play on the screen. She learns of the real heroes behind the screen, the directors; music makers; technicians; the daily helps who earn a pittance on a production that costs millions. She sees the reality behind the facade, and starts valuing a simple ordinary man like Navin, a generous man, a man of principle. To add to it all, Dharmendra and Professor Gupta cook up a few real-life dramas which even Navin knows nothing about. The hero allows Navin to beat him at a game of tennis. He even arranges for Navin to fight him and his uncle disguised as ruffians who "attack" Kusum, if only to prove that he needs no stuntman to fight on his behalf and get hurt in the process. Kusum looks upon him with pride and wonder, but Navin tends to avoid her still. Finally, when he gets the job he was interviewed for, and must leave in a day, Kusum takes the offensive. She slyly sends him off to the terrace in search of his sister who is not there. Catching him alone there, she tries to make peace, but her inexperience only leads to another quarrel. She weeps angrily, and he, after telling her that he loves her and cannot bear this situation, turns to go. "Statue!" cries our weeping heroine, and puts her arms round her frozen hero. Professor Gupta, looking in on the scene, turns his eyes heavenwards and whispers with folded hands: "Glory be to Dharmendra!"

A CHARMING tribute to a real matinee idol, *Guddi* with its unusual storyline was a great success in the days when sex and violence were still not firmly established as the staple of popular cinema. Seventeen years after the film was made, Dharmendra is still a hero of the Hindi screen, so is his eldest son. But in the decade of the seventies he was at the height of his career, and the very human portrayal of the filmstar as an ordinary individual must have done further wonders for his image in the eyes of his audience. The reality behind the screen is shown without radically damaging the fantasy that the cinema stands for. For the hero is still a good man with a great heart and worthy of being a hero. Jaya Bhaduri as the lovable Kusum, became known to the public as the *Guddi* girl, although she was nearer twenty-four than fourteen when she played the role. Jaya Bhaduri's career started in her early teens as a little sister in Satyajit Ray's *Mahanagar*. She later joined the Bombay industry and in spite of her petite looks and lack of obvious sex-appeal, became a highly successful actress till her retirement from the cinema after her marriage to the greatest matinee idol of them all, Amitabh Bachchan.

One of the special attractions of *Guddi* was the array of well-known film personalities who appeared in their real, day-to-day persona in the many studio sequences. For the audience it was a novel experience, almost like meeting them face to face, like Kusum, and carrying a bit of the glamour home with them. Incidentally, Kusum was not the only one to be impressed by the Meera Bai legend. Gulzar, who wrote the story of *Guddi*, and made his little heroine fantasize as a modern Meera, himself directed a moving film a decade later on the life of the poet saint.

GUIDE (The Guide)
colour, 179 minutes, Hindi, 1965

Production: Navketan/ Direction, screenplay and dialogue: Vijay Anand/ Story:
R.K. Narayan/ Camera: Fali Mistry/ Music: S.D. Burman/ Lyrics: Shailendra/
Editing: Vijay Anand, Babu Sheikh
Cast: Dev Anand, Waheeda Rehman, Leela Chitnis, Anwar Hussain, Ulhas,
Jagirder, Rashid Khan, Kishore Sahu

RAJU, ONCE A successful tourist guide, hesitates to return to his home-town
after his release from jail. In the little town where he reigned as an uncrowned
king, he will now be shunned as a thief. Raju decides to search for his
fortunes elsewhere. After many days of aimless wandering, he ends up in a
village temple wearing over his threadbare clothes a saffron scarf which had
once belonged to some passing mendicant, and finds himself suddenly
elevated to the position of a holy man. Six months pass; Raju's mother and
Rosie, a dancer and Raju's erstwhile companion, arrive at the jail to take him
home. The jailor tells them that Raju has been released six months ahead of
time, and Rosie, despite the old woman's hostility, takes Raju's mother home
and relates her own side of the story.

Rosie is the daughter of a *Devdasi*—a professional temple dancer who is
considered little above a prostitute. She has dancing in her blood, but her
mother, in an attempt to give her a respectable existence, marries her off to a
middle-aged archeologist, Marco, who surrounds himself with dead stone and
has no time at all for his flesh and blood wife. He also forces Rosie to leave
dancing as it is not a respectable pastime. On a holiday, they take Raju as their
guide, and while Marco spends his days and nights at an excavation site,
drinking and whoring on the side, the rebellious Rosie tries to commit suicide
in despair. She is saved by Raju who, realizing her inner conflict and seeing
her dance, encourages her to lead a life of her own as an artiste.

One day, after confronting Marco for a last time, when she is humiliated by
him beyond endurance, Rosie comes to Raju's home. Raju refuses to coun-
tenance the taunts of his neighbours for giving shelter to a dancing girl—for
that is what they think Rosie is when they hear the sound of her anklets every
day when she practises her dancing steps in the enclosed courtyard of the
house. Abandoned by all his friends, and neglecting his own career, Raju
insists on grooming Rosie to become a professional dancer. After a terrible
family quarrel, his mother leaves for her brother's home. Hurt but undaunted,
Raju decides to launch Rosie as a dancer, and succeeds beyond his wildest
dreams. Rosie becomes the rage and Raju suddenly finds himself a rich man,
but their personal relationship deteriorates when he takes to drinking and
gambling with rich friends. Rosie moves away from him. Learning that Marco
wants to close a joint account and wishes Rosie to remove her jewels from the
locker, and worried that Marco's sudden generosity can only mean that he
wants Rosie back now that she is famous, Raju forges Rosie's signature in an
attempt to keep Marco away from her. Meanwhile failing to revive the
relationship they used to share, he leaves Rosie and goes back home. Raju's
forgery is discovered by Marco, and he is arrested. Though she initially

misunderstands his motives, Rosie still meets him in jail and promises to wait
for him.

Raju now has got accustomed to being a holy man, but in that role he has
actually helped the village to acquire its own school, hospital and postal
service. The villagers gather round him lovingly one day, and he tells them a
story his mother had told him long ago, of another holy man who had kept a
fast for twelve days to bring rain to a parched land. Unfortunately, before the
story is forgotten, drought hits the village. When the starving villagers attack
the grocer who is hoarding grain and a riot takes place, Raju decides to
intervene. He tells Bhola's half-wit brother who comes with his food, "I
won't eat till the riot is stopped. There is a drought on. Is this any time to kill
each other?" The boy reports his words in a way that leads to the assumption
that Raju will now undertake a twelve days' fast to bring rain for them.
Horrified, Raju calls Bhola and tries to explain that he is no saint, and in any
case has no miraculous powers. But Bhola falls at his feet: "You are our only
hope. Even a jailbird can become a saint. When you have fasted for twelve
days, surely the heavens will crack open and the gods will receive your
prayers." Caught in a bind, Raju tries to escape after two days of fasting, but
taunted by the village Brahmins, he returns. By the time six days pass, people
from other drought-stricken villages pour in to have a view of the saint. For
Raju the playacting becomes the reality. He starts believing that this is a task
assigned to him by god. Looking for his son, Raju's mother too comes there;
so does Rosie. They watch helplessly as Raju slowly drifts towards death.
The rains come at last, and while the villagers dance wildly outside, Raju
reaches another shore where his soul and he are one and nothing else remains
—no joy, nor sorrow; no life nor death; no man nor god—just as he had
visualized it.

WRITTEN IN English by a well-known Indian novelist, *Guide* is an unusual
story. The tale of an ordinary man who is transformed into a saint by the force
of circumstances, it was the ideal role for Dev Anand, who had perfected the
portrayal of the large-hearted, but ungodly common-man hero right through
his career. It was also one of the most successful directorial ventures of his
younger brother, Vijay Anand. Waheeda Rehman, already an established
actress, proved herself a marvellous dancer in the role of Rosie. In spite of the
stereotypical deterioration of Raju as a rich entrepreneur, the disintegration of
his relationship with Rosie is extremely real, and rare in popular cinema. Rosie
never gets a divorce from Marco, but lives with Raju. The relationship which
would still be socially unacceptable in India, is described with enough subtlety
and compassion to avoid censure from the audience.

Raju's reluctant sainthood, a tragic experience both for the viewer and Raju
himself, is redeemed by Raju's own gradual acceptance of selfless responsibility towards his fellow human beings. In a country where gods and holy
men appear at every streetcorner, Raju's understanding of his own sainthood
is essentially heretical; for he knows that by fulfilling the role thrust upon him,
he will attain mystical isolation from all that is human or godly, just as he
knows that it is unimportant if he can achieve a miracle. His task is to sustain
his people till the rains come, and all his being, purified of every other desire,

moves towards that goal, and towards the final nothingness. Though the visual translation of Raju's inner conflict—between the guide and the saint—is far too obvious to be credible, a certain inner force both of the story and its cinematic presentation carries the film triumphantly towards the tragic and sublime finale.

HOLI (The Festival of Fire)
colour, 120 min, Hindi, 1984

Production: Film Unit/ Direction: Ketan Mehta/ Original play: Mahesh Elkunchwar/ Screenplay: Mahesh Elkunchwar and Ketan Mehta/ Camera: Jehangir Choudhary/ Music: Rajat Dholakia/ Art Direction: Archana Shah/ Editing: Subhash Sehgal/ Sound: A.M. Padmanabhan
Cast: Sanjeev Gandhi, Rahul Ranade, Asutosh Gowarikar, Amole Gupte, Om Puri, Naseeruddin Shah, Deepti Naval, Dr Shreeram Lagoo

IN A TYPICAL college in a typical Indian city, the hostel boys are a rowdy lot. The teaching staff suffer from the common apathy of most teachers in similar colleges. The administration has the usual problems, with ill-paid employees periodically going on strike. On the whole, the college is a very normal place. But on this particular day, when the boys rise from their slumber, some with the customary hangover, they are not so perturbed to find no water in the taps again, as when they hear that it is not going to be a holiday after all. Instead there will be a lecture in the auditorium by the Chairman of the Board, on the cultural heritage of India. But it is the day of the festival of fire, Holi, and the boys decide not to attend the classes. The hostel superintendent, the only lecturer with some human links with the students, watches with apprehension their growing restlessness. A notice announcing a further postponement of examinations adds to the bitterness. A fight erupts out of nowhere between the principal's nephew and another student, in which the principal's nephew is hurt and the other boy is promptly rusticated. It is an unjustifiably drastic punishment, and the news spreads like wildfire. Resistance is organized in the library, in the laboratory, in the classrooms and the college grounds. In the auditorium, the first egg hits the Chairman, and pandemonium follows.

To save his own job, the principal decides to track down the culprits. The hostel superintendent politely refuses to help. The principal now blackmails one of the hostel boys, whose father he knows, and who is in any case a loner, and a butt of jokes in the campus. Imbued with a false sense of power, the boy walks into the principal's trap. A large group of boys, all from the hostel, are immediately rusticated, and asked to vacate their rooms by the morning. The boys, not all of them actually guilty of rebellion, are now all in a rage. They make a bonfire of the hostel furniture and their textbooks. Feeling impelled to share his sense of triumph, the informer confides in the boy whom he hates and fears the most, and whose name he has kept out of the list. As a result he is mercilessly humiliated by everyone, and just about manages to rush away from his tormentors and lock himself in his room.

In the gathering dusk, the young rebels sit listlessly on the steps of the hostel, their anger giving way to depression, when one of them discovers the informer hanging from the fan in his room, quite dead. The boys confront faceless policemen who come to investigate the suicide. In the morning, the police van carrying the boys away, is caught in the midst of a rowdy, jostling crowd of merrymakers, playing with colours. The boys stare blankly, hopelessly, out of the barred windows at the shouting revellers, as the van edges its way out.

THE FESTIVAL of "Holi" originated in pre-Vedic times as a spring celebration, involving ritual sacrifice to ensure good crops. Vedic priests subsequently gave their sanction to the celebration, and even later, myths were invented to give the ceremony a Brahminical orientation. In these myths, the sacrificial fire burnt the forces of evil, while whatever was good was retrieved by the gods. Ketan Mehta's *Holi* reverses the original myth. Here the sacrificial fire consumes the vital energies of the youth, after stifling their aspirations within the narrow confines of an unimaginative and regressive educational system.

> We have tasted life here
> We have tasted poison here
> To mend a torn pocket
> We have sewn our hearts here
> The one who knows not himself is giving knowledge away
> What journey is this, where does the path lead?
>
> We are not used to life
> We have no time for death
> There is only a last wish
> To witness the deluge
> What kind of world is it, where we'll be going now?
> What journey is this, where does the path lead?

So sing the boys as they sit tired and spent on the hostel steps, and the words are carried from mouth to mouth. *Holi* recounts a journey without a destination. Within the short span of a day and a night, the students move from one petty disappointment to another, from annoyance to anger, to violence, to death. The survivors, themselves tormented so far, become the new tormentors. Unknown to themselves, they adopt their new roles in the shifting power game of their lives. Apart from being the only serious film so far on the malaise of present day education in India and its consequent student unrest, *Holi* is a parable made up of a total of only forty shots. Mehta's justification for the experiment lies in the economics of film making in the country. Be that as it may, its merit lies in that it goes unnoticed, not a contrivance, but an integral part of the film's internal rhythm.

Commenting on his use of live sound synchronization and long hand-held shots, Mehta says: "First and foremost, it is an experiment. An experiment specially tailored for the topic and structure of this film....You can never quite recreate the mood, the tension, noises, the intonation, later in the dubbing room. This is all the more true when the cast is nonprofessional, which is as I wanted it. And in *Holi*, the camera moves freely, gyrating 360 degrees to capture the buzz, the whispers, the restlessness of a listless collective, all in one take. And the end effect, I think, is that the film achieves unbroken, greater and greater levels of intenseness...Like Ravel's *Bolero*." [In an interview in *Cinema India-International,* October-December, 1984.]

INSAAF KA TARAZU (The Scales of Justice)
colour, 145 minutes, Hindi, 1980

Production: B.R. Films/ Direction: B.R. Chopra/ Story, screenplay and dialogue: Sharad Kumar/ Camera: Dharam Chopra/ Music: Ravindra Jain/ Lyrics: Sahir/ Playback: Asha Bhonsle, Mahendra Kapoor, Hemlata/ Art Direction: Shanti Das/ Editing: B. Mane/ Sound: B.K. Chaturvedi
Cast: Zeenat Aman, Padmini Kolhapure, Dharmendra, Raj Babbar, Deepak Parashar, Shreeram Lagoo, Iftekhar, Simi, Jagdish Raj, Vijay Sharma, Prem Sagar, Om Shivpuri, Sudha Shivpuri, Yunus Pervez, Sujit Kumar, Hiralal

BHARATI, a professional model, first meets Ramesh Gupta, a millionaire's son, at a fashion show where she is crowned beauty queen. Subsequently, he makes his admiration evident by dogging her footsteps. He visits her at a modelling assignment, throws a party on her birthday, presents her with a necklace that he claims is glass but is suspiciously like diamond, and three days after the party insists on personally showing her the photographs taken on that day. Bharati, who lives in a little flat with her school-going sister Nita, and is about to get married to Ashok Sharma, a compere and painter, casually asks Ramesh to drop in with the photographs. In her profession she is used to the admiration of strangers, and to fending for herself as a working girl. Yet she is unprepared for what happens. Finding her alone in the flat, Ramesh rapes her brutally. The ravaged Bharati rings the police, and Ramesh has to stand for trial. Ramesh takes the position that his only guilt was his incapacity to say "no," that it was he who was seduced, that there was no rape. His lawyer ruthlessly blackens Bharati's character and profession, and the judge, in the absence of any real evidence other than the circumstantial, acquits Ramesh.

Shattered, Bharati refuses to marry Ashok. He has stood by her all this while, but his parents are no longer willing to have her as a daughter-in-law. With the scandal that results from the case, Bharati's career takes a downward plunge, and Nita is faced with her friends' curiosity in school. The beleaguered sisters leave Bombay and settle down in Pune, where Bharati takes the first job that comes her way, at an armaments store. Nita finishes school, takes a secretarial course, and starts looking for a job. She is interviewed by a large business concern, and is told that she has been shortlisted for the post of the managing director's secretary, and must come back to be interviewed again by the managing director himself. At the interview, Nita is shocked to see that the man is Ramesh. This time Nita is his victim, and Bharati, finding her sister in a state of collapse at home, and hearing her story, rushes out determined to give Ramesh the punishment that he will escape once again. For how do you legally prove rape? She goes to the shop where she works. Her employer is away and has left the keys with her. Armed with a pistol, she goes after Ramesh, and shoots him dead in front of witnesses.

Bharati makes no effort to escape, and stands in front of the same judge who had two years ago acquitted a guilty man. This time Mr Chandra, who had once defended Ramesh, is the prosecuting lawyer. Bharati reminds them of the earlier case, and identifies herself as the same girl who had accused Ramesh of rape. She says she is not guilty; the criminals are the judge, the lawyer, and their justice that allows a guilty man to go free for lack of legal evidence, and condemns the innocent to a living death. But she does not mention her sister. She admits, however, that this was not revenge for herself, but for another girl in a similar position. When the judge asks who the girl is, Bharati only says that as she knows she must die, she does not want this other innocent to go through the same torture that she had to go through two years ago. Now Nita volunteers to give evidence. Her ravaged innocence, her extreme youth and her despair move even the aggressive Mr Chandra. When Nita collapses in the witness box, Bharati holds her close and turns to the lawyer. "You must have known the truth two years ago, why did you do this injustice to me?" she asks. Bewildered, the lawyer says, "But justice is not my business, that is for the judge to offer. I only did my job, saved my client!" "It could be your daughter next time. Did you save Ramesh for this?" asks Bharati. "Justice that has no power to protect has no right to punish either," pronounces the judge as he frees Bharati and resigns from his position. As the courtroom empties, Ashok comes with his parents. "I'm still waiting for you," he says to Bharati.

MADE AT THE peak of the "sex and violence" era in Hindi cinema, *Insaf ka Tarazu* was hailed by the audience as a spirited defence of innocence in the context of a law that is incapable of providing protection against sexual assault. Yet the arguments used in court against Bharati are so powerful that they establish rather than refute the fact that a rape victim cannot hope for legal redress. Ramesh's lawyer, Mr Chandra, takes recourse to character assassination, and the demand for a witness. The position taken by the woman lawyer appearing for Bharati, that rape cannot possibly have objective witnesses to the event, is not strong enough to prove that Bharati has been raped. The fact that she was tied up, and threatened with a knife, is turned round by Ramesh who says he did as he was told by Bharati, who wanted him to make love to her that way. That she has the guts to confront Ramesh in court, is another fact that goes against Bharati. "Would a good Indian woman ever do such a shameless thing?" asks Mr Chandra. "She would rather die than make a public outcry over rape." In the trial for Ramesh's murder, Bharati reminds the judge that his earlier judgement had only ensured that no other woman would have the courage to do what she had done. And that seems to be the insidious message of the film itself.

For the Indian audience, however sympathetic they may feel about her, Bharati is a woman who belongs to a totally alien world. As a professional model living alone in Bombay, her life is so different from the average Indian woman's, that Mr Chandra's arguments would sound more convincing to them than those of the woman lawyer, or even Bharati. Bharati's appeal is ultimately to the emotions, for the audience have indeed witnessed her rape. They are the only ones in the know. Worse still, a major portion of the audience must have enjoyed the three rapes that the film describes in vivid detail under the guise of sympathy for the victims and outrage at the injustice they must suffer. Each sequence is presented differently, providing additional interest.

The first is a pre-credits sequence, where an unknown woman is raped in shadow-play, behind a screen. The rapist is killed by an army officer who appears in front of the same judge whom Bharati faces twice later on. The words the officer uses in defending himself, are the same that Bharati uses in the last courtroom confrontaton. What happens ultimately to the army officer we are never told. Meanwhile the real story begins. Bharati's rape is the second one in the film, shown in garish daylight, in every gruesome detail. The third rape, that of Nita, takes place in the evening in a plush office room lit by powerful electric lamps. Nita is commanded to take off her clothes and lie down. The process is heartrending, as she gives in step by step. With the Indian censors waiting in the wings, not a single kiss, not a bared breast is shown. The real act of rape is left to the imagination. But the vivid portrayal of the process is far more horrific and titillating than an intercourse on screen can ever be.

Bharati's form of justice is obviously not meant for the average woman who would not have access to a pistol and the rapist together at the right moment. Nor can she hope that the judge will pardon her for an act of wilful murder, and then conveniently resign after making such an unconventional gesture. One of the most blatantly reactionary films in the history of Indian cinema, *Insaf ka Tarazu* too has got away with murder like its heroine. The film's fast pace, the sophistication of its presentation and the powerfully acted courtroom scenes, created for its vivid rapes and insidious reasoning an artificial emotional validity that made it a major success of the Hindi screen.

JAANE BHI DO YAARO (Who Pays the Piper...)
colour, 130 minutes, Hindi, 1983

Production: National Film Development Corporation/ Direction: Kundan Shah/ Story and screenplay: Kundan Shah, Sudhir Mishra/ Camera: Binod Pradhan/ Music: Vanraj Bhatia/ Art Direction: Robin Das/ Editing: Renu Saluja
Cast: Naseeruddin Shah, Ravi Baswani, Bhakti Barve, Satish Shah, Om Puri, Pankaj Kapoor, Satish Kaushik, Neena Gupta, Depak Quazir, Rajesh Puri, Zafar Sanjari, Vidhu Vinod Chopra

VINOD CHOPRA and Sudhir Mishra, two impecunious photographers, borrow heavily to open a photographic studio. After months of sitting idle, they get an assignment from *Khabardar,* a magazine that exposes corruption, to photograph the contractor Tarneja, who even has Police Commissioner D'Mello in his pay. At a site where Tarneja is building a skyscraper, D'Mello, bribed by Tarneja, gives him permission to illegally add another story to the building. But the news is not scandalous enough, and the photographs are still to come. So *Khabardar's* editor Shobha goes to meet the photographers, who take her for an ordinary client and flirt with her outrageously. Though initially annoyed, Shobha forgives them when she sees their work, and takes them with her to D'Mello's beach house where Tarneja comes for a secret meeting. By fooling D'Mello as *Newsweek* reporters, and with Tarneja hidden from them in the bathroom, Shobha and Vinod manage to photograph the tenders they were discussing.

But after they leave, Tarneja discovers that D'Mello's next guest is his arch rival, contractor Ahuja. Slipping out through a skylight, Tarneja tries to shoot Ahuja from the window. But, having just learnt from the "foreign correspondents" how in America they constantly throw food away, D'Mello encourages Ahuja to have some cake and chuck the rest expansively out of the window. The cake hits Tarneja in the eye, deflecting his shot to the electric light and the meeting is adjourned amidst chaos.

Shobha now wants Vinod and Sudhir to spy on the two contractors in Tarneja's bungalow, where they are supposed to work out a compromise. Pretending to be Ahuja's gunmen, the two intrepid photographers manage to disrupt the proceedings. In the middle of it all, enters Srivastava, the Assistant Commissioner of Police, to say that both Ahuja and Tarneja have been duped. D'Mello has given the disputed contract to a third party.

Tired of social service and little money, and reading of a photographic contest, Vinod and Sudhir decide to have a go at it. In the process they land up with a shot of a performing monkey in a park, which when blown up shows Tarneja with a gun in the background, shooting someone. They go there at night and find the body, but it disappears before they know whose corpse it is. Soon Tarneja's new flyover is inaugurated and named after the dead D'Mello! Attending the function, Sudhir picks up a cufflink near the memorial for D'Mello which matches the one they had found in the park near the vanished corpse. At night, from under the memorial they dig out a coffin, and after photographing D'Mello's body, sit down next to it to sort out the bewildering sequence of events that have overtaken them. But a train passes below, the flyover vibrates, and before they know it, the coffin has disappeared. Worse still, a constable takes down their names for loafing at night and removes the few coins they had for their suburban train tickets.

The coffin rolls down to where Ahuja drives up in his car in a state of merry inebriation. Thinking it a stalled car, he tows it away to his garage. Vinod and Sudhir show Shobha their photographs and pretend they have hidden the body. Without telling them Shobha rings Tarneja, blackmails him, and to scare him further, visits him with Vinod and Sudhir. But Tarneja has prepared a special welcome for them. There are time bombs under their chairs. Fortunately, the bombs do not go off in time, and the three escape. That day, the news on television features the collapse of the new flyover. In an interview, Tarneja calls it sabotage and claims that he has only used "foreign" material to build the flyover. To complicate matters, the television interview also features the constable on the beat who mentions meeting two suspicious strangers called Vinod and Sudhir near the flyover before its collapse. Shobha says now she will have her revenge on Tarneja and never mind about the constable. All she needs is the body of D'Mello.

Trying to explain how they lost the body, Vinod and Sudhir realize that Shobha is more interested in blackmailing Tarneja than in exposing corruption. They leave in disgust, but seeing Ahuja's car at her press the next day, spy on them and soon realize where the body is. Tarneja's agents, spying on Ahuja, see Vinod and Sudhir rush away. They follow, and Ahuja, Shobha, Tarneja and Srivastava soon join the chase. After lugging the body on rollerskates through many an adventure, including a party of burkha-clad Muslim ladies and a costume drama on stage, Vinod and Sudhir finally get to the police. But while they wait for truth and justice to triumph, Srivastava unites the warring crooks and arranges to save the situation by penalizing the two photographers as saboteurs. After all, they were seen on the flyover by the constable before it collapsed.

With a ringing chorus of "We shall overcome" on the soundtrack, Vinod and Sudhir walk up to the camera in their prison clothes, mime their demise and drop below the frame.

A WILDLY funny film, harking back to the days when slapstick was king, *Jaane bhi do Yaaro* is also a sad comment on present day India. It contains allusions to actual events in Bombay, narrated within an absurd and farcical framework. Bombay, till recently, did have a doughty Police Commissioner with a Portuguese name who is now floundering among the terrorists in Punjab, and one of the flyovers in the city did collapse some years ago while being built. Explaining it away, Ahuja tells Shobha in the film: "You see, we mix sand with our cement, but Tarneja mixes cement with the sand."

The film is also full of little private jokes. Vinod Chopra and Sudhir Mishra, both real-life filmmakers, not only lend their names to the two innocents who lead the cast, but are also involved in the production of the film. Kundan Shah had earlier worked as production manager in Vinod Chopra's film, *Sazaye Maut*. His association with another director of the new cinema movement, Saeed Akhtar Mirza and his film, *Albert Pinto ko Gussa kyon Ata Hai?*, is recalled in the sequence where Vinod fools Tarneja's agent Ashok by pretending to be a "Deep Throat" called Albert Pinto. Naseeruddin Shah, who plays Vinod in *Jaane bhi do Yaaro*, actually acted as Albert Pinto in Mirza's film. The park where D'Mello is supposed to have been murdered, is named Antonioni Park, and the two photographers must blow up their photograph of the monkey to discover the monkey business taking place in the bushes behind them.

"I react to life like the common man on a suburban train," says Kundan Shah. "On his way home he reads the newspaper, but can do nothing if the news angers him. So he throws back his head and laughs. That is how humour is born. In fact, comedy reflects this very frustration." [*Indian Cinema 83/84*, Directorate of Film Festivals, 1984]

JAI SANTOSHI MA (In Praise of Mother Santoshi)
colour, 3877.50 m, Hindi, 1975

Production: Bhagyalaxmi Chitra Mandir/ Direction: Vijay Sharma/ Story: Pandit R. Priyadarshi/ Camera: Shobhendu Roy/ Music: C. Arjun/ Lyrics: Pradeep/ Playback: Manna Dey, Mahendra Kapoor, Usha Mangeshkar, Pradeep/ Art Direction: Hirabhai Patel
Cast: Anita Guha, Ashish Kumar, Kanan Koshal, Trilok Kapur, Mahipal, Manhar Desai, B.M. Vyas, Bharat Bhushan, Anant Marathe, Rajan Haksar, Dilip Dutt, Johnny Whisky, Shree Bhagwan, Kundan, Radheshyam, Rajnibala, Leela Mishra, Asha Poddar, Lata Arora, Padma Rani, Neelam, Bela Bose, Surendra Mishra

GANESHA, the elephant-headed god, son of Lord Shiva, is approached by his family and Narada the ascetic god, to create a daughter. He obliges, and a little girl appears on a lotus. Narada calls her Santoshi—the one who brings satisfaction. On earth, in Sonpur village, Santoshi's devotees sing to her image. Leading the prayer is Satyavati, daughter of a village priest. On her way home, Satyavati meets a stranger and it is love at first sight. The stranger is Birju from Mirpur, the youngest of seven sons of a widow, who spends his days singing devotional songs. Asked to sing at the temple in Sonpur, Birju meets Satyavati again, and rescues her when she is attacked by the local ruffian, Banke. Soon the families get together and Satyavati is given in marriage to Birju. In heaven, the wives of the holy trinity—Brahma, Vishnu and Shiva—are teased by Narada to feel jealous of Santoshi and her growing number of admirers which include their own husbands. On earth, after a day of ill-treatment from her sisters-in-law, Satyavati dreams of the three goddesses warning her not to worship Santoshi any more. She humbly refuses their command, and next morning Birju has a confrontation with his brothers and leaves home promising to come back a rich man. The three goddesses now raise a storm on calm waters to drown Birju's boat. Satyavati wakes up at night. "Look after my husband," she prays, and Santoshi herself goes into the river to rescue Birju. News comes of Birju's drowning, but Satyavati refuses to believe that her husband is dead.

Looking for a job, Birju reaches another temple of Santoshi far away, where he revives an old man who is suddenly taken ill. The man takes Birju home and makes him the manager of his jewellery business. Meanwhile Satyavati, tortured by her sisters-in-law, and driven to suicide, is saved by Narada who tells her that by praying to Santoshi for sixteen Fridays, she will get all she wishes. To try her further, the three goddesses now make Birju forget his wife and he is drawn to Gita, the old man's daughter, who loves him. Satyavati is also harassed by Banke but the goddess appears and frightens the ruffian with the vision of a venomous snake till he falls off a cliff. Many Fridays pass, and Narada tells the goddesses that Satyavati will soon have her wish, for tomorrow is the sixteenth Friday. The goddesses unsuccessfully try to stop Satyavati from completing her cycle of prayers. With the help of a few miracles, Satyavati reaches the temple. "My husband has forgotten me," she cries to Santoshi, "remind him of my existence." In the jeweller's home, Birju suddenly calls out to Satyavati. Gita and her father are surprised to learn that Birju has a wife. But to vindicate him, a heavenly voice tells Birju that his forgetfulness was a curse of the three goddesses. Back home, finding his wife in rags crying for a piece of bread, the horrified Birju takes her away and builds a separate home.

Satyavati, now happy and secure, wants to unite the family and invites them to a temple celebration. In heaven, Narada teases the three goddesses. "Here is your last chance," says the naughty ascetic and whispers in their ears. On the day of the celebration, Birju's sisters-in-law poison the offerings to the goddess. In heaven the angered Santoshi makes the thrones of the gods rock like boats on a stormy sea. On earth children die after eating the poisoned offerings, a fierce wind blows, and the two sisters-in-law are stricken by leprosy. Accused of being a murderer and a witch, Satyavati sings in prayer. The storm passes, and the goddess appears. At Satyavati's request, the dead come back to life, and the sisters-in-law are cured. They confess their misdeeds and pray for mercy. In heaven, Narada takes the three goddesses to appease the wrath of Santoshi, but they laugh when they get to her. "We know her, Narada," they say gleefully. "She's our granddaughter. We were only testing the devotion of her followers." The holy trinity appear near Santoshi, and Narada requests them all to bless Santoshi so that her name too is henceforth immortalized like their own.

A FASCINATING story, especially for the uninitiated, the film established a hitherto unknown goddess in the homes of millions of Indians, and made a pile for its producer. Released the same year as the now legendary *Sholay,* and without a star cast or any of the technical sophistications that were the hallmark of the other film, *Jai Santoshi Ma* became a legend in its own right. Today Santoshi is regularly worshipped by women from all walks of life, from computer programmers to housewives. Hindus have always had their innumerable gods to fall back upon, but perhaps by the year of the film's release it had suddenly become imperative to have an omnipotent leader, who could right all wrongs at the snap of her heavenly fingers, something that our more familiar divinities, as well as our political leaders, seemed reluctant to do.

Referring to Umberto Eco's *Travels in Hyper-Reality* (Picador 1987), critic Iqbal Masud writes: "The Pax Americana is breaking down and the barbarians are threatening civilization. Insecurity is the key word. Such a climate generates outcasts, mystics and adventurers. The grip of rationality and reason is loosened. This does not mean that institutionalized religion is coming back. What is emerging is vulgarised, crude adoration, a sense of terror, and an irresistible fascination for the powerful and the omnipotent: This analysis is applicable to the influences on our cinema. We have our own variations of our adorations and of the omnipotent." Masud goes on to analyse the new mythology as it expresses itself in *Jai Santoshi Ma* in relation to the mythological experiences of early Indian cinema: "The first difference is the emotional tone of the film. Neither in *Harishchandra* nor *Tukaram* was the divine element humanised the way it is in *Santoshi Ma.* The frenetic and excited quarrels of Satyavati's sisters-in-law are exactly paralleled in the heavens. It is as if the exigencies, the hardships and harshness of the seventies were forcing themselves into mythology. The anger of Santoshi Ma at the offence to her particular ritual and the resulting mass deaths have a certain savagery absent from earlier mythological films.

"A second difference is the importance given to rape scenes. There are two attempted rapes on Satyavati. The second is more explicit. The camera focuses on breasts and stretched legs....A last feature of the film is its crass surrender to materialism. When Birju is raised to riches by Santoshi Ma, he makes a crude display of wealth. From beggary, Satyavati is raised to an expensive sari-clad, big mansion-living status. The contrast with *Sant Tukaram* of 50 years ago where the saint gently chides his wife and children on their greedily grasping the finery sent by the king could not be more obvious." [*Cinema in India,* January-April 1988]

With its cardboard miracles and shrewish goddesses, its marketplace delineation of the abode of the gods, its simplistic division of people into blacks and whites, its deliberate sacrifice of reason, *Jai Santoshi Ma* appealed to that instinct for blind surrender. If your husband dallies with another woman, it is because the gods are trying you. If you are tortured by your in-laws, it is for the same reason. And if you have faith and are a saint, everything will be all right at the end. Except that fasting and prayers on sixteen Fridays cannot make all women saints. So it is not the fault of the gods if your prayers go unheard and your wishes remain unfulfilled. Either way, you cannot win. The most unfortunate outcome of the film, however, is not the identification of the crude materialism of the seventies with godhead, but the acceptance of Santoshi by great numbers of Indian women as the final arbiter of their lives.

Incidentally, the ascetic god Narada, the prime mover behind all the intrigues against Mother Santoshi, is supposed to be the proverbial mischief-maker among mortals and immortals alike.

KAGHAZ KE PHOOL (Paper Flowers)
b&w, 148 minutes, Hindi, 1959

Production: Guru Dutt Films Pvt. Ltd/ Direction: Guru Dutt/ Screenplay and dialogue: Abrar Alvi/ Camera: V.K. Murthy/ Music: S.D. Burman/ Lyrics: Kaifi Azmi/ Art Direction: M.R. Achrekar/ Editing: Y.G. Chauhan/ Sound: S.V. Raman
Cast: Waheeda Rehman, Guru Dutt, Baby Naaz, Johnny Walker, Veena, Tun Tun, Mehmood, Minoo Mumtaz, Mahesh Kaul

IN A DESOLATE film studio, Suresh Sinha, once a famous filmmaker, remembers his past.

Young Suresh is a very successful director who can dictate his own terms to a producer, or reject a popular star who refuses to deglamorize herself even when the role demands it. At home, however, his marriage is a failure. His wife Bina and her father, an old aristocrat, do not consider his profession respectable enough. Separated from his wife, Suresh is not even allowed to meet his daughter Pammi who is sent away to a boarding school in Dehra

Doon. Once on a wet, cold morning, having drowned his sorrows in alcohol the night before, Suresh takes shelter under a tree in a park. There he meets Shanti, a homeless girl, and offers her his coat to keep her warm. Back at work he is confronted with a crisis when his heroine demands drastic changes in a film under production. Faced with a choice between the star and his director who strongly opposes the changes, the producer opts for Suresh. The film is *Devdas,* and Suresh must now find a new heroine who has both the strength and the simplicity inherent in the character of Parvati. When Shanti walks into the studio to return his coat, Suresh realizes with a shock that she is the Parvati of his imagination. He makes an actress out of the reluctant girl, in spite of the opposition of the producer who wants a star. *Devdas* is a hit, and so is Shanti.

Rumours about Shanti and Suresh's friendship reach the press, and Pammi, teased by her classmates, comes back to Bombay in the hope of reuniting her parents. Pammi appeals to Shanti to stay out of her father's life and allow the marriage another chance. Moved by her earnestness, Shanti relinquishes her new career and the fame and fortune attending upon it, to go and teach in a village school. With Shanti out of his life, Suresh loses interest in his work and increasingly seeks solace in alcohol. His films begin to fail and he is sacked by the producer, who will only take him back if Shanti agrees to return to films. Shanti is willing to come back for his sake, but Suresh refuses to make use her to revive his career. An alcoholic now, he loses his right to keep Pammi in a bitter courtroom battle. The years pass, and Suresh, penniless and forgotten, tries to survive by taking a job as an "extra" in the same studio where he was once the most sought after person. But the film has Shanti as its heroine, and in despair, Suresh flees from the studio. Returning to the empty studio, Suresh now breathes in the smell of the dusty sets, recalling his days of glory. When the crew return and the doors are opened, they discover him lying dead in the director's chair.

THE LAST FILM to be directed by Guru Dutt, *Kaghaz ke Phool* was a financial disaster. Subsequently, till his death, Dutt only produced and acted in films. But a film like *Sahib Bibi aur Ghulam,* supposedly only produced by him, has always been attributed to him for its artistry and lyricism. Highly autobiographical in its theme, *Kaghaz ke Phool* presented the filmmaker's own dilemma with great poignancy, but failed to get a response from the mass audience who found the film too slow, and too personal. A virtually unknown actress, whom Guru Dutt happened to see in a dance sequence in a Telugu film and summoned to Bombay, became his heroine in his earlier and tremendously successful directorial venture, *Pyaasa.* He fashioned her into a star and an overnight success, much as Suresh Sinha had done for Shanti. Two years later in *Kaghaz ke Phool,* Waheeda Rehman as Shanti, in many ways re-enacted the role she played in Guru Dutt's own life. She remained a popular star long after Guru Dutt, unhappy in his personal life and suspicious of his own professional and artistic abilities, committed suicide. Today, rediscovered by a new generation of filmmakers and film viewers, *Kaghaz ke Phool* has become part of film nostalgia. Its intense romanticism, its lyrical camera, its deeper understanding of the subtleties of cinematic acting, and its homage to the world of

the big studios of another age, all combine to immortalize a director who was
convinced that he had failed.

KANCHANJUNGHA
colour, 100 minutes, Bengali, 1962

Production: N.C.A., Calcutta/ Direction, Script and Music: Satyajit Ray/
Camera: Subrata Mitra/ Art Direction: Bansi Chandragupta/ Editing: Dulal
Dutta
Cast: Chhabi Biswas, Karuna Banerjee, Pahari Sanyal, Subrata Sen Sharma,
Anubha Gupta, Anil Chatterjee, Alaknanda Roy, N. Viswanathan, Arun
Mukherjee, Haridhan Mukhopadhyay

INDRANATH Choudhury, a Bengali aristocrat, recipient of a British title, and
a man of immense authority, is on a holiday with his family at the hill-station
of Darjeeling in northern West Bengal. Though it is the last day of their stay,
they have still not had a glimpse of the celebrated snow-covered peak of
Kanchanjungha. But away from their normal surroundings, isolated amidst
the sweeping mists and pine forests, they finally face themselves, discovering
and admitting truths they have long denied in their lives. Indranath's wife,
Labanya, a fading beauty and a gentle, sensitive woman, has always accepted
her absolute submission to her husband's will. His elder daughter Anima,
unhappy in her marriage to Shankar, a marriage that was arranged by her
father, has found her own compromise with her circumstance. It is now the
turn of Monisha, the younger daughter, and in deference to changing social
mores, a suitable and rather pompous young engineer has been encouraged by
her father to woo her. Monisha, shy and reserved, is revolted by the brash
arrogance of her suitor, Pranab. But she knows that the final decision lies with
Indranath. There are only two people who do not come under Indranath's
direct surveillance—his son Anil, a playboy who has never managed to
outgrow his adolescence; and his brother-in-law, Jagadish, an eccentric bird-
watcher who, with quiet compassion, observes humanity as well.

Into this closed upper-class world of suppressed tensions, intrudes the
grotesque figure of Sibsankar Roy, once private tutor to Anil, who has come
to provide a change of air to his widowed and ailing sister-in-law. With him is
his unemployed young nephew, Ashok. Roy is the archetypal schoolmaster,
underpaid, unsuccessful, fawning and pragmatic. Lower in the social scale, in
Darjeeling they can only find place in a hotel physically lower down the hill
slopes. Puffing up to the Mall, he comes upon his ex-employer and introduces
Ashok to him in the hope of a job. In the meanwhile, a series of events
overtake the family.

Anima realizes that her husband has always known of her clandestine affair
with another man. They confront each other with the truth for the first time in
their life together, and for the sake of their child, take faltering steps towards a
more honest relationship. Monisha decides not to marry Pranab, even if it
means flouting her father's wishes. She strikes up a warm friendship with

Ashok in spite of the fact that he is unemployed, socially inferior and bitterly critical of her own class. The passive, submissive Labanya, who is not yet aware of Monisha's rebellion, but understands her dilemma, determines to stand by her daughter's decision on the marriage, whatever it may be. Ashok, at first eager to impress Indranath, is ultimately revolted by the man's hypocrisy and refuses the offer of a job. Indranath finds himself suddenly alone. The patriarch, the aristocrat, the chairman of five companies, feels his authority slipping away. When the Kanchanjungha reveals itself at last in all its glory, Indranath has no time for it. He goes looking frantically for his family in the hope of consolidating his lost empire.

KANCHANJUNGHA was Ray's first film in colour, and the second for which he composed the music. It was also his first attempt at using his own story. The only other film based on his story and meant for an adult audience, is *Nayak* . Structurally, and in their narrative contrivances, the two films have a great deal in common, elements that separate them from the body of his work. In *Nayak,* the incidents take place in the confined time and space of an overnight train journey. Establishing a pattern which is followed in *Nayak* four years later, *Kanchanjungha* records incidents which reveal and partially resolve the inner dichotomies of a handful of people on the last day of their holidays in the mountains. The dramatic constraints of time and space are sublimated with the help of a mobile camera eye. At the thematic level, the film pushes away the confining walls of authoritarianism, to let in the first breath of change and establish the inevitable passing away of the old order.

When the film reached America fifteen years after it was made, David Ansen wrote in the *Boston Real Paper* : "With a gentle resonance worthy of Chekhov, Ray sees in the family a microcosm of the social tensions pulling India apart. His film unfolds with such quiet, transparent artistry that one is astonished how deep his thematic roots spread; how fully one comes to know those people; how much of Indian history is suggested in the fleeting conversations of an afternoon. Without forcing the point, Ray shows us the equation between colonial and patriarchal power; but though Indranath may be a tyrant, fatuous and corrupt, Ray allows him his stature—you can understand his feeling of accomplishment, his dream of an Anglophile civilization. Like the madly proud aristrocrat in *The Music Room*, also played by Chhabi Biswas, Indranath is both victim and villain, a man whose historical time is running out. For Ray, an aristocratic Indian steeped in European culture, the celebration of change is always, in his early films, accompanied by a note of elegiac remorse, and his ambivalent feelings give *Kanchanjungha* an added poignance."

Most critics also noted the luminous quality of colour in the film. Ray and his cameraman, Subrata Mitra—who was twenty-two when he shot his first feature film, *Pather Panchali*—captured on the screen every subtle shade of mood and moment in the translucent mist that drifts across the screen, the dense green of the pine forests, the picturesque and colourful bungalows dotting the hillside, the holiday clothes of the rich, and when the clouds lift, the glorious emergence of the silver peaks of the Kanchanjungha. Unfortunately, the real colours of the film are lost forever. The original negative was damaged accidentally, the locally made prints faded very fast. For years the film has not been in a shape to be shown. The only more or less acceptable print and a two-inch videotape copy prepared by the BBC for telecasting are at the National Film Archive of the British Film Institute. Recently the National Film Archive of India has prepared a print which still falls short of the films original splendour.

KISMET (Fate)
b&w, 131 minutes, Hindi, 1943

Production: Bombay Talkies/ Direction and screenplay: Gyan Mukherjee/ Dialogue: P.L. Santoshi, Shaid Latif/ Camera: R.D. Pareenja/ Music: Anil Biswas/ Lyrics: Pradeep/ Editing: Dattaram N. Pai/ Sound: S.B. Vacha
Cast: Ashok Kumar, Mumtaz Shanti, Shah Nawaz, V.H. Desai, Chandraprabha, Kanu Roy, Jagannath Aurora, Prahlad, David, Haroon, Baby Kamala, Mubarak

SHEKHAR, a handsome young thief, notices someone stealing a watch from an old man. He picks the thief's pocket, and follows him into a jeweller's. The jeweller, a receiver of stolen goods, introduces the thief to Shekhar as Banke. Having discovered that he has been outwitted by Shekhar, Banke now wants to establish a partnership with him. Outside the shop, Shekhar meets the same old man who has come to sell his watch, and discovering that it has been stolen, says he wanted the money to go to a show. Feeling sorry for him, Shekhar takes him to the theatre. There he learns that the main singer on the stage is the daughter of the old man who once owned the theatre. In a fit of drunkenness, he had forced his child, Rani, to dance till she dropped from exhaustion. Rani has never danced since and needs a crutch to walk with. The present owner, Indrajitbabu, who used to work under the old man and is now his creditor, sits in a box nearby. Shekhar notices an expensive necklace round his wife's neck.

When the show is over, handing him a small garland of flowers for his daughter, the old man melts into the crowds. Rani trying to reach her father is snatched from the path of a car by Shekhar. Having seen him with the old man, she takes him for her father's friend. Soon the owner appears with his wife, and Shekhar steals the necklace, but with the police close by, hides it in Rani's carriage. When he comes to retrieve it, the carriage has gone. He manages to steal into Rani's home, takes the necklace, places the forgotten garland next to Rani's pillow, but is seen by passers by as he is leaving. The noise wakes Rani who, believing that Shekhar came with her father to leave the garland, insists that he must stay the night. Next morning, Indrajitbabu's manager harasses Rani for the payment of her father's loan and Shekhar, feeling sorry again, suggests that he rent a room in the house to help her pay it off.

At Indrajitbabu's home, the police Inspector comes to discuss the theft, and accidentally discovers the tragic story of his eldest son. Brought up by an indulgent stepmother, Madan was naughty and spoilt. One day, in a fit of temper, he was rude to his stepmother, and Indrajitbabu threw him out of the house just as he was sitting down to a meal. Madan never returned home, and the family still keeps a plate of food on the table for him.

Indrajitbabu's younger son Mohan is in love with Rani's sister, Lila, but does not have the guts to tell his father. Meanwhile Shekhar, whom Rani looks upon as a god, pays off her loan by stealing money from Indrajitbabu's bullying manager. He also accidentally realizes that the necklace he has stolen was a gift to Rani from her father, which had to be sold. Shekhar brings back the necklace for her, and they both admit their feelings for each other. Rani tells him of her dream of walking without a crutch again. Shekhar talks to a doctor who quotes a large sum to treat the patient. At Lila's insistance, Rani wears the necklace to the theatre, even though Shekhar had forbidden her to. Learning about it, he rushes off to the theatre, but by that time, Indrajitbabu's wife has spotted her necklace and called the police. The same Inspector, a kind-hearted man, asks Rani to reveal who had given her the necklace. But refusing to believe that Shekhar is a thief, Rani is silent. When the Inspector threatens to arrest her, Shekhar enters the room and admits to the theft. In her disillusionment and shame, Rani disowns him. On his way to prison, Shekhar escapes and joins Banke who now works as a servant in Indrajitbabu's home.

Meanwhile, Mohan is sent off for higher studies. He does not know that Lila is pregnant. The two sisters, bereft of all support, are also repulsed by Indrajitbabu when they try to tell him about Lila and Mohan. Though Rani goes through the operation and is cured, she is horrified to learn that it was Shekhar who paid for it with money stolen from Indrajitbubu. But by now, the Inspector, who has been on his trail for a long time, puts the pieces of the puzzle together and discovers that Shekhar is no other than Madan, Indrajitbabu's long lost son. The case against him is promptly withdrawn and a family reunion takes place, where Rani and Lila are accepted as the fututre daughters-in-law, and everyone is happy at last.

THE HAND of fate—*kismet* —is seen at every turn of this tortuous story. Rani's father says that it was fate that brought his ruin. Shekhar admits that every time he tries to go straight, fate gets in the way. And discovering that her god in human form is only a common thief, Rani sings dolefully of unkind fate that has only brought her sorrow. The audience must willingly suspend their disbelief to enjoy the film. However, it is not a difficult task, since the handsome, happy-go-lucky crook is such an endearing fellow, the pretty singer is so sweetly helpless and meek, and they both sing so effortlessly well. One of Ashok Kumar's early successes, *Kismet*, with its totally unreal but romantic story was the stuff of dreams for the public who lapped it up enthusiastically. It had eight "hit" songs, and ran for over three years in Calcutta.

Bombay Talkies, under whose banner the film was produced, had been founded by the legendary pioneer Himanshu Rai and his extraordinarily beautiful actress wife, Devika Rani. Ashok Kumar joined the company as a laboratory assistant, and was picked up by Himanshu Rai for a screen test when he heard the young man sing. In *Jeevan Naiya,* with Devika Rani as his heroine, Ashok Kumar sang his own songs on the screen and also established himself as an actor of some standing. He followed it up with blockbusters like *Achhut Kanya*, also with Devika Rani, and has remained in the industry ever since. Most romantic heroes in popular cinema are never given the opportunity to prove their abilities in any other kind of characterization. Ashok Kumar is one of those lucky exceptions who has managed to continue with important supporting roles, and has had a great variety to choose them from. Though he has always been given fairly serious roles, he shifted to comedy in later years, and was an equally great success. Today, at much more than three score and ten, he is still the most youthful actor of the Hindi screen.

KSHUDHITA PASHAN (Hungry Stones)
b&w, 120 minutes, Bengali, 1960

Production: Eastern Circuit Private Limited/ Direction and screenplay: Tapan Sinha/ Story: Rabindranath Tagore/ Camera: Bimal Mukherjee/ Music: Ustad Ali Akbar Khan/ Editing: Subodh Roy
Cast: Arundhati Mukherjee, Chhabi Biswas, Radhamohan Bhattacharya, Dilip Roy, Robin Banerjee, Bina Chand, Padma Devi, Rasaraj Chakraborty

A GOVERNMENT tax collector comes across an old ruin of a palace standing in solitary spendour with green hills rising beyond, and a river flowing nearby. This, as he discovers, was the pleasure palace of the Emperor Mahmud Shah II, built two hundred and fifty years ago. It was also once the scene of countless dramas of unrequited passion and wild lust, and the young collector is warned by the locals that years of thwarted hope and heartache have made each stone of the palace hungry for revenge, and no man can survive within its walls.

Yet every night the young man is drawn to the house by some inexplicable force. He hears the sound of bells and laughter, of music and dance. He is tortured by fleeting images from an unknown past which put such a spell on him that his nights and days take on separate realities. During the day he goes about his work in a daze, worn out from lack of sleep. At night he relives his dreams, and in the grip of some strange intoxication is transformed into a personage from a lost leaf of history. However hard he tries to extricate himself from this absurd situation, he remains bewitched by the old palace. His visions take on a set pattern, and one night he succeeds in locating the cry of pain that has come back to haunt him again and again. It is the cry of a girl chained in a dungeon. Rushing to her rescue, he stumbles and falls, losing consciousness.

When he awakes, he is back in history, cared for lovingly by the girl he had tried to save. They leave the palace and there are two horses waiting for to carry them away. He is now Imtiaz Ali, a trader, who in one of his missions had bought a slave girl for his emperor, and then fallen in love with her. He had tried to rescue her from the palace, and failed, leading to his banishment from the land. Reliving the past, Imtiaz falls from his horse, and the tax collector wakes up in the present. His questions have finally been answered, his search has ended, but only with the repetition of his failure in another time. He leaves the palace desolate in his awareness.

TAGORE'S famous short story was a most suitable framework for Sinha's own special talent for cinematic story-telling. A beautiful and haunting fantasy, *Kshudhita Pashan* has stirred the imagination of countless admiring readers. Sinha uses the story mainly as an exploration into a mind severed by two realities, one of the elusive and forgotten past, the other of the tangible present. In his dry, day-to-day existence, the young tax collector lives in the realms of the ordinary. His visions from the past lend him the mantle of romance, yet, in the perspective of history, the roots of Imtiaz Ali's failure lie in the fact that he too was ordinary, helpless to combat the forces that ruled his life. In translating the haunting quality of Tagore's prose into the language of the cinema, Sinha makes full use of the black and white medium. Night and day become metaphors for the shadowy past and the harsh present; and history is shrouded in darkness, with sudden flashing glimpses of a lost awareness.

In keeping with the classical associations of the story, Sinha used a famous exponent of Hindustani classical music as his music director, Ustad Ali Akbar Khan. This was much in the tradition of Satyajit Ray who, in his early films, depended on well-known classical musicians, Ali Akbar Khan having been the last of them with his musical score for Ray's *Devi* made the same year as *Kshudhita Pashan*.

MADHUMATI
b&w, 163 minutes, Hindi, 1958

Production: Bimal Roy Productions/ Direction: Bimal Roy/ Story and screenplay: Ritwik Ghatak/ Dialogue: Rajinder Singh Bedi/ Camera: Dilip Gupta/ Music: Salil Chowdhury/ Lyrics: Shailendra/ Art Direction: Sudhendu Roy/ Editing: Hrishikesh Mukherjee/ Sound: Dinshaw Billimoria
Cast: Dilip Kumar, Vyjayantimala, Johnny Walker, Pran, Jayant, Tiwari, Misra, Baij Sharma, Jagdish, Sagar, Tarun Bose

ON A STORMY night, Devendra, an engineer, drives down a hill road with his friend, to fetch his wife and child from the railway station. A landslide blocks their path and the friends take shelter in an old mansion just off the road. Devendra finds the house uncannily familiar. In the night he hears a woman's cry and the sound of anklet bells. In the large front room he finds an old portrait which he recognizes. His friend and the old caretaker join him, and Devendra, amidst flashes of memory from another life, sits down to tell his story while the storm rages outside.

Anand comes to Shyamnagar timber estate as its new manager. An artist in his spare time, he roams the hills and forests with his sketching pad and falls in love with Madhumati, a tribal girl whose songs have haunted him from a distance. Intrigued by her father's hostility towards him, Anand questions

Charandas, his servant, and learns that Madhumati's father was once the tribal king till the timber estate owner forcibly took over most of the land, oppressed the tribal population, and stabbed the king's son in the back when he protested.

Soon Anand meets his employer, Ugranarayan, a ruthless and arrogant libertine. Contemptuous of the man, Anand refuses to fawn on him like the others, and incurs his wrath. Anand also has enemies among his staff who have been fudging the accounts till his arrival. Sent away on an errand suddenly, he returns to find that Madhumati has disappeared. Both he and Madhumati's father, who now trusts him, search for her in vain. Half out of his mind, Anand learns from Charandas how Madhumati had been taken to the landowner in his absence. He confronts Ugranarayan whose men beat him unconscious, and are taking him away in a cart when they are stopped by the tribal king. In the fight that follows, Charandas manages to escape with the cart straight to the hospital.

Anand's life is saved, but his mind wanders. One day in the forest he meets a girl who looks exactly like Madhumati. She says she is Madhavi, but Anand refuses to believe her, and is beaten up by her companions when he tries to plead with her. They realize the reason for Anand's peculiar behaviour when they find a sketch of Madhumati in the forest, for Madhavi has never met him before. Madhavi takes the sketch to the resthouse where Anand now stays, and is deeply touched to learn his story from Charandas. Meanwhile Anand is haunted by the spirit of Madhumati who tells him that Ugranarayan is her killer. Seeing Madhavi at a dance recital where she dresses as a tribal girl, he appeals to Madhavi to help him get a confession out of Ugranarayan for the police to take action on.

Returning to Ugranarayan's palace, Anand apologizes to the landlord for his earlier defiance which cost him his job, and begs permission to do a portrait of him. Next evening with a storm brewing outside Anand paints the landowner. At the stroke of eight, the wind blows out the lamps and the front door creaks. Outside stands a shadowy figure. Anand calmly lights the lamps, one by one. Ugranarayan sees Madhumati in front of him. Shaken, and goaded by Madhumati, he confesses the truth. The police who have been waiting outside the room to hear the confession, now come and take him away. In the silence that follows, Anand suddenly realizes that the leading questions the false Madhumati asked were on matters unknown to him. How did Madhavi know where Madhumati was buried? The girl just smiles, and moves towards the stairs. As he follows her up, through the open door rushes in Madhavi dressed as Madhumati. She is late, for the car failed on the way. Deaf to Madhavi's calls, Anand runs up to the terrace where the shadow of Madhumati beckons him from the edge. She had fallen from the same terrace and died to escape Ugranarayan. Now Anand follows his beloved.

Devendra's story is over. "But," he says to his astonished friend, "I finally did have Madhumati as my wife. In this life." Just then news comes that the train in which his wife was travelling has met with an accident. The road has been cleared, and the two friends rush to the station. From one of the coaches, Devendra's wife Radha appears unhurt with her baby. Radha bears an uncanny resemblance to Madhumati.

MANY OF the key people behind *Madhumati* had appeared in the credits of another film made a year before. *Musafir* was directed by *Madhumati's* editor, Hrishikesh Mukherjee, and used a story by Ritwik Ghatak, with dialogue by Rajinder Singh Bedi, art direction by Sudhendu Roy, lyrics by Shailendra and music by Salil Chowdhury. They both have Dilip Kumar in a leading role. Yet the real similarity between the films lies only in the compactness of their scripts, and the fact that they both use the minimum number of sets. *Musafir* is set almost right through in a small flat, in the same three rooms and the balcony in front. *Madhumati* mostly uses the outdoors, so that except for the lavish front room of Ugranarayan's palace, there are only two or three other simple interiors that were necessary.

Unlike *Musafir*, the simple story of a little apartment that witnesses many a drama of joy and sorrow, Bimal Roy's film is one long lyrical experience. The rolling mists on the terraced landscape, the brooding monsoon in the hills, the silent death of a decadent age and a joyous primitive culture, and the haunting girl, all come together in the form of a unique vision of the past. The role of Devendra-Anand is ideal for an actor like Dilip Kumar, the only master of the understatement in popular Indian cinema. The songs in the film have not lost their charm in the thirty years that have followed the release of the film. *Madhumati* is also a classic example of the best traditions of the ghost story, whose credibility lies in the powers of story-telling, in the expectant sound and silence of each passing moment, in the fearful wait for the lifting of the veil when the truth will reveal itself. It belongs to that twilight zone where the real meets the unreal across temporal barriers, and Radha and the tribal girl are one at last.

MASOOM (Innocent)
colour, 165 minutes, Hindi, 1983

Production: Krsna Films Unit/ Direction: Shekhar Kapoor/ Screenplay, dialogue and lyrics: Gulzar/ Camera: Pravin Bhatt/ Music: R.D. Burman/ Art Direction: Bijohn Das Gupta/ Editing: Arunavikas/ Sound: Hitendra Ghosh
Cast: Shabana Azmi, Naseeruddin Shah, Saeed Jaffrey, Tanuja, Supriya Pathak, Urmila, Aradhana, Rajan, Jugal Hansraj, Satish Kaushik, Pran Talwar, Anila Singh, Aziz Qureshi, Ram Gopal Bajaj, A.K. Chaturvedi

A PHOTOGRAPH of a happy family shows D.K. Malhotra, a successful young architect, his wife Indu, and his two daughters, Rinky and Minnie. One day a telegram from his old schoolmaster, Gurdayal Singh, summons D.K. to Nainital. Surprised, he calls the school, and speaks to a man called Tiwari who tells him that Singh wants D.K. to fetch his son. But D.K. has no son. When a letter arrives from Singh, D.K. realizes it is the son of Bhavna, a young girl now dead, whom he had met in Nainital at a school reunion. He tries to tell Indu about the incident, which had happened after he was married. Horrified, Indu refuses to have the child in her home, but D.K. has no alternative when another telegram comes to say that the boy is already on his way.

Suddenly the happy home is plunged into uncomfortable silence. The girls, too young to understand, are puzzled but ultimately happy when Rahul arrives to stay, though Indu is coldly hostile. Indu pours her heart out to Chanda, a friend who has left her husband and son, and is now a successful businesswoman. Chanda's anger sharpens Indu's resistance. D.K. meanwhile unburdens himself to his friend Suri, telling him about the elusive charm of Bhavna who nurtured the grief of her parents' death by accident, and knew she would die soon herself. He had known her only for a few days in Nainital, and after that one moment's weakness when her frailty had drawn his love, he had never met her again, never known that she had borne him a son eight years ago.

While the relationship between Indu and D.K. deteriorates, the girls, now very fond of Rahul, tell him that their mother loves him too, but feels shy to show it. As a result, for her birthday, Rahul happily makes her a box to keep her bangles in. It is a beautiful box, and Indu is moved, but finds it impossible to admit it. At night she steals into Rahul's room, but finding near his bed photographs of Bhavna, tells D.K. to take the child away immediately. D.K. reluctantly takes Rahul to Nainital, but Gurdayal Singh is dead, and D.K. tries to enter Rahul in his old school. Waiting for the formalities to be finalized, Rahul and D.K. spend a lot of time together, and the boy's generous love which he openly expresses, warms and sustains D.K. But he still cannot admit to Rahul that he is the father the boy has been searching for. Rahul is unhappy at the thought of going to boarding school, leaving the family he has learnt to love. When he is back in Delhi briefly before his final departure, Chanda comes to visit Indu. But it is a different Chanda; not the hard-headed businesswoman, the angry feminist. She has come to tell her friend that she is returning to her husband. Her son wants her back, and she cannot resist the call of motherhood. Watching her bubbling with joy, Indu is surprised and a bit annoyed. Chanda now even seems to approve of the children's acceptance of Rahul.

Taken to D.K.'s office, Rahul accidentally reads Gurdayal Singh's letter, and realizes that D.K. is his father. He is hurt even more when D.K. introduces him to his boss as a friend's son. That night Indu discovers him missing, and while D.K. goes on a frantic search, a policeman on the beat, finding Rahul with Singh's letter in his pocket addressed to D.K., brings him home. After the hours of worry and guilt, Indu angrily scolds the child. "Can't you even say sorry?" she shouts, "Do you know how worried your father and I—" and stops midway. Before she can correct herself, Rahul admits that he knows the truth. When D.K. returns and tries to talk to Rahul, the boy maintains his hurt silence. Sending her tired husband to bed, Indu goes into Rahul's room. For the first time, she stretches her hand towards him in a gesture of affection, and opening his eyes, Rahul says meekly, "Sorry, Aunty." Unable to control herself, Indu rushes out to sit on the stairs and cry her heart out for this motherless, homeless waif whom she can no longer deny her love. But in the morning when she takes the girls to school, D.K. takes Rahul to the station. Finally admitting to the boy that he is his father, D.K., distraught at having to send him away, rushes back to his car to fetch a forgotten waterbottle. He reaches the platform just as the train gathers speed. Going back to the car despondently, he finds his whole family in it, including a grinning Rahul. Indu has managed to rescue him at the last minute, and the girls say triumphantly, that he will now live with them forever.

There is a new photograph in the Malhotra home now, showing Rahul held by Indu in a loving embrace along with the rest of the family.

MASOOM is a typical Gulzar story, with the right mixture of family love, sentiment, and good clean fun. Though reminiscent of similar themes in contemporary American cinema, it retains its Indianness and even manages to make Rahul's illegitimacy acceptable to a basically orthodox audience. However, there are two potent questions that come to mind. In India, where most abandoned children are female and where prenatal tests more often than not lead to abortion in the case of girl children, one wonders what would have happened if Rahul was not a boy. In fact, there are many moments in the earlier part of the film where it is established that all D.K. needs to be really happy is a son. The only exception is Indu, who undoubtedly responds to Rahul's innocence; not to the fact that he can be a son to her. But then she is a woman. And that brings us to the next question. What if the child had been an illegitimate offspring of the woman instead of the man? Would the audience have found it equally easy to forgive her momentary surrender to infidelity? Even Chanda's change of heart seems a wry comment on independent women who are actually unhappy and longing to find a man to lean on. Nevertheless, *Masoom*, made with a certain professionalism and competence, was a success for its young director; and coming in the wake of an explosion of sex and violence in mainstream cinema from Bombay, it was a refreshing change.

MAYA MIRIGA (The Mirage)
colour, 120 minutes, Oriya, 1983

Production: Lotus Productions/ Direction and Screenplay: Nirad Mohapatra/ Camera: Raj Gopal Mishra/ Music: Bhaskar Chandavarkar/ Art Direction: Sampad Mohapatra/ Editing: Bibekanand Satpathy
Cast: Bansidhar Satpathy, Manimala, Binod Mishra, Manaswini, Sampad, Sujata, Bibek, Tikina, Kunumuni, Shrirangan, Kishori Debi

RAJ KISHORE, ex-freedom fighter and headmaster of a school in a sleepy district town of Orissa, lives in a rambling old house that has seen better days. Tuku, his eldest son, works as a lecturer in a local college. His wife Prabha, pregnant with their first child, helps her mother-in-law to run the household. Tutu, the ambitious second son, comes back from Delhi having passed the written examination for the Indian Administrative Service. Now it is only a matter of getting through the orals, and he will be on the first rung of a promising career. The younger brothers, Bulu and Tulu are in college, and the little sister, Tikina, still in school. Raj Kishore's mother, a toothless, decrepit old woman, the last representative of a passing era, is now a silent observer in the daily life of the household.

But there is a current of change flowing through this gentle stream of existence. Prabha, tied down by her husband's family loyalty and lack of ambition, is unhappy with a life of endless drudgery. Once her baby is born, she gently but persistently urges her husband to look for a better job, and a home of their own. Meanwhile Bulu, whose graduation marks disappoint everybody, sinks into a depression and refuses to look for employment. Tulu, the youngest boy, defies his father and comes home at all odd hours. Tutu, having entered the Indian Administrative Service, is soon married off to the daughter of the Secretary of the Education Department, who even provides a fat dowry. The house gets a fresh coat of paint after years, a large fridge and a formica-topped dining table adorn the home and Tutu's room looks prosperous and modern with its new furnishings. A week after the wedding Tutu goes away for training. His wealthy wife goes back to her parents' home against the family's wishes. For the first time, Tuku the eldest son, seriously thinks of looking for a job outside the little town.

Raj Kishore retires after thirty-five years of service. He occasionally talks to an old friend whose only son has gone abroad for further studies. In his absence, his father is turning into a bitter and neglected old man. Raj Kishore reasons with his friend and in the process tries to adjust to his own changing circumstances. The old grandmother dies peacefully, watched over by the family. Tulu does remarkably well for his graduation and is determined to go to Delhi to specialize. When Tutu visits home on his way to his first posting, Raj Kishore expresses the hope that his older children will now help the younger ones with their future careers. But Tutu, the most fortunate of the lot, refuses to help Bulu find a job, and has no intention of paying for Tulu's stint at the university. Even the responsible and loyal Tuku, is unwilling to share a new burden. In an uncharacteristic display of anger, Raj Kishore reminds them of his own sacrifices for their sake, and tells them of his resolve to sell his plot of land in the village to pay for Tulu's education. The two elder sons, sensitive to the hurt beneath their father's anger, agree to help Tulu. But nothing will be the same again for Raj Kishore's family.

Tutu and his wife leave the next morning. Tulu goes away to Delhi. Tuku and Prabha will soon be going to Bhubaneswar, where Tuku has found a new job in the university. Waiting listlessly for her release, Prabha refuses to light the fire for the family meal. Raj Kishore and his wife carry on with the life they have chosen, with Bulu and young Tikina looking towards an unknown future.

NIRAD MOHAPATRA trained in the Film and Television Institute of India in Pune and taught there before taking up film making. *Maya Miriga* , his first feature film, arose out of his personal experience of the extended family in Orissa. The pace is slow, the people are ordinary. The underlying drama of change takes place without fanfare, but with a certain inexorability. It is something that happens every day in middle-class homes all over India. If *Maya Miriga* investigates disintegration, it also explores continuity with equal objectivity. Therein lies its gentle charm. A tone of grey uniformly shades all the characters. Prabha's desire for a little privacy, a life of her own is not unreasonable, nor are Raj Kishore's need to cling to older codes of family loyalty, and his wife's occasional assertion of matriarchal authority. Tutu may have a selfish wife, but she belongs to a different culture and cannot be expected to conform. She brings a large dowry, and the family seem to expect it as payment for Tutu's professional success. There is no attempt to hide their disappointment when Prabha gives birth to a girl. Only the old grandmother, marginalized in the natural course of existence, says the baby will bring good fortune to the family. But no one really believes her. In Raj Kishore's conversations with his friend, the old order continues, though faltering under the buffetting winds of change. While his friend grinds out his daily complaints, Raj Kishore attempts to rationalize his own compromises with a changing world. The transition is inevitable, and each generation tries to meet it with calm resignation. Mohapatra views his characters in all their simplicity and poignancy, through the shadowed frames of pillars and doors of the old gracious house, each one isolated in time and space, each merging with a larger, more complex pattern of life.

Along with winning a National Award, *Maya Miriga* received the Grand Prix in the Third World section of the Mannheim Film Festival in 1984.

MEERA
colour, 155 minutes, Hindi, 1980

Production: Premji/ Direction, screenplay and dialogue: Gulzar/ Camera: K. Vaikunth/ Music: Ravi Shankar/ Playback: Vani Jairam, Dinkarji/ Art Direction: Desh Mukherjee/ Editing: Vaman Bhonsle, Gurudutta/ Sound: Essa M. Suratwala
Cast: Hema Malini, Vinod Khanna, Shreeram Lagoo, Amjad Khan, Vidya Sinha, Om Shivpuri, Bharat Bhushan, Dina Pathak, Dinesh Thakur, T.P. Jain, Sudha Chopra, Shammi Kapoor, Gauri Kamat, Shahu Modak

MEERA, the niece of Biramdev, the Rathor king of Merta, is given in marriage to the Sisodia king Bikramjit's younger brother Bhojraj, as a political move towards bringing peace to the strife-torn Rajput lands. The alliance would help to unify the Rajput kingdoms against growing Mughal domination. Even though the Mughals, Muslim rulers of Afghan extraction, have already spent three generations in India, they are still considered usurpers by the fiercely independent Rajput race. Though born in a Rajput royal family, Meera has grown up believing that she is married to Krishna, the amorous dark god, and her earthly marriage to Bhojraj is something she can submit to, but not accept. All Bhojraj's efforts to win her fail, but he cannot bring himself to force the issue even when his sister Uda openly criticizes Meera's strange behaviour. As a bride in Chittor, she refuses to serve meat at a ritual feast though it is meat of a goat sacrificed to the goddess in the palace temple by the royal priest. With her companion Lalita, she goes to a neglected temple of Krishna and sings and dances in a trance, watched with reverence by the common people.

In the palace too she keeps with her the image of the god she had at home and spends her time adorning it or writing love songs for Krishna. Facing constant rebuke from the family, she even gives up wearing the ornaments that a woman of a royal household would wear, and tells Lalita of her desire to leave home and wander in search of Krishna.

Frustrated by his own rejection and goaded by his aggressive sister and the hostile royal priest, Bhojraj tells Meera to go back to her father's home and wait till he asks for her back again. Gratefully accepting the freedom she has longed for, Meera goes home, but her uncle is away at war, and his son, still hostile towards the Sisodias, sends her away from the doorstep. "You belong to the Sisodias now," he tells her. Carrying the *ektara* (a single-string musical instrument) which was a gift of Raidas, a low-caste tanner and poet, Meera now goes wandering alone, leaving even Lalita behind. She finds the door of the Krishna temple locked by the orders of the royal priest. Given another chance to repent by keeping a ritual fast the next day for her husband, Meera says she will fast for her divine husband till the door of the temple opens again. Bhojraj, hearing of her vow, is worried for he knows how obstinate Meera can be. But Uda is elated, and to try Meera further, she sends food twice a day to the temple where Meera waits in a hut. The servants who carry the food also bring a lamp every evening and hang it near the locked door, away from the wind. But one night, when Meera, weakened by her fast, sleeps like the dead, a storm lashes against the temple. The lamp rocks and spills oil on the wooden door, setting it on fire. In the morning the people of Chittor join Meera to look lovingly upon the image of Krishna revealed behind the burnt-down door.

Bhojraj takes Meera back to the palace where he has built a separate temple for her. But while he is away at war, Uda secretly arranges to throw the image of Krishna in the well. Meera, for whom the palace becomes a prison, leaves, carrying her book of songs and her *ektara,* and wanders in Dwarka, Mathura, Vrindavan, towns where Krishna was supposed to have spent his life. One evening, as she sits singing in front of a small temple, Akbar and his Hindu friend and courtier, the great singer Tansen, come in disguise to listen to her. Unable to hold himself back, Tansen sings with her, and Akbar, knowing by her response that she has seen through their disguise, leaves with her a pearl necklace as his offering to her god. When Bikramjit learns of the incident through his spies, in great fury he sends his soldiers to bring Meera back to Chittor where she is tried by a religious court headed by the royal priest, but attended by the people of the city along with the royal household and the courtiers.

Meera refuses to defend herself and is condemned to death for infidelity, treason and heresy. In spite of Bhojraj's efforts, she refuses to recant, and accepts the cup of poison offered to her. The people of Chittor follow her as she walks to the temple where she had fasted for the door to open. The sky reverberates with her song. Uda breaks through the crowd to enter the temple after her. The incense burns in front of the image, the *ektara* lies with Meera's *mangalsutra* (a bead and gold necklace worn as a sign of marriage) on it, her book of songs lie nearby with the quill pen poised in the inkpot. But Meera is no longer there.

MEERA BAI, Rajput princess of Merta, belonged to the tradition of Bhakti poets in medieval India, who expressed their love of god through common, day-to-day imagery and the analogy of human relations. In keeping with Lord Krishna's amorous image, Meera imagined herself a rival of Krishna's earthly lover, Radha, and her songs, immensely popular all over India, speak of her human longing for the god. There were many legends created around this extraordinary woman who left her princely home against the conventions of the time, to wander as a mendicant. Her life was supposed to have spanned nearly a century (1450?-1547?), though the dates are uncertain. History mentions that she was widowed after five years of marriage, and probably left her husband's home after that due to constant persecution by the family. In 1546 the ruling king of Mewar, her husband's kingdom, tried to bring her back home. Reluctant, she entered a Krishna temple in Dwarka to spend a last night there, and was said to have disappeared in the morning. Her songs mention two attempts on her life, including the poisoned cup from which she drank without harm. The Meera story has inspired more than one Indian film, the most famous being the Tamil and Hindi version in which M.S. Subbalakshmi, the renowned exponent of Carnatic music, acted as Meera and sang her songs.

Some of the events in Gulzar's version are taken from the miracles ascribed to Meera, but there has been a definite effort to explain them rationally as far as possible. Even Meera's disappearance can be explained away as a real escape. Perhaps the poisoned cup held no poison, for by the time she was convicted, her calm perseverance in her faith and her simplicity had moved all who attended her trial. Gulzar's film falls far short of the historical assumptions made about Meera. But it was not his intention to translate history onto the screen. "Would it be wrong to say," he asks, "that inspired by Meera's life, I have set her to my own tune?...The end of the film is a dramatic expression of Meera's personality. It should be accepted as a symbol, understood as a metaphor...perceived as Meera's message. It is certainly real, but not realistic.... If for the sake of making it realistic, Meera's entire life as a widow, and the years she survived—83, or 90 or 97 years—were all covered in the film, it would have been a film on the 'years' of Meera, not on her 'life'." [*Meera: Katha, Montage, Anusandhan aur Patkatha*, Radhakrishan Prakashan, Delhi, 1979] Poet, lyricist and filmmaker, Gulzar is yet to produce another film with the same beauty and brevity of expression. Meera's message of divine love, universal equality and tolerance certainly belonged to another age. Today it can only survive as an abstraction to be pruned to the needs of the times. By abandoning the miracles and making Meera into not so much a saint as a warm, loving, flesh and blood woman, Gulzar gives her a contemporaneity that makes her real in the way that all moving experiences are real. Like Anarkali in Asif's *Mughal-e-Azam*, Meera too absolves the royal priest of the guilt of murdering her before she touches the poisoned cup to her lips.

A well-known sitarist of the Hindustani classical genre, Pandit Ravi Shankar's music not only adds to the majesty of the theme and the background, but also transforms Meera's songs into a celebration of love. Stylistically, the film juxtaposes Meera's inner calm with the tumult of history; the even pace of the story with sudden dramatic action; the gentle surrender of

Meera to her god when the temple door burns down, with the sharp whiplash movement of Bhojraj's hand as he flings a shawl round his shoulder and rushes out of the palace to bring his wife back home.

MEGHE DHAKA TARA (The Cloud Capped Star)
b&w, 120 minutes, Bengali, 1960

Production: Chitrakalpa/ Direction and Screenplay: Ritwik Ghatak/ Story: Shaktipada Rajguru/ Camera: Dinen Gupta/ Music: Jyotirindra Moitra/ Art Direction: Ravi Chatterjee/ Editing: Ramesh Joshi/ Sound: Satyen Chatterjee
Cast: Supriya Choudhury, Anil Chatterjee, Gyanesh Mukherjee, Bijon Bhattacharya, Gita De, Gita Ghatak, Dwiju Bhaawal, Niranjan Ray, Satindra Bhattacharya

IN THE LATE 50s, a refugee family from East Bengal, victims of the Partition, struggle for survival in the outskirts of Calcutta. Shankar, the eccentric and irresponsible eldest son, is only concerned with his music and dreams of being a well-known singer one day. Nita, his sister, works as a private tutor while continuing her studies. The younger children, Gita and Montu, are still students. The old father teaches in a small school for a pittance. In Nita's drab life, there is only one thing to look forward to: the return of Sanat, a young scientist she hopes to marry. Sanat comes back from higher studies, and remains unemployed, struggling to continue his research. Nita encourages him, even helps him with money from her meagre earnings. But unknown to her, Sanat finds himself drawn to her sister Gita, whom he had known as a child and who has now blossomed into an attractive young woman.
The increasing needs of her family lead Nita to abandon her studies and take up a full-time job. Soon her father is too ill to work, and Montu drops out of college to work in a factory against everyone's wishes. He starts despising the unemployed Shankar who is also the target of their parents' wrath. Meanwhile, without telling Nita, Sanat gives up his research, takes a new flat, and prepares to marry Gita. Their mother is not unhappy, for the family needs Nita's salary. But Shankar feels outraged and leaves home, while their father, disabled with illness, can only fall back upon self-recrimination.
Emotionally shattered, Nita attempts to carry on with life; but Montu has an accident and has to be hospitalized. Nita seeks and accepts help from Sanat, but spurns his attempts to salvage their old friendship. With Montu unable to earn, the entire burden is on Nita, who falls ill with tuberculosis. She segregates herself at home, but continues to drag herself to work. Her parents accepts her isolation and fail to realize the seriousness of her ailment. At this point Shankar returns home; he has made good in Bombay. Montu is released from hospital and offered compensation by his employers. It is Shankar who discovers how ill Nita really is. When he tells the family, Nita's father, crazed with grief, tells her to leave before she becomes a burden in this home which has used and neglected her. Shankar finds her in the rain outside, and takes her to a sanatorium in the hills. He visits her, with news of happiness and

hope. With the shadow of death in her eyes, Nita suddenly expresses her urge to live.

Back home, Shankar sees another Nita, an unknown girl walking down the same road after a day's work, with a familiar bag hanging from her shoulder. The strap of her worn out sandal snaps, as Nita's had done long ago. She stops to look, and with a tired smile, walks on, dragging her feet. The local grocer stops Shankar. "Poor girl, she carried her burden till her back broke," he says.

THOUGH GHATAK the theoretician wrote at length about the femininity principle in the Hindu religious tradition in Bengal, and how it infused his work, especially *Meghe Dhaka Tara*, it was another, more easily comprehensible archetype that the lay audience could respond to in the film. Ghatak the filmmaker was no less conscious of the human and the universal in his works, and it is his words that best describe the essential charm of Nita: "A girl, a very ordinary girl, tired after her day's work, waits often near my house at the bus stop, carrying a lot of papers and a bag. Her hair forms a halo around her head. Loose strands stick to her sweating cheeks. I discover history in the subtle lines of pain on her face. My imagination reaches out to the most ordinary, yet unforgettable drama in her strong, firm and determined, yet soft and touching, and infinitely patient life." [*Chitrapat* , 10.]

For the discerning critic, however, *Meghe Dhaka Tara* provided unique intellectual stimulation. "The triangular division, taken from Tantrik abstraction, is the key to the understanding of this complex film," wrote Kumar Shahani. "The inverted triangle represents in the Indian tradition, fertility and the femininity principle. The breaking up of society is visualized as a three-way division of womanhood. The three principal woman [*sic*] characters embody the traditional aspects of feminine power. The heroine, Nita, has the preserving and nurturing quality; her sister, Gita, is the sensual woman; their mother represents the cruel aspect.

"The incapacity of Nita to combine and contain all these qualities...is the source of her tragedy. This split is also reflected in Indian society's inability to combine responsibility with necessary violence to build for itself a real future. The middle-class is also seen in triangular formation, at the unsteady apex of the inverted form." [*Filmfare* , 1976.]

Complexities notwithstanding, *Meghe Dhaka Tara* reaches out to the audience with its directness and simplicity of presentation, and its unique stylistic use of melodrama. Melodrama as a legitimate dramatic form, has long ceased to exist in the urban Indian milieu except in its distorted manifestation—the tear-jerker. But it has continued to play a vital role in rural Indian theatre and folk dramatic forms. Ghatak goes back to these roots in his presentation of a familiar struggle for survival which has lost its dramatic identity and essential pathos through repetition in real life. In *Meghe Dhaka Tara,* day-to-day events are transformed into high drama: Nita's tormented romance is intensified with the harsh sweep of the whiplash on the soundtrack; Shankar's song of faith in a moment of despair is carried to the height of emotional surrender with Nita's voice joining his; and the consumptive girl's urge to live becomes a universal sound of assertion reverberating in Nature, amidst the distant peaks of the Himalayas.

MOHAN JOSHI HAAZIR HO! (A Summons for Mohan Joshi)
colour, 130 minutes, Hindi, 1984

Production: Saeed Akhtar Mirza Productions/ Direction and Story: Saeed Akhtar Mirza/ Screenplay: Saeed Akhtar Mirza, Sudhir Mishra, Yusuf Mehta/ Camera: Virendra Saini/ Music: Vanraj Bhatia/ Lyrics: Madhosh Bilgrami/ Art Direction: Nachiket and Jayoo Patwardhan/ Editing: Renu Saluja/ Sound: Jagmohan Anand
Cast: Naseeruddin Shah, Deepti Naval, Rohini Hattangady, Bhisham Sahni, Dina Pathak, Amjad Khan, Mohan Gokhale, Satish Shah, Pankaj Kapoor

MOHAN JOSHI is a foolish old man. So what if the sewage pipe leaks through the year and the plaster peals off the ceiling without notice? At least he is one of the privileged few who actually have a home in the crowded city of Bombay. Standing in the queue at the milk booth one day, Joshi overhears a conversation that changes his life. He decides to get his landlord to pay for the running repairs of his flat where his family has lived for three generations, and paid the rent regularly too. And if the landlord does not agree, Joshi will sue him. Like the man in the queue.

But the corpulent Kapadia, surrounded by sinister building promoters, would rather allow Joshi's tenement to collapse, and construct a hi-rise building in its place. So Mohan Joshi goes looking for a lawyer. Out of a pack of hungry wolves, Gokhale and Malkani emerge as victors, and the deluded Joshi becomes their first client. The case begins, and stretches through months and years. The old couple part with their meagre savings to the disgust of their elder son. Kapadia hires Desai and Rani, smart lawyers who lead the Joshis a merry dance with an assault case and an eviction suit to complicate matters. The neighbours watch their humiliation with glee. Then, threatened by Kapadia's hired ruffians, and harassed by his lawyers, the elder son and his wife too join the battle.

Meanwhile Joshi's lawyers, Malkani and Gokhale, progress from a desk in the corridor to a luxurious office. In the landlord's camp, Rani marries Desai, but carries on a clandestine affair with Malkani. Between the four of them the case drags on, while the promoters wait patiently for their chance to build a sea of buildings from Bombay to Dubai. Judges come and go to the clash of sections and sub-sections in the courtroom. Tossed between impatience and despair, even Joshi begins to see through the hoax. Finally, pressurized by the whole family, Malkani makes a passionate appeal, and the judge agrees to come and see things for himself. All of a sudden Mohan Joshi is a hero to his jeering neighbours. After all, when the judge comes, he will see everybody's home.

But the tenement dwellers have counted without Kapadia and his lawyers. An army of workmen descend on the crumbling building, propping it up with painted poles and covering cracks. Though the tenants resist, the building wears an undeniably festive look when the judge arrives. The two sets of lawyers now take over the show. The tenement dwellers watch helplessly as one more interminable legal wrangle ensues, with the vacillating judge in its centre. Joshi's son tries to intervene, but the judge is no longer interested. In desperation, Mohan Joshi ends the dispute permanently by shoving hard at the painted props till the house comes crashing down on his head.

SAEED AKHTAR MIRZA came to film making after graduating from the Film and Television Institute of India and eight years in advertising. A vociferous spokesman for the parallel cinema movement in the country, Mirza's documentaries and features have focused on urban problems in a variety of fields. The movement from his two earlier feature films to *Mohan Joshi Haazir Ho!* has been one of growing maturity in craftsmanship and story-telling. The slow paced visual formalism of *Arvind Desai ki Ajeeb Dastan*, which portrayed the alienation of upper middle-class urban youth, gave way to the freedom of anger in *Albert Pinto ko Gussa Kyon ata Hai,* the story of a working class boy hemmed in by the aspirations and morality of his small community in a permissive and exploitative metropolitan city.

In *Mohan Joshi Haazir Ho!,* Mirza experiments with an allegorical form, lending poetry to the sordid and mocking tale of the tenements where old Mohan Joshi gains heroic proportions in his battle for human dignity. "Mohan Joshi is mythological," he says. "I use mythology not in its obscurantist form, but as a cross-reference in today's context. Today, the entire world—specifically Bombay city—is working towards a kind of desensitization to its own living conditions. To this, Joshi says: No. He is not a conventional hero. He is an old pensioner. He is not eccentric, he is demanding what everybody needs to demand—dignity according to our Constitution." Mirza's concern as a film maker is with creating, what he calls, "a cinema of struggle as opposed to the cinema of the status quo," an idea that unfortunately does not have much appeal for the pragmatic film distributors in the country. Yet it seems strange that the economics of film marketing in India should not be able to support this vivacious and colourful tale and present it to a wider public.

MUDHAL MARYIADHAI (A Matter of Honour)
colour, 160 minutes, Tamil, 1985

Production: Manoje Creations/ Direction and screenplay: Bharathi Rajaa/ Story: S. Selvaraj/ Camera: B. Kannan/ Music: Ilaya Raja/ Sound: S.P. Ramanathan
Cast: Sivaji Ganesan, Radha, Vadivukkarasi, Ranjani, Janaka Raj

WORN OUT with age and illness, Malaichamy awaits death in a small hut at the edge of the river, refusing to die in his own ancestral home. His shrewish wife Ponnatha raves at him, but Malaichamy does not even open his eyes.

Many years ago, Malaichamy was a robust and merry man, and a benign landowner. But his crude, shrewish wife cared neither for him, nor for their home. His daughter, ill-treated by her husband, stayed with her father. Malaichamy's young nephew Chellakannu looked after his cattle and wooed the local cobbler's daughter Sevili. One day a fisherman and his daughter Kuyil came to stay in the village. Gradually an odd friendship grew between Malaichamy and the pretty lass with a sharp tongue. He looked upon her as a naughty child, but Kuyil was no child. Like the villagers, she too was aware of Malaichamy's unhappy home life. An excellent cook, she would call him into her hut often to share a meal. It all changed as a result of a silly joke. She had wagered that if Malaichamy lifted the heavy stone near her home, she would marry him. He had joined in her laughter, but every once in a while had given it a try secretly, just to prove to himself that he was still young. One day he succeeded, but never thought of telling Kuyil. What he did not know was that Kuyil had seen him, and from that day there was no other man in her life. Though she too kept her silence, she took every opportunity to give him her support and her compassion. She reasoned and argued with him till his anger faded over Chellakannu and Sevili's romance, and he allowed the boy to marry the low-caste girl.It was a tragic alliance. The pregnant Sevili was found floating in the river, dead, her ornaments torn from her body. Chellakannu lived for a while in a daze, then haunted by his beloved, walked into the river after her. Soon after, Malaichamy's son-in-law came to take his wife home. But before he could do so, Sevili's father showed Malaichamy a part of a human toe that was found bitten off in Sevili's mouth. Malaichamy noticed that his son-in-law had a toe missing, and with a heavy heart called the police.

The enraged Ponnatha now attacked Malaichamy with new weapons. She invited the villagers home and incited them by casting doubts on Malaichamy's friendship with Kuyil. For the first time, his daughter heard Malaichamy angrily defend himself. She learnt that her mother was carrying another man's child when Malaichamy married her because her saintly father had begged him to save their family honour. But Ponnatha got her way. The villagers publicly accused Malaichamy of keeping Kuyil as his mistress. In sudden anger, he accepted the lie. When he tried to explain to Kuyil, she told him about her love, but Malaichamy could not accept her offering either. Depressed, Kuyil left the village.

Rowing a boat across the river, she was taken for the ferry-girl by a man who said he was going to visit Ponnatha. Suspicious of his brashness, Kuyil agreed to row him across. On the way, the man brazenly admitted that he had seduced Ponnatha twenty years ago, and was now coming to claim her, after his release from prison. To preserve Malaichamy's honour, Kuyil hit out at the man with the oar. Malaichamy, looking for Kuyil, saw her silently facing the police, while Ponnatha stared with horror at the familiar dead face on the sand. Kuyil went to prison in silence. Malaichamy finally got the story out of her, but only after he had promised to keep his silence too. He kept his word, though Kuyil's sacrifice filled him with sorrow. "I will wait for you to come to me," he told her.

Now, after long years of waiting, old Malaichamy refuses to die till Kuyil comes. The villagers arrange to fetch her under police escort. Malaichamy opens his eyes and smiles faintly as Kuyil sits holding his hand. He can die in peace at last.

IN SOUTH INDIA, where Brahmins have traditionally been identified with the Aryan invaders who imposed their rule on the older Dravidian civilization, the non-Brahmin alliance grew during the last decades of the British *raj* into a consolidated political movement that culminated in the anti-Hindi agitations after independence and the formation, in Tamil Nadu, of the Dravida Munnetra Kazhagam (DMK)—the Dravidian Forward Movement—in 1949. Of all the southern states, Tamil Nadu possessed a language furthest from the Sanskrit roots from which the northern languages had sprung. The founder of the DMK was dramatist and actor C.N. Annadurai who around the same time joined the film industry. His special attraction lay in his flair for vivid imagery and alliteration in writing dialogue for the cinema, which he turned into the most powerful vehicle for propaganda. In 1952, M. Karunanidhi, his trusted lieutenant and a later Chief Minister, scripted *Parasakthi,* an amalgam of family drama and DMK propaganda, which was a thundering success. Its hero, a lesser known stage actor, with an amazing ability to reel off long passages of alliterative, jaw-breaking, high flown Tamil in a single take, shot into fame overnight. This was Viluppuram Chinniahpillai Ganesan, called "Sivaji" for his powerful portrayal of the Maratha leader on stage. Consequently, with the combination of Ganesan's odd talent and the fervour of DMK propagandists like Karunanidhi, popular Tamil cinema developed a tradition of extremely talkative talkies, an absolute explosion of words, which continues to this day.

Ganesan who is himself no stranger to politics, has based his immense popularity on his florid acting style, with melodramatic eyes under exceptionally mobile eyebrows, a stentorian voice and oratorical delivery of dialogue. Even today, when South Indian cinema is veering towards realism, Ganesan is a force to contend with, and directors are said to find it difficult to control the ferocious overacting of the veteran star. However, Bharathi Rajaa, who in the last ten years has established himself as a popular director with a difference, considerably tempered and toned down the star's portrayal of Malaichamy in *Mudhal Mariyadhai.* Ganesan plays the role with relatively mild exaggeration, and a great deal of spontaneity, though the quivering brows are only occasionally stilled. Luckily for Rajaa, South Indian actresses who used to be grossly overweight are now slimming down to compete with (and in the hope of entering) the Bombay industry; in addition, the South Indian popular cinema takes pride in its technical finesse; elements that have combined to make *Mudhal Mariyadhai* a milestone in the mainstream cinema of the region.

MUGHAL-E-AZAM (The Great Mughal)
b&w and colour, 172 minutes, Urdu, 1960

Production and direction: K. Asif/ Screenplay: K. Asif, Aman/ Dialogue: Kamal Amrohi, Aman, Ahsan Rizvi, Vajahat Mirza/ Camera: R.D. Mathur/ Music: Naushad/ Lyrics: Shakeel Badayuni/ Playback: Bare Ghulam Ali Khan,

Mohammad Rafi, Lata Mangeshkar, Shamshad Begum/ Dance: Lachchu
Maharaj/ Art Direction: M.K. Sayed/ Editing: Dharamvir/ Sound: Shaikh
Akram
Cast: Prithviraj, Durga Khote, Dilip Kumar, Madhubala, Nigar Sultana, Ajit,
Kumar, Murad, Jillo Bai, Vijayalaxmi, S. Nazir, Sheela Delaya, Surinder,
Johnny Walker, Jalal Agha, Baby Tabassum, Gopi Krishna

MUGHAL EMPEROR Akbar walks barefoot on the burning sands to pray for a
son at the feet of Salim Chishti, a Muslim saint who lives in Sikri, more than
twenty miles west of Agra, the imperial capital. With the saint's blessings,
Jodha Bai, the Rajput wife of Akbar, gives birth to Salim. A maid brings the
news to Akbar and is rewarded with a royal ring, and the promise that by
presenting the ring, she can demand from the emperor one special favour.
Salim grows up a debauch, pampered by the palace women till his despairing
father sends him to the battlefield at the border of his expanding empire.
Having proved himself as a warrior, Salim is recalled to the palace where
Jodha Bai orders her closest companion, Bahar, to prepare a celebration and
engage a sculptor to create an image of great beauty in her son's honour. The
sculptor, with a curious obsession for truth, and disdain for pomp and power,
provocatively presents a real slave-girl as a stone image. Amused, Akbar
requests Jodha Bai to accept the girl as part of her entourage, and names her
Anarkali, the flower of the pomegranate.
   The next day, by the emperor's orders, Anarkali sings and dances in the
palace celebrations and charms the prince with her performance. Thus begins a
romance that shakes the Mughal throne and nearly destroys Akbar's empire.
The heir to the Mughal inheritance promises a slave-girl that she will be queen
of Hindustan one day. When the jealous Bahar conveys to Akbar news of his
son's indiscretion, the outraged emperor imprisons Anarkali. Faced with
Salim's defiance, Akbar orders Anarkali to convince Salim that she has never
loved him. Anarkali, who fears that her love can only harm Salim, submits to
the emperor's wishes. But before she can carry them out, Bahar tells Salim
that unable to bear her chains, Anarkali has accepted Akbar's suit. She will
celebrate her release with a dance before giving herself to the emperor. Salim
rages at a silent Anarkali. Yet, dancing in the hall of mirrors watched by the
royal family, Anarkali sings a song of fearless love which will survive even
death. The message is clear, and she goes back to the dungeons. When Salim
protests, he is ordered back to the battlefield. Salim is defiant till his faithful
Rajput follower, Durjan Singh, promises to guard Anarkali with his life while
the prince is away. The moment Salim leaves, however, Akbar arranges
Anarkali's marriage with the eccentric sculptor, who promptly reveals to Salim
what his father is plotting. Salim sends a message to Agra, proclaiming
himself emperor. If his father disputes the claim, they will meet on the
battlefield.
   Akbar orders the execution of Anarkali and visits Salim at his camp to plead
with him for a last time. But when a bleeding Durjan enters the tent with
Anarkali, the furious emperor declares war. Salim's army is routed, and while
Durjan escapes with Anarkali, Salim is taken prisoner, tried, and condemned
to death for refusing to surrender the girl. Hiding in a temple with Anarkali,

Durjan hears the verdict and though mortally wounded, tries to rush out only to fall dead at the feet of the goddess. People gather sorrowfully at the public execution. Akbar himself fires the canon facing his son, but Man Singh, Jodha Bai's brother and Akbar's trusted general, deflects the shot just as Anarkali rushes up to the crowd and faints on hearing the blast. Akbar is ready to pardon Salim if Anarkali will take his place. Ordered to be walled up alive, Anarkali states her last wish: she wants to be queen for a night, so that the prince may keep his word. Akbar agrees, but insists that she must, when the night is ending, give Salim a drugged flower to make him unconscious. If she does not do so, Salim will not let her die, and Akbar will not let her live, says the emperor. Anarkali sits dressed as a queen in the hall of mirrors with her prince. Bahar sings to entertain them, but the hidden barbs in her song on what the morning will bring, distresses Anarkali. She accepts the inevitable, and holds the drugged flower near her lover's face. As Salim sinks into unconsciousness, he realizes the truth, but has no strength to resist the black cloaked men who drag Anarkali away.

Years ago, at Salim's birth, the maid to whom the emperor had given a ring as a reward, now comes to Akbar. "She is my daughter; save her life," she pleads. Akbar pretends not to remember his promise and the maid is removed forcibly from his presence. But later, the emperor himself leads the maid bilndfolded into an underground chamber where waits Anarkali. He shows her the tunnel through which she must take her daughter away from his city. Salim must never know that Anarkali still lives. Anarkali recedes into the darkness of the tunnel wordlessly, to a living death.

MUGHAL-E-AZAM has the curious distinction of being a black and white film that uses colour in the two long sequences set mostly in the Sheesh Mahal, the famous hall of mirrors. A travesty of history, the film transforms a sordid political power struggle between father and son into a battle between temporal duty and immortal love. The romance of Salim and Anarkali has become a literary legend like many another such doomed alliance. It is futile to question the historical truth of the story, for it has through the years gained its own veracity. By literary convention, however, Anarkali is indeed walled up before Salim can save her. An earlier film version of the story, *Anarkali,* with Pradeep Kumar and Bina Rai in the leading roles, had ended thus, in tragedy. Asif, in *Mughal-e-Azam*, provides a new and less horrifying ending that serves two purposes. It re-establishes the greatest of the Mughals as a merciful man whose hands are tied by the responsibility he bears towards his great empire; and it gives his audience the satisfaction of seeing the beautiful, romantic, self-sacrificing slave-girl saved from a dire destiny.

Asif's version of Salim's adolescence is more like Akbar's own beginnings, when he came to the throne at the age of thirteen in 1556, and after a period of tutelage under his guardian Bairam Khan, spent two years of his youth "behind the veil," caring for nothing but sport. The last years of Akbar's life were complicated by the treachery of his eldest son Salim, the child of so many prayers, who continued in open rebellion till all his rivals to the throne were eliminated by natural or not so natural causes. Later, as emperor Jahangir, addicted to drinks and opium, he allowed his queen, Nurjahan,

"Light of the World," to become the *de facto* sovereign of Hindustan. The daughter of a Persian refugee, she was married to Sher Afghan, who had received from Jahangir the *jagir* of Burdwan in Bengal. When her husband fell from favour and was killed as a rebel, Nurjahan came to the imperial court as an attendant in the royal harem.

Mughal-e-Azam was the culmination of the trend for the spectacular which began with Vasan's *Chandralekha*. It was nine years in the making and was said to have cost its producer as much as *Chandralekha* had grossed. The gorgeous sets, recreating the splendour of the Mughal court at its height of power, served as the backdrop for an intense drama played out between two powerful men, acted by two of the most dynamic performers of the Hindi screen. Visually, the Sheesh Mahal sequences are the most interesting, with the dancer reflected in a million pieces of glass fragmenting the screen. Asif's instinct for drama is revealed in the numerous confrontations in the film between royal responsibility and individual love. But the most moving perhaps is the sequence where, having agreed to allow Anarkali one night of royal splendour, he must crown her a queen. It is an immense degradation for Akbar and he dismisses her immediately. But, with the veil pulled low over her beautiful face, and her proud head bearing the crown, she has the last word. "For this invaluable gift," she tells him, "this slave-girl absolves the emperor of the crime of murdering her."

MUKHAMUKHAM (Face to Face)
colour, 107 minutes, Malayalam, 1984

Production: General Pictures/ Direction, Story and Screenplay: Adoor Gopalakrishnan/ Camera: Ravi Varma/ Music: M.B. Srinivasan/ Art Direction: Sivan/ Editing: M. Mani/ Sound: Devadas
Cast: P. Ganga, Balan K. Nair, Kaviyoor Ponnamma, Krishna Kumar, Karamana, Thilakan, Vishwanathan, Ashokan, Lalitha

IN 1957 the Communist Party was voted into power in Kerala in South India and ruled the state for a brief period. In 1964 the party was split in two, the Communist Party of India and the Communist Party (Marxist) of India. Later other extremist splinter groups emerged. The first part of the film is set in the decade ending 1955; the second part begins ten years later.

We first see Sreedharan, the legendary trade union leader, sitting in front of the gates of the tile factory where the workers have struck work under his leadership. Mechanization in the factory threatens to take away the livelihood of the workers. A confrontation with the management leads to a prolonged strike. The party starts collecting funds as the workers' families face starvation. Sreedharan remains the key figure in the struggle. The man who runs the tea stall, the beedi shop owner, the common man in the street, rally round his leadership. Young Sudhakaran, still a boy, listens to him avidly and schools himself in the intricacies of political idealism. One night an old farmer discovers Sreedharan lying bleeding after an attack by faceless strangers in the dark. He brings him home, where his daughter Savitri tends to the wounds. The enforced familiarity transforms into a more intimate relationship. Sreedharan is accepted as the old man's son-in-law and stays on in his home. But when the proprietor of the tile factory is found murdered, Sreedharan and his comrades have to go underground.

Years pass, and Sreedharan's son, Sreeni, born soon after his disappearance, is now ten years old. In the intervening years Sreedharan's comrades have returned one by one and made their compromise with the changing face of left politics in the country. Sreedharan, believed dead, has become a legend and a permanent fount of inspiration. Only Sreeni, who has never known his father, awaits his return. One night Sreedharan crosses the gulf of ten unknown years, and walks into his home. He comes carrying the weight of ten years of exhaustion and promptly falls asleep. The news spreads, and the old familiar faces crowd around for a glimpse of the man whose memory sustained them in troubled times. But is this the same man? He talks to no one, regularly drinks himself into a stupor, steals money from his wife for more alcohol to dull an acute physical pain. But they still cannot dismiss him as a common alcoholic. The rival factions of the party vie with each other for the use of his image, his name. Sreedharan responds with silence. The ideal revolutionary becomes an embarrassment. Sreeni's friends throw stones at him, his old admirers, the common people, mock him publicly. Then one day he is found mysteriously killed. No one knows who killed him or why. No one wants to know. In death, the beloved leader returns to his people. The rival parties parade the streets together, resurrecting their hero, transforming the image into reality.

BETWEEN THIS image and this reality lies an area of search. Who is Sreedharan? A firebrand revolutionary who has fallen upon bad times, a man in the throes of self-doubt, or just a common drunkard with a political past? In death Sreedharan reverts back to his heroic image. But the living Sreedharan, victim of an imperilled ideology, provides no simple answer. Where does the truth lie? Did Sreedharan betray the revolution, or did the revolution betray the man?

Gopalakrishnan, who lives and works in Kerala, faced immense criticism locally for his fourth feature film in twelve years. He also received a great deal of admiration from serious film viewers who have been watching with interest the evolution of his highly personalized style coupled with detailed and careful craftsmanship. The shadowed lamplit interiors, the sharply etched figure of the silent Sreedharan outside the house viewed through the darkening frames of doors and awnings, the long moments of silence that end with the softly rising swell of a single note of music, the creaking door that announces Sreeni's cautious survey of his sleeping father, are all part of an elaborate and highly cohesive artistic scheme. *Mukhamukham* was taken by some to be a clear indictment of the dubious character of left politics in Kerala today. For Gopalakrishnan it went far beyond that. It was an investigation, a search, for the dormant spirit of revolution that may, if entreated by the people, shake a spiritually inept and morally corrupt society out of its slumber. In the film, "the man of the image turns out to be a bitter disappointment," says

Gopalakrishnan. "He acts and behaves like themselves—withdrawn, indifferent, evasive, confused, even defeated....He is in fact a projection of their own selves—a very inconvenient, embarrassing and menacing revelation. Naturally they do not want to accept this for it is pointing the finger at themselves. Soon the status quo is maintained by destroying the real and resurrecting the blemishless, venerable image of the ideal."

MUSAFIR (Traveller)
b&w, 149 minutes, Hindi, 1957

Production, direction and story: Hrishikesh Mukherjee/ Screenplay: Ritwik Ghatak, Hrishikesh Mukherjee/ Dialogue: Rajinder Singh Bedi/ Camera: Kamal Bose/ Lyrics: Shailendra/ Music: Salil Chowdhury/ Song: Lata Mangeshkar, Kishore Kumar, Shyamal Mitra, Shamshad Begum, Manna Dey, Dilip Kumar/ Art Direction: Sudhendu Roy/ Editing: Das Dhaimade/ Sound: Essa M. Suratwalla
Cast: Suchitra Sen, Sekhar, Bipin Gupta, Durga Khote, Nirupa Roy, Kishore Kumar, Nazir Hussein, Keshto Mukherjee, Hira Sawant, Daisy Irani, Dilip Kumar, Usha Kiron, Paul Mahindra, Mohan Choti, David, Rajlaxmi, Baby Naaz, Rashid Khan

SOMEWHERE in the middle of a teeming city, there is a little single-storyed house, with a small stretch of verandah, and a patch of green near the entrance. The flat is on rent. Tenants come and go, unfolding the drama of their lives for a little while within its walls. Our story begins with Shakuntala, who has run away on her wedding day with the man she loves. Shakuntala and Ajay are married the next day, but Ajay is worried about how his parents will take it. A month rolls by, with no reply to Ajay's letter. Shakuntala, herself an orphan, is impatient to be a part of his home. But it is not to be. The day the landlord is expected to collect the month's rent, Ajay goes out to the market, and an elderly couple appear at the door. Taking them to be the landlord and his wife, Shakuntala welcomes them in and is so warm and winning, that Ajay's parents (for that is who they are) are completely disarmed. When they leave, they take Ajay and Shakuntala with them, and the little house is vacant once more.

The next tenant is Madhavbabu whose eldest son has died recently, leaving a pregnant young wife behind. Madhavbabu's younger son, Bhanu, is a fun-loving young man who has just sat for his final examinations and while he waits for the results to be out, tries his best to keep his sister-in-law from falling into a depression. Once the results are out, Bhanu starts looking for a job, for his father has money to last for the next two months only. Many interviews later, Bhanu is a changed and chastened man. His father has started questioning his ability to ever get a job at all, and suspects him of frittering away whatever money his sister-in-law had given him from her meagre store. Scolded and thrown out of the house one day, Bhanu returns home at night with a small bottle of poison, which he duly consumes after leaving a suicide note and before going to bed. In the morning, a telegram comes—Bhanu has got a job! The suicide note is discovered, and Madhavbabu has just started beating his breast when Bhanu sits up on the bed! Everything is adulterated nowadays, even poison. His sister-in-law gets her baby and they all rejoice. Bhanu's job is in another town, so the family move with Bhanu and the house is empty again.

Next comes Vakilsahab, the advocate, with his widowed sister and her paralysed little son, with the purpose of taking a second opinion on the boy's disability. Vakilsahab goes out of town on a case, and Uma waits for the doctor's report. At night she hears the haunting notes of a violin. The previous tenants too had heard it and wondered about the mysterious musician, and this time the boy from the local teashop agrees to get the man across to play for the child. Uma is astonished to recognize Raja, the man she was to marry, who broke her heart in her youth. Raja apologizes, for he did not know he was coming to Uma's home. When he leaves, Uma questions the boy from the teashop and learns that Raja is homeless, and is slowly drinking himself to death. She insists that he stays with them when he comes next, but the Vakilsahab comes back and insists that he leaves, though it is evident by then that Raja is a very sick man. Raja leaves a letter for Uma, explaining how, on the eve of their wedding, he had learnt that he was dying from a terrible disease, and to make it easy for her, had rejected her ruthlessly. In the morning the sun gleams through the window next to the little boy's bed, and large flowers bloom at last on the tree that Shakuntala had planted a long time ago. It is a miracle, thinks the little boy, for Raja had promised him that he would walk the day the flowers appear. With renewed hope, the boy takes his first steps to health. But outside, under the tree, Raja lies dead.

THE SUCCESS of *Musafir* was no surprise, considering it had all the ingredients needed to appeal to the popular viewer. Hrishikesh Mukherjee was already established as a well-known director of "family dramas." Incidentally, till recently, apart from being a respected film-maker, he was the Chairman of the National Film Development Corporation, and still known for his skills as a film editor. Assisting him with the script was Ritwik Ghatak, an unknown filmmaker who had till then made only one film which was never released. Today, eight films later, and more than a decade after his death, Ghatak is known as one of the masters of serious Indian cinema. If Salil Chowdhury was known for his innovative use of folk music and orchestration from all over the world, Shailendra was already a successful lyricist. Rajinder Singh Bedi, who wrote the dialogue for the film, was himself a highly respected novelist, and a thwarted filmmaker. All these men had, at one time or another, been associated in varying degrees with the Indian Peoples Theatre Association, a left-wing cultural organization which had taken a leading role in the nationalist movement and gave the country a gold mine of talents, many of whom are still active in their respective fields. There were also three very famous stars in the three episodes of the films: Suchitra Sen, who was Shakuntala in the first episode, was the heart-throb of millions in Calcutta; Kishore Kumar, who was Bhanu in the second episode was, till his death recently, one of the most successful playback singers of the Hindi screen; and

Dilip Kumar, who was the doomed Raja in the last episode, had already perfected the role of a tragic hero and is described by Indian film journalists today, somewhat quaintly, as the Thespian, perhaps because of his effortless forays into high drama. Obviously made within a strict budget, the film cleverly uses the same sets to tell three stories in one film, stories that have the right doses of humour and pathos and tragedy, packed neatly within a single narrative framework.

NEW DELHI TIMES
colour, 123 minutes, Hindi, 1985

Production: P.K. Communications Private Limited/ Direction: Ramesh Sharma/ Story: Ramesh Sharma, Gulzar, K. Bikram Singh/ Screenplay and dialogue: Gulzar/ Camera: Subrata Mitra/ Music: Louis Banks/ Art Direction: Nitish Roy, Samir Chanda/ Editing: Renu Saluja/ Sound: Robin Sengupta
Cast: Shashi Kapoor, Sharmila Tagore, Om Puri, Kulbhushan Kharbanda, A.K. Hangal, Manohar Singh, M.K. Raina, Farookh Mehta

VIKAS PANDE, the Executive Editor of an English language daily, *New Delhi Times,* has been following with interest the career of Ajay Singh, a rising new politician in a neighbouring state, who is locked in a power struggle with its Chief Minister, D.N. Trivedi. But before the latest news on it can reach the front page, information comes from Ghaziabad of a ghastly illicit liquor tragedy leading to the death of many migrant labourers. Kedar, the reporter who talks to local liquor manufacturers, repeatedly hears a much feared name, Moghul. Warned that his life is in danger, Kedar makes an appointment with Vikas, but is killed in an accident before they can meet. Vikas is convinced that Kedar has been murdered. Meanwhile, Vikas's lawyer wife Nisha meets an old man from Ghazipur, whose daughter, who was being harassed for more dowry, has been reported missing from her in-law's home. Nisha promises to help find the girl.
  Bhale Ram, a leader of the scheduled caste MLAs and a staunch supporter of Trivedi, is shot dead in Ghazipur. The police arrest a local businessman, Iqbal, known to be Ajay Singh's man, who surprisingly claims that Singh arranged the killing. Singh's supporters go on a rampage when the news is made public, and a bloody communal riot follows. Vikas discovers that Iqbal is none other than Moghul, a powerful smuggler, who was supporting Singh in his effort to buy off Bhale Ram. Iqbal soon retracts his statement, claiming that it was made under police pressure. But Vikas is convinced that Iqbal and Singh are involved in both the murder and the liquor tragedy. Disturbed by his articles, Singh meets Vikas, but ends up abusing and threatening him. Subsequently Vikas and Nisha are assaulted by strangers on the highway. Next day Poddar has a heart attack and his son who takes over from him, refuses to publish an article by Vikas openly accusing Singh of the murder. Rebellious, Vikas threatens to resign.

While Vikas gets threatening calls over the telephone, the disputed article is published when Poddar, the grand old advocate for a free and honest press, intervenes from his sickbed. The same day Nisha is visited by the old man from Ghazipur whose daughter she had helped to find. The girl was placed in a lunatic asylum by her in-laws. The old man mentions that when he went to fetch her, he met people there who were not really mad at all, including the missing guard of the Circuit House in Ghazipur. Vikas manages to get access to the guard and learns that Bhale Ram had indeed sold out to Ajay Singh that night. The murderer was the guard's own son who, unknown to his father, was Trivedi's spy, and had been appointed to kill Bhale Ram if he sold out to Singh. As the pieces of the puzzle finally fall into place Vikas realizes he has been manipulated all along by Trivedi. Worse still, while he has been pursuing Singh, Trivedi has reached a compromise: the evening's news flash on the television announces that Trivedi has accepted Singh in his cabinet. Vikas also gets a telephone call to say that the guard has committed suicide in the asylum. His friend Anwar, a photo-journalist, who can understand his sense of shock, nevertheless points out that it does not make a difference who was the killer and who the killed. There is nothing to distinguish between men like Ajay Singh, Bhale Ram and Trivedi.

Vikas continues with his investigations, but even if his stories lead to the setting up of a commission of enquiry, will the report ever be made public?

NEW DELHI TIMES obviously follows the vogue of films on investigative journalism from the West. That it does so efficiently and realistically is what makes the film important. Corruption and its political whitewash have been targets of attack by newspapers that do not belong to the ruling party's camp. A now established journalist who had exposed a state scandal against its Chief Minister some years ago, and was later shunted out of the newspaper he worked for, has been reinstated as its editor recently. His employer has a reputation very like Jagannath Poddar. Though the story of the film does not have a direct counterpart in reality, its close resemblance to what appears daily in the news makes it uncomfortably real for the viewer.

Ramesh Sharma, the young director with a reputation for good documentary filmmaking, attempted to make a serious film for a mass audience. He used popular stars for the key roles, gave a certain gloss and finish to the film by using one of the best cameramen in the country, told a story that is shockingly credible, and told it well. The critics found *New Delhi Times* disturbing and stimulating; but the mass audience felt no enthusiasm for this all too real piece of screen fiction. Shown during the Filmotsav (the non-competitive international film festival in India) as one of the best twenty-one films of the year, Sharma's first feature gained brief notoriety when Doordarshan (Indian television and a government concern) temporarily withdrew from its commitment to broadcast the film. It was eventually broadcast after much criticism of Doordarshan's censorious attitude, but had as little effect on the moral fibre of Indian politics as its protagonist Vikas Pande's exposures. In a way that is the dismal message of *New Delhi Times*. In a country where the press is still free, it is allowed to be free only because it has little or no effect on the powerful forces of political corruption.

NIRMALYAM (The Offering)
b&w, 134 minutes, Malayalam, 1973

Production, direction and story: M.T. Vasudevan Nair/ Camera: Ramachandra Babu/ Music: K. Raghavan
Cast: P.J. Antony, Kaviyoor Ponnamma, Ravi Menon, Sukumaran, Sumitra, Sankaradi, Devidasan

IN THE ANCIENT temple, the village oracle dances before the goddess with his sacred curved, broad-bladed sword. It is his livelihood and the expression of his obsessive faith. He is in a trance till someone touches him, and he offers his sword to the goddess. With the money he earns from the village faithful, he must feed his wife and four children as well as a dying father. He is also the faith healer of the village, and householders often ask him to attend to a sick child. The priest of the village temple leaves in disgust for the trustees have no interest in maintaining it. One of the trustees sends his Brahmin cook's son as the new priest. The boy is preparing for an examination and takes the assignment with great reluctance. Ammini, the eldest daughter of the oracle, helps to settle him down in his new quarters, and a friendship develops between them which soon moves towards greater intimacy.

   Appu, the unemployed son of the oracle, spends most of his time with the village gamblers. While his father goes seeking alms to feed his family, Appu attempts to sell off his sacred sword and the temple bells to pay his gambling debts. The oracle returns home just in time to save his holy possessions which are part of his livelihood as well; and Appu leaves the village the same day. Meanwhile Ammini continues her relationship with the new priest, sharing his ambitions of a future in the city. At home, the oracle, tired and worn with worries waits for the day when he believes the temple will be as it was in his youth, and he himself will once again live with dignity.

   There is an outbreak of small-pox in the village. The villagers prepare to organize the annual celebrations of the goddess with greater fanfare to propitiate her, for it is her curse that has brought the disease to the village. The oracle's day of glory is here at last. He attends the festival that has already begun, then goes home to fetch his sacred sword, anklets and bells to dance in front of the goddess. The house is silent. He shouts for his wife and daughter, but no one answers. Then, from an inner room, emerges one of his creditors. As he leaves without a word, the oracle's tired, embittered wife appears at the door of the room. She has sold herself to pay his debts. Furious, he shouts at her, but she is defiant. "When my children are hungry, does your goddess bring rice for them, or money?" she asks. The oracle leaves his home and walks with firm steps towards the temple. He bathes in the river and comes out of it shaking, already in a trance. At the festival where the crowds have gathered, the oracle rushes past the noise and the lights in a frenzy, past rows of lamp-bearing women devotees, hitting himself on the head with his holy sword. Someone tries to control him, but he brushes him aside and runs into the temple. In a wild lunge, he hits himself with the sword again for the last time, spits at the goddess who has only betrayed him, and falls down dead at her feet.

THE FIRST feature film of a distinguished journalist from Kerala, *Nirmalyam* won the best feature film award for 1973. Unlike Adoor Gopalakrishnan's *Swayamvaram* which was made just a year earlier and displayed a rare restraint along with disciplined craftsmanship, *Nirmalyam* relied for its appeal on the passion and strength of its portrayal of the village oracle. Vasudevan Nair's sense of the dramatic is as acute as that of his actor, P.J. Anthony. Not surprisingly, Anthony came into films from the stage, and brought with him the ability to convincingly create and sustain a larger-than-life persona for his role. *Nirmalyam's* oracle may be dramatic, but he is not theatrical. A remnant of the feudal past, he is fast losing his identity and his spiritual relevance in an industrial society where even the villages are gradually going through a transformation. There cannot possibly be a furture for the oracle, nor will the past suddenly rejuvenate itself. His offering of hatred to the goddess who can no longer sustain him, is for the oracle his last act of defiance against a world which has already left him behind.

ONDANONDU KALADALLI (Once Upon a Time)
colour, 156 min, Kannada, 1978

Production: L.N. Combines/ Direction: Girish Karnad/ Story and screenplay: Krishna Basrur, Girish Karnad/ Camera: Apurba Kishore Bir/ Music: Bhaskar Chandavarkar/ Art Direction: Jayoo Nachiket/ Editing: P. Bhaktavatsalam
Cast: Shankar Nag, Sundar Krishna Urs, Akshata Rao, Sushilendra Joshi, Ajit Saldanha, Rekha Sabnis, Anil Thakkar, Vasant Rao Nakod

MEDIEVAL Karnataka, after the Hoysalas and before the Vijayanagar empire. With no strong central government, the land is ruled by greedy little men squabbling for more power. Fortune seeking soldiers pour in from all over India, for Karnataka is now the home of the martial arts, and Kannada warriors are in demand as far away as in Nepal. In a little kingdom on the border between the Maland jungles and the plains of the Deccan, two brothers war endlessly in the hope of taking over each other's land. On Kapardi's side there is the aging general, Permadi, whose shrewdness and skill gives him an edge over his brother, Maranayaka. Ganduguli, a wandering mercenary, joins Maranayaka. His cynicism about a soldiers life is in direct opposition to Permadi's traditional loyalty to his master. As antagonists, they are well-matched in spite of the difference in their age and experience, and their confrontation begins cautiously, like a game of chess.
If Permadi finds Ganduguli's mercenary status distasteful and immoral, to the younger man the aging general is a laughable anachronism, who refuses to accept the reality that soldiers go into battle not for honour but to fill their bellies. Yet, when both of them are humiliated by their respective masters, they form an alliance against the brothers, who are driven into each other's arms in this confrontation between the two classes. But each man continues to be suspicious of the other. The story of betrayal, cruelty and cowardice ends when young Jayakeshi, the rightful owner of the throne, returns to power,

brings with him the hope of a new and better life, the idealism of a new generation.

ONDANONDU KALADALLI is, by Girish Karnad's own description, his tribute to Kurosawa. The first exuberant exposition of the martial arts in India, the film is essentially an excellent entertainment, in a manner that has nothing in common with its vulgarized counterparts in mainstream Indian cinema. Martial arts are not unknown to India, where they were practised by Buddhist priests who were not allowed to carry arms, but had to protect themselves against the attack of bandits when travelling long distances overland. Well researched in its historical context, the film convincingly recreates thirteenth century Karnataka in all its political instability and lawlessness, but gives the narrative the rhythm and objectivity of a ballad. The fights, which form the dramatic focus of the film, are brilliantly choreographed without taking away from the historical authenticity of the characters and the situations. Shankar Nag, who plays Ganduguli with great vigour, is a stage and screen actor who has recently taken to directing his own films. Bhaskar Chandavarkar, who provides the musical score for the film, is himself a noted scholar of Indian music, has taught film music in the Film and Television Institute of India, and writes extensively on the subject. The art directors, Nachiket and Jayoo Patwardhan, are by profession a husband-wife team of architects, who have not only specialized on period cinema, but directed their own films with great success.

ORIDATH (Somewhere)
colour, 112 minutes, Malayalam, 1986

Production: Suryakanti Film Makers/ Direction, Story and Screenplay: G. Aravindan/ Camera: Shaji/ Art Direction: Namboodiri/ Editing: Bose/ Sound: Devadas
Cast: Nedumudi Venu, Sreenivasan, Thilakan, Vineet, Krishnankutty Nair, Surendra Babu, Kunhandi, Chandran Nair, Surya, Sitara

A REMOTE village in the erstwhile Travancore Cochin state in the mid-fifties, when the new republic was looking towards technological advancement as the "catalyst for social change." Following the initiative of the local Panchayat Board headed by the Brahmin landlord, the government decides to bring electricity to the village, with the noble intention of leading the poor, ignorant villagers from darkness to light. The village is not so backward after all. Within the framework of the old world, it presents a lively variety of characters: the Communist tailor given to rabble-rousing speeches; Kuttan the odd jobs man, always hitching himself to the latest bandwagon; the elderly school teacher with a wealth of traditional wisdom; the adolescent boy, Jose, sharing his insatiable curiosity about life with the little girl next door. Each family has its own story to tell, but their lives are interwoven, with the festivals at the local temple as their focal point.

The executive engineer from the Electricity Board comes to survey the village. He brings with him an overseer with an eye for the girls, and Kuttan becomes his loyal slave. But not for long. With progress round the corner, a doctor sets up a dispensary in the village and soon Kuttan is hanging about his doors. The overseer ceases to be a figure of awe, and gets involved in forming an amateur group of players. They start preparing in earnest for the coming festival, with a play about separated lovers. Young Jose plays the heroine. But in all the bustle and excitement, bad omens hover over the village. Neighbours and old friends quarrel over where the electric poles are to be located. Crows fall dead, and then a cow, electrocuted by the wires. Kuttan's girl finds that she is pregnant. Kuttan who cannot support her, takes her in a panic to the doctor for an abortion. It turns into a nightmare when her body is found in the temple pond, and the doctor is revealed as a quack and a bigamist. Kuttan's nemesis is complete when his sister is seduced by the overseer.

At the temple festival, playing his traditional role of the black goddess, Kali, Kuttan decides to wreak vengeance on the overseer whom he now sees as the instrument of all calamities in the village, a symbol of imminent destruction of the peaceful old way of life. But it is young Jose, with his dreams and ambitions of a future in the city, who gets electrocuted by mistake, his cries drowned by the noise and dazzle of the temple fireworks. A short circuit at the same time adds to the show as the electric poles spark and crackle and go up in flames. As the fiery forces of change consume the village, the screen freezes on a parachuting mannikin hovering between heaven and earth in eternal limbo.

"I WAS BORN in a small village," says director G. Aravindan, "and up to the age of ten I hadn't seen electricity. I still remember with nostalgia those times, when people moved through the night with burning flares. When electricity came, they went out."

Painter, cartoonist, writer and musician, Aravindan has been actively involved in folk theatre as well. Surprisingly, he also spent many years as an officer in the government Rubber Board, a job that was tempered by his popular cartoon serial during that period in a well-known Malayalam weekly, on the trials and tribulations of a small man in a big world. Aravindan films, however, rarely use direct caricatures, though the cartoonist's precision of lines is evident in the portraits he paints on the screen. Documentary realism in time and space is often juxtaposed with an inner existence, and forms a recurring motif in all his films, unfolding layer upon layer of perception. If *Oridath* contains caricature, its tragi-comic use merges it with the real, and carries it forward to a broader, surreal viewpoint of modernization and change, where technology is transformed into a new Frankenstein.

"The first half of the film—gay and satirical—is in sharp contrast to the sombre second half," says critic Iqbal Masud. "The various episodes are held together by the thread of the disruptive assault of modernity. The finale is rather abrupt, even facile. But in the fabric of the film, Aravindan has masterfully questioned the impact of one kind of 'development' on a rooted and integrated—however unjust—society.

"Is Aravindan an 'enemy of the modern?' Rather he emerges as a mystical—transcendental, Burkean conservative who in a very concrete fashion warns against the shibboleths of 'change' and 'progress.'" [*Indian Express*, 16 November 1986.]

Oridath won Aravindan the National Award for the best director of the year.

PAAR   (The Crossing)
colour, 120 minutes, Hindi, 1984

Production: Orchid Films Private Ltd./ Direction, Camera and Music: Goutam Ghose/ Story: Samaresh Bose/ Screenplay: Partha Banerjee, Goutam Ghose
Cast: Naseeruddin Shah, Shabana Azmi, Utpal Dutta, Om Puri, Mohan Agashe, Anil Chatterjee

EVENING falls on a small village in Bihar. In the homes of the poor Harijan labourers the hearths are being lit when motorbikes and jeeps break the silence of the night. The huts are set on fire, their inmates gunned down. Only a handful escape in the cover of darkness, among them Naurangia and his pregnant wife, Rama. The day after the massacre come the protectors of the people—the police, the press, the local administration. The story that the village headman relates is as old as the hills.

The village schoolmaster, an idealist of the old order, encouraged a Harijan to stand for the Panchayat (village level administration) elections. He also began a movement for minimum wages in the area. When the landlord refused to respond, the labourers, in protest, stopped work in the fields. A Harijan winning the Panchayat elections came as an additional insult, and the landlord's hot-bloooded young brother decided to take matters in hand. The schoolmaster met sudden death on the roadside, but even eyewitnesses could not convince the police that it was murder. The feud would have ended right there, if Naurangia and his friends did not take it upon themselves to mete out equally sudden justice to the landlord's brother one dark evening. The massacre was its aftermath.

Fugitives from the law, Rama and Naurangia begin their odyssey at the home of the schoolmaster's widow who sends them off with a letter to a friend in a nearby town. From there, armed with a note to another unknown benefactor, they set off for Calcutta. At the jute mill near Calcutta, they find the man's home, but he has left for his village. Naurangia spends futile days looking for a job. With all their money gone, and starvation round the corner, Naurangia takes on an absurd offer—to take a herd of swine across the river. The ferries refuse to take animals. With the hope of money on the other side, money that will at least take them back to their beleagured home, Naurangia wades into the river with his pregnant wife.

It is a long and arduous journey. With their money secure, they lie down under a shed for the night, when Rama suddenly fears for the baby, still and silent within her. Her first child drowned in the village well. Will this one go too? In the darkness, Naurangia puts his ear against his wife's rising belly.

"Wait, listen. There he is. I can hear him cry." Rama relaxes as Naurangia listens avidly to the small silent voice of life in his wife's womb.

PHOTO-JOURNALIST Goutam Ghose started making award-winning documentaries in his early twenties. His first feature film, *Ma Bhoomi,* based on the extremist movement in Andhra Pradesh, was made in Telugu in 1980, and brought him a National Award as the best regional film. His second feature film, *Dakhal,* made in Bengali in 1981, on a tribal people's battle with exploitation, won him the President's award for the best feature film of the year and the Grand Jury Prize in the XI International Human Rights Film Festival in France. *Paar* won his actor, Naseeruddin Shah, the best actor's prize at the 41st International Film Festival in Venice. But critical success often remains a blind alley in India. As with his earlier films, *Paar* has not reached the wider Indian public, and this despite the fact that it was made in Hindi rather than in a regional language.

Whatever may have been the extent of Ghose's earlier leftist involvements, politics in *Paar* is overshadowed by its human drama. With two of the best young artistes of the Hindi screen as his protagonists, Ghose soon shifts his attention from the wider rural arena to a probing close up of human endurance. Shabana Azmi and Naseeruddin Shah are among the earliest recruits of the parallel cinema. Daughter of a highly respected Urdu poet, Azmi (Rama in *Paar*) joined the popular cinema soon after her debut in Shyam Benegal's films. She has been equally at home in the social realism of Benegal's *Ankur* and *Mandi,* Mrinal Sen's *Khandhar,* Satyajit Ray's *Shatranj ke Khilari,* as in the rumbustious fantasies of Bombay's film industry. The remarkable range of her portrayals has probably not been matched by any other actress on the Indian screen. Shah who plays Naurangia, has had an equally interesting career spanning both the stage and the screen. He still runs a dramatic troupe with his actress wife, and has recently extended his professional identity beyond the serious cinema, to more lucrative appearances in occasional popular films.

PAKEEZAH (Pure Heart)
colour, 4327.55 m, Hindi, 1971

Production, direction and story: Kamal Amrohi/ Camera: Joseph Wirsching/ Music: Ghulam Mohammed, Naushad/ Lyrics: Kaif Bhopali, Majrooh Sultanpuri, Kaifi Azmi, Kamal Amrohi/ Playback: Lata Mangeshkar, Mohammad Rafi/ Art Direction: N.B. Kulkarni/ Editing: D.N. Pal/ Sound: R.G. Pushalkar
Cast: Meena Kumari, Ashok Kumar, Raaj Kumar, Veena, Sapru, Kamal Kapoor, Vijay Laxmi, Jagdish Kanwal, Nadira

SOMETIME near the beginning of the century, Sahabuddin, a son of a North Indian aristocratic family, brings home Nargis, a courtesan, as his bride. His father, a patriarch of the old order, refuses to accept her. Shamed by his insults, but unwilling to return to her earlier life, Nargis runs away and takes shelter in a graveyard; while Sahabuddin spends his days going from town to town, searching for her among the courtesan community. One day a woman brings a bracelet to sell to Nargis's elder sister Nawabjaan which she recognizes as her own. The woman tells her about the golden-haired stranger with a little daughter, dying among the gravestones, on whose behalf she is selling the ornament. Nawabjaan hastens to her sister; but by the time she reaches the graveyard, Nargis is dead. Telling the woman to sell her sister's meagre possessions, Nawabjaan takes the child home.

Seventeen years later, a book of poems that belonged to Nargis, is picked up from a roadside stall by an old scholar, who discovers in it a letter ready for posting. That is how Sahabudding learns of his daughter, and comes to take her home. Believing him guilty of betraying her sister, Nawabjaan tells him to come back the next day, and meanwhile takes her niece, Sahebjaan, away to another town. Sahabuddin comes back to find the door of Nawabjaan's dwelling locked. Sahebjaan and her aunt spend the night on a train; in the morning, Sahebjaan finds a note between her toes which says, "Forgive my intrusion. I am a stranger who found refuge for a brief while in your compartment. I saw your beautiful feet. Do not let them touch the ground, or they will be soiled."

To hide Sahebjaan from her father, Nawabjaan buys Gulabi Mahal—the Rose Palace—where under the stern eye of Goharjaan, its previous owner, Nargis's daughter becomes a much sought-after courtesan. Sahebjaan often wonders about the stranger on the train. The note in a golden box hangs on a chain from her hair, and she runs to the verandah each time a train crosses the bridge nearby. Among the men visiting Gulabi Mahal is Zaffarali Khan, a local aristocrat, who showers her with expensive gifts. Forced to accept an invitation to his launch, Sahebjaan gets a reprieve when a herd of wild elephants attack and destroy the launch. Drifting to the shore alone, she sees an empty tent where in a diary she finds a mention of that strange meeting on the train. She waits in apprehension for the man she has never met but who has completely taken over her imagination. When he comes, he recognizes her at once and is overjoyed; but remembering her own low status in society, and fearful of losing him once she reveals her identity, Sahebjaan pretends to be suffering from amnesia. It is no lie, for her life has long lost its reality, ever since that night on the train.

The man is a forest officer, and leaves in the morning for work, promising to be back before dark; but soon after, Goharjaan comes looking for her ward on a boat. Dragged back to Gulabi Mahal, Sahebjaan finds it impossible to perform as a courtesan. The angry Goharjaan sends a common trader into her room. When he falls into a fountain frightened by a snake, Sahebjaan runs away and is found unconscious on the railway tracks by the forest officer. This time he takes her home to his family. When his grandfather returns from Hyderabad with his ailing son Sahabuddin, both Sahebjaan and her father are unaware of the coincidence. Sahebjaan's protector is Salim, her father's nephew. The old patriarch now commands Salim to abandon a girl who has no past, nor family. Refusing to be a puppet in the hands of his grandfather, Salim leaves home. Back in the hills where Salim works, Sahebjaan admits the truth about herself and her love for him. After only a moment's hesitation, he draws her into his arms. Salim now faces constant humiliation because of Sahebjaan, but refuses to leave her. Instead, he arranges a *nikah* (Muslim wedding) at a mosque. When, as part of the ritual, the priest asks her name, Salim replies, "Pakeezah," the pure of heart. But asked if she accepts Salim as a husband, Sahebjaan, unable to condemn him to a life of shame, runs away again.

She returns to a now empty Gulabi Mahal and lives in virtual isolation. One day a letter arrives from Salim, a sarcastic note, inviting Sahebjaan, as a celebrated courtesan, to perform at his wedding. While Salim waits in agony for a meeting that will pain them both, Sahebjaan comes with her companions and her aunt to celebrate the death of her dreams. Unable to stand the anguish in her song, Salim leaves the place. The distraught Sahebjaan, with a sweep of her arm, throws a chandelier to the ground, dances in a frenzy on the broken glass, and collapses exhausted in the arms of her aunt. Nawabjaan, seeing Sahabuddin in the audience, calls upon him with scorn and sorrow: "How shameful it is that your daughter whom you should protect is exposed to everyone as a courtesan in your own home." As Sahabuddin runs to Sahebjaan, the old patriarch, taking a gun, shoots his son who will no longer obey him. Lying in Sahebjaan's arms, the dying Sahabuddin tells Salim that she is indeed his daughter. "She will only be your daughter when, as her father, you give her away in marriage from the courtesan's home," says Nawabjaan, haunted by her sister's fate. Salim promises Sahabuddin that he will be there to give his daughter away.

In Gulabi Mahal, the bridegroom's family comes with Sahabuddin's coffin, and the *nikah* is performed before it. As they leave carrying the bridal palanquin down the narrow lanes, Nawabjaan stands alone, watching from the open verandah of the courtesan's home.

KAMAL AMROHI came to Bombay in 1938 as a lad of twenty, and in fifty years, directed four films, two of which were blockbusters, the other two total failures at the box-office. Of the blockbusters, *Mahal* was his first film, made in 1949, and *Pakeezah* his third, made eighteen years later and starring his third wife, Meena Kumari. After he had completed shooting five reels of the film, *Pakeezah* was stalled for seven and a half years, mainly due to Amrohi's differences with Meena Kumari which eventually led to their separation. When it was finally taken up again, Meena Kumari was already an alcoholic and the film was one of her last. She died soon after its release; yet it is impossible to find any lack of consistency in her portrayal, or any sign of the passage of the years.

Recreating a lost era of decadence, and the world of high-class courtesans who were artistes in their own right, the film weaves an incredible romance which cannot be contained within a rational or a causal framework. Sahabuddin cannot find Nargis though she is in the same town, in a public place, for ten months. Similarly, once he finds Nawabjaan's door locked, he gives up looking for his daughter. In the course of her adventures, Sahebjaan moves from one town to another seemingly with no money at all, and alone, in days when women were hardly ever seen outside the *purdah*. Goharjaan, who sells her house to Nawabjaan because of her debts, appears to wield a great deal of power over Sahebjaan even though she is living off the younger girl.

Geographically too, *Pakeezah* seems totally confusing, with hills, lakes, mountain springs and railway lines appearing all over the place whenever the story requires one of them. And what about the mysterious snake that appears wriggling in an earlier sequence, vanishes without explanation, only to reappear and become an almost mystic redemption for the trader who was called in to teach Sahebjaan a lesson? The coincidences that form the motive force of the story are as numerous as they are unreal. But the ambiance of the film is such that all details are swept away by the overwhelming emotional drama of the two central characters. It is possible to be so moved also by the spectacle, the songs, the little cameos of life in another world—in the courtesans' dwellings, in the inner sanctums of the aristocrat's home; it is easy to accept the unreality of the narrative as long as the men and women who people this world are undeniably real. And so they are, from the weak, gentle Sahabuddin to the proud, relentless Nawabjaan; and in the centre of them all, Sahebjaan, "Pakeezah," virgin and courtesan, pure yet tainted forever, loving yet fearful of receiving love, a haunting image and the stuff of every man's dreams.

PARAMA
colour, 139 minutes, Bengali and Hindi, 1985

Production: Usha Enterprises/ Direction, story and screenplay: Aparna Sen/ Camera: Ashok Mehta/ Music: Bhaskar Chandavarkar/ Sound: Bejoy Bhoge
Cast: Rakhee Gulzar, Sandhya Rani Chatterjee, Aparna Sen, Mukul Sharma, Dipankar De

PARAMA, a beautiful woman, married early into an old fashioned, upper-class, extended family, has through the years unconsciously moulded herself into the various roles that her family demands of her. At the autumnal *puja* ceremony, a major event in the household which she supervises, Parama meets Rahul, a photographer friend of a young nephew. Rahul, who lives abroad, is travelling through India in search of photographic material for magazine features. Parama's beautiful, quiescent face becomes a challenge for him. An Indian, yet an outsider in Indian society, Rahul perceives what is hidden behind her peaceful, submissive exterior, something that Parama herself has long forgotten. With the permission of her mother-in-law, Parama reluctantly allows herself to be photographed. Rahul also wants her to show the old city. She goes with him, once again reluctantly.

Gradually, Rahul's freedom from the mores of the society that binds her, his unrestrained friendship and compassion, begin to reveal to herself her own hidden persona. Parama comes alive in a way she has never known. The brief, one-sided love making of her husband while he worries about his promotion, the demands that each member of the family makes on her, her daily routine, everything that had found a slot in her life, now become insignificant compared to the growing awareness within her. Her dormant sensitivities, her love of music and poetry, her passionate response to nature, her sexuality, become agonizingly real to her, and disrupt the smooth, even flow of her existence. Her inevitable love affair with Rahul leaves her completely shattered, for she has broken two of the most rigid taboos of traditional Indian society: a married woman cannot have a physical relationship with anyone other than her husband, and a woman cannot love a younger man. Added to this is the realization that at forty, she is considered far too old for such dallying.

Rahul leaves; Parama goes through her daily chores listlessly, waiting for his letters. And then the blow falls. In his usual impulsive manner, Rahul sends a magazine with an intimate portrait of Parama and a message of love scrawled on it. Parama is ostracized at home. Her husband, who is not above making an occasional pass at a secretary, calls her a whore when she tries to talk to him. The children are kept away from her. Her friend Sheela, a divorcee and a working woman, the only person who had known of the affair and offered cautious sympathy, shows her a news item about Rahul who is missing in some strife-torn country in another part of the globe. Parama tries to kill herself, but is discovered in time and removed to a nursing home.

As she convalesces, her family gather around her feeling vaguely guilty, unable to understand her silence. Even the news that Rahul has been found and is safe, fails to stir her. The affair is over. Parama resolves to take a very ordinary job with the help of Sheela, as she is not trained for anything better. Her husband who has always provided for all her material needs and more, is bewildered. When the kindly family doctor suggests psychiatric care to help her recover from her deep sense of guilt, Parama suddenly breaks her silence. "But I don't feel guilty at all," she says with dawning self-assurance. While the men search frantically for a suitable response, Parama's teenage daughter, with instinctive compassion, comes to sit with her mother and share the wonder of the first flower in a potted plant that Rahul had brought for her a long time ago.

MADE BY A woman director, *Parama* is very much a woman's film. What it lacks in artistry or cinematic craftsmanship, it makes up for in the obvious sincerity of its statement. The Bengali version of the film, released in Calcutta, raised a furore among the orthodox middle-class, but surprisingly, also found some staunch supporters among them. For the western audience, unaware of the hidden barriers of modern Indian society, the theme of the film may seem trivial. Adultery is nothing to make a fuss about. But for Sen and her Indian viewers it is much more than extra-marital sex.

Parama explores three primary areas of social existence for an Indian woman. First among them is the role a woman plays in the family and outside the home. Before her marriage, she is sister and daughter; after her marriage she is sister-in-law, mother, aunt. Her relationships with men outside the family are always identified by these symbols, just as they are within the family. (Parama is initially disturbed by the fact that a nephew's friend refuses to address her as aunt.) Hidden below these symbols, many a clandestine relationship has flourished through generations. But on the surface, women are worshipped, not desired. The double standards of social morality extend to the second area: marital relationship is sacred for the woman, not so for the man. A man may want an occasional diversion, but a woman fulfils her own needs by surrendering to the needs of her husband. The third area is what is still the most controversial: a woman's sexuality, if such a thing exists at all, is something to be sublimated, not indulged. Involuntarily, Parama attacks the veracity of all three assumptions. She learns to accept Rahul's friendship as something outside her predetermined space as a married woman and a mother. She learns that apart from being worshipped or being casually used, a woman has a third alternative: being appreciated for what she can give or receive, intellectually, emotionally and sexually, as an equal. She also learns that sex is not a duty, that she herself can feel desire as much as arouse it.

That she discovers all this near the end of her youth and through her encounter with a younger man, only serves to make the experience more incredible for the Indian public, a large section of whom, both men and women, either dismissed the issue as sensationalist, or registered their sense of outrage against such overt encouragement of promiscuity. Sen, who had conceived *Parama* not as feminist propaganda, but as wider social comment, found in the raging controversy a confirmation of the film's validity, at least in the environment it was made for. The film did well regionally, though the Hindi version is yet to be released. Meanwhile Sen has begun work on her third film, this time about a woman caught in the web of the regressive morality of another age.

PARASH PATHAR (The Philosopher's Stone)
b&w, 102 minutes, Bengali, 1957

Production: L.B. Films International/ Direction and Screenplay: Satyajit Ray/ Story: Based on a short story by Parashuram/ Camera: Subrata Mitra/ Music: Ravi Shankar/ Art Direction: Bansi Chandragupta/ Editing: Dulal Dutta
Cast: Tulsi Chakravarty, Ranibala Devi, Kali Banerjee, Gangapada Basu, Mani Srimani

RETURNING home from work one rainy afternoon, Paresh Dutta, an elderly bank clerk, picks up a stone from the pavement, the alchemic properties of which he soon discovers. Within four years, Paresh is mysteriously rich, and a much respected citizen of Calcutta. From the little hovel in a backlane of the city, the childless couple move to a mansion with all the trappings of opulence. Paresh now has a secretary to look after his work, Priyatosh Henry Biswas, a young man who spends most of his time talking to his girlfriend over the brand new telephone. The anonymous little man has become a public figure, sought after in social and political circles. No one knows the source of his sudden wealth, which he carefully invests in various industrial and business enterprises.

But success has its pitfalls. Paresh goes to a cocktail party in a rich businessman's home, and is betrayed by his first taste of alcohol. The guests are given a free magic show by the inebriated Paresh, who proudly demonstrates the powers of his precious stone. It may be entertainment for the guests, but for his host, a shrewd businessman, it is a revelation. However, his native cunning restored the next morning, Paresh manages to fool the businessman when he tries to extract more information. In revenge, he alerts the police.

In a panic, Paresh gives the stone to Priyatosh, and tries to make a dash for it in his car. He is caught by the police who hold him on a charge of smuggling gold. To prove his innocence, Paresh must produce the stone in court. But Priyatosh who has just been jilted by his girl, once again over the telephone, decides to end his life by swallowing the strange stone. For the police doctor it is an amazing case. Repeated X-rays show that the stone is slowly disintegrating in the labyrinths of Priyatosh's digestive canals! The healthy young man digests the stone, and all Paresh's gold turns back into iron. Paresh and his wife heave a secret sigh of relief.

PARASH PATHAR, Ray's third feature film, translates into cinematic idiom a story written by probably the only true humorist Bengal has ever produced. Humour, written or spoken, tends to be localized and dependent upon the nuances of the language, and *Parash Pathar* has remained an essentially Bengali film. Although the fundamentals of the story are familiar and universal, even its Bengali audience found it difficult to assimilate the subtle inward movement of its humour, tinged with the pathos of an impossible dream. Yet the film remains an example of Ray's inimitable style, detailed, carefully crafted, gently mocking at human frailty with an unsurpassed lyricism. Paresh, with his childlike wonder, pride and bewilderment, is a masterly portrayal by one of the veterans of the Bengali screen, Tulsi Chakravarty, who was the hilariously temperamental schoolmaster in Ray's first film.

"One will always remember the scene in which the couple go through the long wait at the police station," writes film critic Chidananda Dasgupta. "When the clerk explains the limits of his ambition, his pathetic, impossible desire to stop at the end of his needs, and shows his knees full of injuries received in alighting from crowded buses, we see his sudden wealth only as an insight into his poverty. 'I have never harmed anyone,' Paresh Dutta says in defence of his unexpected wealth, which the police, more than anyone, so resent. He seems acutely aware, more convinced than all his angry observers, that he has done something shameful in becoming rich. It is a sin he must expiate. Finally his guilt is washed clean when his wife's face is lit up by a wonderful smile, as the gold turns back into iron." [*Satyajit Ray,* Directorate of Film Festivals, 1981.]

PATALA BHAIRAVI (The Goddess from below the Earth)
b&w,   minutes, Telugu, 1951

Production: Vijaya Productions/ Direction: K.V. Reddy/ Story and dialogue: Pingali Nagendra Rao/ Camera: Marcus Bartley/ Music: Ghantasala/ Editing: Jambulingam, Mani/ Sound: A. Krishnan

Cast: N.T. Rama Rao, S.V. Ranga Rao, C.S.R. Relangi, Balakrishna, Padmanabhan, Malati, T.G. Kamala, Lakshmi Kantham, Hemalata Amma Rao

A GARDENER'S son, Thota Ramudu, is in love with the princess of the land. His love is reciprocated by the princess Malathi, but her father, the King, will not marry her to anybody unless he is equally rich. Thota Ramudu, therefore, spends a great deal of time pondering on how to get rich quickly. In the same kingdom lives a sorcerer who is greedy for greater magical powers and riches. He knows that if he appeases the goddess of the underworld, Patala Bhairavi, with human sacrifice, he will become the most powerful man in the kingdom. But the sacrifice must be a very special man. With the help of his magical powers, the sorcerer identifies Thota Ramudu as the most eligible man for the purpose and he knows exactly how to snare him. He takes an empty bowl and magically produces money from it. When Thota hears of the magic bowl, he steals it. The sorcerer catches the thief, and takes him into the deep forests where there is an abode of the dreaded goddess.

To purify himself before the sacrifice, Thota is asked to have a bath in the forest pond. But in the pond lives a ferocious crocodile who attacks the young man. Thota, who is stronger than most men, vanquishes the crocodile, who turns into a divine being released from a curse. She blesses him and tells him how to outwit the sorcerer. When the sorcerer asks him to prostrate himself before the image of the goddess, Thota Ramudu pretends that he does not know how to. The sorcerer lies down to show him the proper way, and Thota at once chops off his head in front of the goddess. The goddess, pleased with the sacrifice, appears before Thota, blesses him, and gives him an image of herself as a talisman. Thota goes home carrying the talisman, grows rich beyond his imagination, and prepares to marry the princess.

Meanwhile, the sorcerer's disciple, having found his master's decapitated body, revives the corpse with the healing power of magic roots from the forest. Furious at being outwitted, the sorcerer now gets the King's foolish brother-in-law to steal the talisman from Thota, and even manages to kidnap the princess. Thota's riches vanish, and he is once again the poor gardener's son. Determined not to be defeated, Thota follows the sorcerer into his forest hideout, and wrests the image back from him. He returns home in triumph and is married to the princess. Now that he no longer needs the talisman, Thota calls upon the goddess and returns it to her. Patala Bhairavi is pleased by Thota's lack of greed, and blesses the couple before disappearing with the talisman.

AN EXTRAORDINARILY meaningless modern myth, *Patala Bhairavi* is the ultimate in kitsch; the whole purpose of the film being to project its hero suffering incredible ups and downs of fortune to win his lady love. Jungles of studio foliage and ornate cardboard castles are his playground. The hero is of course no other than the charismatic Telugu actor, N.T. Rama Rao, today the controversial Chief Minister of Andhra Pradesh. Born in a landed family, Rama Rao joined government service after graduation, and started his own theatre group at the same time. His success as an actor led to his first screen role in 1947. By 1950 he was enough in demand to be employed on a monthly salary by Vijaya Productions, a new enterprise at the time, where Rama Rao played the lead in some of their most successful films. *Patala Bhairavi,* for example, celebrated 100-day runs in 34 cinema halls, silver jubilees in 13 of them, and a golden jubilee in one. It broke all previous box-office records in the Telugu film industry. Vijaya soon made a Tamil version of the film, and Gemini Studios a Hindi version, both with Rama Rao as the hero.

Rama Rao started his own production company soon after, where he not only acted in his own productions, but also directed them on occasions. His phenomenal popularity as the mythological hero is evident in most Andhra homes, where portraits of N.T. Rama Rao in the roles of various divinities and saints, have taken the place of paintings of gods. Rama Rao tends to make the most of his screen image, and has often played more than one role in a film, the culmination being in *Dana Veera Sura Karna,* a mythological produced under his own banner. The story of a romantic and tragic character from the *Mahabharata,* the film has Rama Rao playing three roles—that of the upright Karna, his dubious ally Duryodhana, and his arch enemy Lord Krishna. Having won the Chief Ministership of his state on a wave of popularity, and evidently as a result of his identification in the popular mind with the most revered of the gods, Rama Rao today has no time for films. As the head of the Telugu Desam party, the leading opposition party in the parliament, he is under direct attack from the ruling party, and at present the centre of much political controversy.

PATHER PANCHALI (Song of the Road)
b&w, 115 min, Bengali, 1955

Production: Government of West Bengal/ Direction and screenplay: Satyajit Ray/ Story: Bibhutibhushan Bandyopadhyay/ Camera: Subrata Mitra/ Music: Ravi Shankar/ Art Direction: Bansi Chandragupta/ Editing: Dulal Dutta/ Sound: Bhupen Ghosh
Cast: Karuna Bandyopadhyay, Kanu Bandyopadhyay, Chunibala Devi, Uma Dasgupta, Subir Bandyopadhyay, Runki Bandtopadhyay, Reba Devi, Aparna Devi, Tulsi Chakravarty, Rama Gangopadhyay, Haren Bandyopadhyay

HARIHAR RAY, an impoverished brahmin, lives with his wife, Sarbojaya, and his little daughter, Durga, in his ancestral home in the village of Nishchindipur. Of a scholarly bent of mind, he is more interested in writing plays than earning a livelihood. Whatever land the family had, has been usurped by the neighbouring landlord, as payment for an old inherited debt. The house is in bad shape, needing many repairs. They live off what little Harihar earns as the family priest of a few households in the locality. There is never enough for the three of them, and Sarbojaya resents having to share her home with an old and infirm aunt, Indir. There are constant quarrels between the two, and Indir leaves home periodically, carrying her meagre belongings, to take refuge in the home of some distant relative.

Sarbojaya's life swings between hope and despair. A son is born to them, Harihar gets a job as an accountant with the rich neighbour. For a while the struggle seems to ease a little, though, to Sarbojaya's annoyance, Indir is back again in her section of the house. Harihar dreams of new verses, new plays that will immortalize him. Sarbojaya hopes to send little Apu to school, and find a good husband for Durga. Maybe now they can pay off all their debts and repair the house. But six years pass, and nothing really changes. Sarbojaya still quarrels with Indir who is becoming more of a liability. The children watch hungrily as their rich neighbour distributes sweets. And Durga is accused of stealing a bauble from a playmate to the great humiliation of her mother. After months of waiting, Harihar comes home with his overdue salary, and the hope of additional earnings by taking over the priestly duties in a landed household in another village. Indir, who has left home once again, comes back one afternoon, when Sarbojaya is alone in the house. Sarbojaya refuses to have her back in the family, and the children discover the old woman dead among the bamboo groves at the end of the day.

Harihar goes away for a week in search of work, but stays away for months. His first letter disheartens Sarbojaya, for the job he was hoping for has not materialized. A long silence follows, and the family faces abject poverty. Sarbojaya, too proud to ask for help, sells the last of her brass vessels to feed the children. Harihar's second letter arrives after five months of anxiety and despair. "It seems our luck has turned at last," he says. But before he can come back home, the monsoon arrives in the village. Durga dances wildly in the rain, and comes home with fever. The monsoon winds blow outside as Durga languishes in bed. Then comes the night of the storm. A fierce gale devastates the house, and as the sky turns grey in the first light of the morning, Durga dies. Harihar, coming home at last with his earnings and gifts for the family, is unprepared for the tragedy that awaits him. A sense of defeat leads him to accept a suggestion made by Sarbojaya long ago. He decides to abandon his home and go to Varanasi, a temple town, where he might make a better living as a priest.

HOW DOES one describe a film that is a phenomenon? Much has already been written about the unknown young commercial artist and film buff who joined the ranks of the greatest directors of the world with his first film, irrespective of the fact that Francois Truffaut could not bear to sit through it. Made on a shoestring budget, mostly shot outdoors in a real village, with a majority of unknown faces playing the key roles, a story that lacks drama, and none of the usual "entertainment" offered by a potentially successful Indian film, *Pather Panchali* found its own audience wherever it went. Even today, more than thirty years after it was released, it is impossible to come away from one of its screenings without a rather unexpected sensation of complete involvement and identification. The documentary realism of the film does not detract from its wider fictional reality and broad, inclusive character. The struggles of an impoverished family in a Bengal village of more than half a century ago have successfully crossed the boundaries of time and space, of culture and environment, and come to be recognized as a universal human experience. The film was based on a very famous novel of the same name, which, added to the spectacular ancestry of Ray (his father and grandfather were well-known Bengali writers) and his own apprenticeship as an artist in Shantiniketan, lent his effort an unusual respectability. Yet, none of this could ultimately explain the mastery with which a totally inexperienced filmmaker, and a virtually equally inexperienced team, took a simple human story and made of it one of the classics of world cinema.

Ray chose *Pather Panchali* "for the qualities that made it a great book: for its humanism, its lyricism, its ring of truth." In an article he wrote two years after the film's release, he recalled an interesting fact about the novel, which seems to find a parallel in his own experience with the film: "Bibhutibhushan Banerji's *Pather Panchali* was serialized in a popular magazine in the early 1930s....The manuscript had been turned down by the publishers on the ground that it lacked a story. The magazine, too, was initially reluctant to accept it, but later did so on condition that it would be discontinued if the readers so wished. But the story of Apu and Durga was a hit from the first instalment. The book, published a year or so later, was an outstanding critical and popular success and has remained on the best-seller list ever since." And so it happened with the film, which went on to win an award for being "the best human document" at the Cannes festival. *Pather Panchali* not only changed Ray's own life, it left its mark on the lives of the people who were associated with its making, and on filmmakers and critics of a whole generation to follow.

PHANIYAMMA
colour, 115 minutes, Kannada, 1982

Production, direction and screenplay: Prema Karanth/ Story: M.K. Indira/ Camera: Madhu Ambat/ Music: B.V. Karanth/ Art Direction: K.S. Sridhar/ Editing: Arunavikas
Cast: L.V. Sharada Rao, Baby Pratima, Pratibha Kasaravalli, Archana Rao, Dashrathi Dixit, H.N. Chandru, Vishwanath Rao, Kasargodu Chinna, Sri Pramila

IN KARNATAKA, in the latter half of the last century, little Phani helps the older women with the household chores while her brothers go to the village school. In their village, Hebbalige, the titles of Mail Runner and Postmaster are important ones in British times. Phani's uncle is a Mail Runner, and they live in a palatial, sixteen-pillared house. When she is nine, a suitable bridegroom is found for her with the help of matching horoscopes, and Phani is married to a young relative. The two children go through the wedding uncomprehendingly. After the festivities are over, Phani's little husband goes back to his village, while she remains in her uncle's home to wait till she reaches puberty. Though she was supposed to have been born at a most auspicious moment, Phani is widowed in six months' time. Unaware of the implications of widowhood, she is suddenly faced with them at puberty: her bangles are broken, her head is shorn of the long locks and she is given a plain white sari to wear as widow's weeds. Her days are suddenly full of harsh penances, and the girl grows up withdrawn and silent, unable to understand the "crime" for which she must suffer life-long punishment.

As she grows into womanhood, however, Phani gradually overcomes the emptiness within by giving to others the love and compassion she had been deprived of so early in her life. In the villages around, she comes to be known as the wise and loving Phaniyamma, forever ready to help or advise. From somewhere deep within her comes the conviction that the time for obsolete norms is passing away. Herself an upper-caste Hindu, she helps in the difficult delivery of an untouchable woman. When a childless woman is ill-treated consistently by her husband, Phaniyamma encourages her to take the unheard-of step of leaving him. Dakshayini, a sixteen-year-old widow, rebels against the customary humiliations that society and her family are eager to shower upon her. She refuses to shave her head or wear widow's weeds. When the elders of the village are horrified, Phaniyamma alone stands by her. The times have changed, she says. We must move with them. Dakshayini not only manages to hold her own against her in-laws, but eight months later when she is obviously pregnant, declares that she will marry her brother-in-law, the father of her child. More than half a century ago, little Phani had helplessly obeyed the cruel customs of a society that believed in depriving their widows of any right to survive like other human beings. Today, at the age of seventy, Phaniyamma protests firmly and confidently on Dakshayini's behalf against the obsolete norms of an orthodox society.

At the end of a lifetime's service to the people, irrespective of caste and creed, Phaniyamma dies as gently as she lived, passing forever into the loving memory of the ones she had cared for so well.

PHANIYAMMA, who lived from 1870 to 1952 in the village of Hebbalige in Malnad, Karnataka, had indeed lived through almost a century of change. With none of the advantages of formal learning, she supported her essentially humane convictions with innate wisdom and compassion. Her biographer, M.K. Indira had first met her as a child of ten, when Phaniyamma had come to help her mother during childbirth. Phaniyamma had related her experiences to Indira's mother who passed them on to Indira when she grew up. For Prema Karanth, the first woman to write, direct and produce a film in Kannada, *Phaniyamma* is not a film about women's liberation. It is a quiet tale of a woman who with grace and humility accepted the need for change in society, and had the strength to support that change at a time when it was twice as difficult to talk about progressive ideas in relation to women. Unlike young Dakshayini, Phani does not stand for revolt. But her strength of conviction, her humanity and her wisdom cannot keep her bound to the obsolete traditions she had submitted to in her own youth. To play the role of the adult Phani, spanning at least fifty years, Prema Karanth chose L.V. Sharada Rao, a young actress who had already proved her mettle in serious cinema. Her portrayal is remarkable for its authenticity: she moves with ease from youth to old age, from slow awakening to gradual comprehension, from passive submission to a full flowering of wisdom. It is a transformation that is all the more remarkable for its credibility.

Phaniyamma received the National Award for the best regional film of the year, as well as awards at Mannheim and the International Women's Film Festival in Paris.

PRESIDENT
b&w, 153 minutes, Hindi, 1937

Production: New Theatres Limited/ Direction, screenplay and camera: Nitin Bose/ Music: R.C. Boral, Pankaj Mullick
Cast: K.L. Saigal, Leela Desai, Kamlesh Kumari, Jagdish Sethi, Bikram Kapoor, Nawab, Prithviraj

EVER SINCE sixteen-year-old Prabhavati took over as the President of the cotton mills left to her by her father, the business has prospered enormously. Today she is respected by all her staff for her unusual management capabilities and her knack for making the right decisions. Yet she has obviously made a mistake in quarelling with Prakash, a young worker. Prakash has designed a machine which he claims is better and safer that the one he has been working on in the mill. Refusing to accept that her own machine is unsafe, Prabhavati dismisses Prakash from his job. But the worker who takes his place is badly injured in an accident with the same machine soon after.

While out of a job, Prakash accidentally meets a sprightly young girl, Sheila, who happens to be Prabhavati's younger sister. As their friendship moves inevitably towards romance, Prabhavati reinstalls Prakash in the cotton mills, this time as the head of the design unit. Prakash's machine is also installed, replacing the old one. Prabhavati is too shrewd a businesswoman to allow her pride to stand in the way of profit. The business prospers further with Prakash's input, and he gradually rises to the position of the General Manager. The President of the company, still unaware of her sister's relationship with Prakash, finds that she is falling in love with the dynamic young man. Her new vulnerability suddenly makes Prabhavati gentler, more feminine, almost submerging her practical and businesslike exterior. Sheila notices the change, and one day, when the two sisters finally confide in one another, they realize with a shock that they love the same man.

For the sake of her elder sister's happiness, Sheila walks out on Prakash. Deeply hurt and confused, Prakash takes out his frustrations on his work. In the process he becomes a grim autocrat driving the workers hard till they are grossly overworked. Their growing resentment soon turns into rebellion. Unified against Prakash's tyranny, they storm the factory and even threaten to kill him. Prabhavati, realizing that it is Prakash's terrible unhappiness over his separation from Sheila that is wrecking the business and threatening his life, blames herself for it all. In desperation, she enters her office, and locks the door. There will be no peace in her familiar world till she dies.

PRESIDENT is a curious mixture of the radical and the reactionary. It is one of the very first portrayals of a liberated, educated, dynamic woman operating professionally and successfully in a predominantly male world. It is also a story of feminine vulnerability, womanly sacrifice, and female submission to the superior, scientific, male mind. Prabhavati's transformation from a totally angular, humourless woman to a bundle of very feminine nerves, happens through her love for Prakash. The assumption obviously is that for a woman to succeed in a man's world, she has to be intimidating and grimly masculine—an assumption that has persisted to this day even in developed societies. Her fall (as it must be construed) is therefore the greater once Cupid's arrow pierces her heart. The arrogant, aggressive businesswoman becomes a mere simpering female, and neurotic to boot.

Prabhavati's role has been recreated unchanged over and over again in the last fifty years of popular Indian cinema—an indication of how tenacious the traditional attitude towards women can be. However, the film created quite a stir, with the emancipated woman as a novelty and K.L. Saigal, already a rage as Devdas, in the role of Prakash, wearing his usual neat wig to cover an unredeemably bald head. Visually there are many interesting moments, among the machines and in the gathering of protesting workers. But the grim determination with which the President and her hero act out their roles make them appear less than human in the eyes of today.

PYAASA (Thirst)
b&w, 146 minutes, Hindi, 1957

Production: Guru Dutt Films Pvt. Ltd/ Direction, story and screenplay: Guru Dutt/ Dialogue: Abrar Alvi/ Camera: V.K. Murthy/ Music: S.D. Burman/ Lyrics: Sahir Ludhianvi/ Art Direction: Biren Naug/ Editing: Y.G. Chauhan
Cast: Guru Dutt, Mala Sinha, Waheeda Rehman, Rehman, Kumkum, Shyam, Johnny Walker, Leela Misra, Mehmood

VIJAY IS a young poet who is yet to find recognition. His poetry speaks of human suffering, and editors and publishers, who still prefer superficial romantic stuff, throw Vijay's work in the refuse bin. At home, his brothers, angered by his refusal to take an ordinary job and contribute to the family expenses, sell his poems as waste paper. Vijay leaves home in desperation to live on the streets of Calcutta. Searching for his manuscripts, he learns that a woman has taken them away from the grocer to whom his brothers had sold them. Roaming the city, Vijay is hears the voice of a woman singing one of his poems. She is Gulab, a prostitute, who lures Vijay in, thinking him a client. When she discovers her mistake, she throws him out, but soon realizes that Vijay is indeed the author of the poems that have won her heart. Full of remorse, Gulab tries to befriend Vijay who now spurns her, but out of their hesitations and uncertainties, a rare friendship blossoms between them.

At a function held for the ex-students of his college, Vijay meets Meena, the girl whom he used to love. Now Meena is married to a successful publisher, Mr Ghosh, whose wealth had proved more attractive to her than the love of a struggling poet. Suspicious of Meena's relationship with Vijay, and curious to know more about her past, Mr Ghosh gives Vijay a small job in his office. Humiliated by Meena at a party in their home, Vijay is sacked by her husband, and starts drifting once again. He hears of his mother's death, and depressed by his own failure, aimlessly wanders through brothels and bars till he decides to end it all. Gulab, who has tried to give him solace, finds him missing one day. The papers announce Vijay's death by accident and Gulab, the only person who has believed in his talents, spends her life's savings to get Vijay's poems published by Mr Ghosh.

But Vijay is not dead. On his way to eternity that night, he had stopped to give away his coat to a beggar. When he threw himself under a train, the beggar, in an attempt to save his benefactor, died. His body was identified by Vijay's coat. Recovering in a hospital, Vijay learns about the great success of his book; but when he claims to be its author, his brothers and his publisher who are reaping the profits refuse to identify him and he is sent to an asylum for the mentally ill. It is only with the help of an old friend, a poor masseur, that Vijay escapes from the asylum.

Attending a meeting in the city hall to pay homage to the dead poet, Vijay is struck by the irony of the situation, and is provoked to denounce the organizers as hypocrites. Beaten up as a gatecrasher, he is rescued by one of the publishers who had earlier rejected his works, and who now has hopes of future profits. Another meeting is called to prove that Vijay is alive, but despite Meena's pleas to admit the truth, Vijay now claims to be an imposter, embittered by the mercenary attitude of the people around him. Rejecting the world that has so long refused him recognition, Vijay decides to go away, taking Gulab with him.

"IT IS NOT difficult to make successful films which cater to the box-office alone," Guru Dutt had once said. "The difficulty arises when purposeful films have to be shaped to succeed at the box-office." With its rare synthesis of the commonplace and the profound, *Pyaasa* was a tremendous success with the audience and with it Guru Dutt emerged as a major director. An archetypal story of a struggling young poet's thirst for fame and love, *Pyaasa* also projected the director's own inner turmoil, and his uncertainties about the future of his career.

One of his close associates, Abrar Alvi, has described Dutt as "the Hamlet of films." More appropriately, he has been likened to P.C. Barua, whose obsessive dissatisfaction with his own work he shared. In a later film, *Kaghaz ke Phool*, Dutt played a role that was reminiscent of Barua, of a director making a new version of *Devdas*. The hero of *Kaghaz ke Phool*, defeated in his struggle as a creative filmmaker, takes to drinking and goes into a decline much like Barua did in real life. So did Devdas, though for a different reason. And Dutt's hero in *Pyaasa*, not unlike Devdas, builds a relationship with a sensitive, warm-hearted prostitute. Gulab is the new Chandramukhi, who in spite of her traditional submission to the man she loves, is able to actually win him for herself in the end. As for Dutt himself, disappointed by the failure of *Kaghaz ke Phool* in the box-office, he never directed another film, though he continued to act and produce them till his death at the age of thirty-nine from an overdose of sleeping pills.

RAMSHASTRI
b&w, 108 minutes, Marathi, 1944

Production: Prabhat Film Combpany/ Direction: Gajanan Jagirdar/ Camera: Pandurang Naik/ Music: G. Damle/ Art Direction: S. Fattelal
Cast: Anant Marathe, Baby Shakuntala, Gajanan Jagirdar, Meenakshi

NEARLY three hundred years ago, in western India, a little Brahmin boy, Ram, plays around with his child bride in his widowed mother's home. His father had been a man of great learning. But after his death, Ram's mother found it difficult to give the boy even the ordinary education that all Brahmin children received. Goaded by mockery and insult from other members of the closed-in community, Ram determines to become as learned as his father. One night he steals away from his home and travels all the way to Benares, the city of Hindu learning, where privileged young apprentices sit and learn at the feet of well-known scholars. It is a hard life, for the pupils have to relinquish everything at the feet of their teachers, and serve them day and night to receive knowledge. Rejected at first by all scholars, with tremendous perseverance, Ram attaches himself to a teacher at last, and proves worthy of his attention. Years pass, and the day comes when Ram returns home as Ramshastri, the renowned scholar. His mother has been waiting for this day. But the struggle for survival has worn her out and she soon dies, leaving her son and daughter-in-law to move to the city of Pune.

Pune is the seat of the peshwas, the rulers of the once powerful, but now decadent Maratha empire. The upright character and scholarly reputation of Ramshastri attracts the attention of Peshwa Madhavrao, who appoints him Chief Justice of the kingdom. In an atmosphere of constant court intrigues and eternal political wranglings, the fearless and incorruptible Ramshastri becomes a symbol of truth and justice for the common man.

When Peshwa Madhavrao dies, fierce disputes take place among his courtiers over the succession to his throne. Madhavrao's younger brother, Narayanrao, still a mere boy, is set up as a puppet and proclaimed the Peshwa under the guardianship of his uncle, Raghunathrao. But Raghunathrao's ambitious wife, Anandibai, is not satisfied with her husband's *de facto* powers. In her greed, Anandibai plans the assassination of Narayanrao. The boy is murdered by her covert instructions within the palace and Raghunathrao is proclaimed the Peshwa.

Aware of the truth behind Narayanrao's death, Ramshastri refuses to accept this travesty of justice. The populace are coerced into silence; but Ramshastri voices his protest by denouncing the murderers publicly. Raghunathrao is proved guilty. A weak man who has given in to his wife's ambitions and his own greed for power, he now feels remorse, and decides to do penance for the murder of his nephew. But for Ramshastri the only real penance for the evil doer would be his death. He declares a death penalty for the accused, and disgusted with the inherent dishonesty of the ruling clan and their courtiers, announces that he will not stay any longer in this kingdom of sin. He leaves Pune with his family, no longer the Chief Justice, but a common man who has always been true to himself and to God.

RAMSHASTRI was obviously not the work of one director. The initial half of the film was the first independent directorial venture of Raja Nene, who started his career in Prabhat as an assistant director under V. Shantaram and later worked under Damle and Fattelal. At some stage, Vishram Bedekar took over the direction of the film. Gajanan Jagirdar, who plays the role of the adult Ramshastri is, however, the only person mentioned as the director in the credits of the film. Perhaps that would explain the episodic structure of *Ramshastri* and its uneven quality. The film was also made at a time when the company was going through difficult times. Damle, the backbone of the organization, was seriously ill and would die in another year's time. Fattelal, the artistic support of Prabhat, found the burden of the organization an irksome one to bear. Outside the walls of Prabhat, the industry was getting increasingly competitive, and the studio system was being swiftly replaced by stars who owed allegiance to no one but themselves. *Ramshastri,* with its extravagant sets and costumes, became one of the last successful productions from Prabhat, followed by nine agonizing years till the company went into liquidation in 1953.

The position of the peshwa was created by Shivaji, the founder of the Maratha empire in western India in the seventeenth century. The peshwa was then the chief minister who headed a council of eight ministers. In later Maratha history, under the rule of Shivaji's grandson, Peshwa Bajirao I, a Chitpavan Brahmin, secured hereditary succession to the post for the first time. Gradually, the powers of the peshwa grew to such an extent, that the Maratha ruler became a cypher. But the peshwas too were soon destroyed by internacine power struggles. Weakened by constant intrigues, the hostility of other Maratha chieftains, and pressures from the East India Company, the last peshwa died in exile under British protection in a small fortress near Kanpur, far away from his original home. Thematically, *Ramshastri,* made during the war years, reflected the political confusion and the changing values of the times. It was as if sanity could only be restored in the world if a man like the film's incorruptible protagonist was at the helm of affairs.

SAMSKARA   (Funeral Rites)
b&w, 100 min, Kannada, 1970

Production and direction: Pattabhi Rama Reddy/ Story: U.R. Ananthamurthy/ Screenplay and dialogue: Girish Karnad/ Camera: Tom Cowan/ Music: Rajeev Taranath/ Art Direction: S.G. Vasudev/ Editing: Steven Cartaw, Vasu
Cast: Girish Karnad, Snehlata Reddy, P. Lankesh, Dashrathi Dixit, Lakshmi Krishnamurthy

NARANAPPA belongs to the close-knit community of the Madhva Brahmins. He lives in a Brahmin village, but eats meat, drinks and keeps a low-caste mistress, Chandri. A constant reminder to the other Brahmins of the pleasures they will never know, Naranappa's rebellion is a source of intense resentment and hatred in the community. When he dies of the plague, no one is willing to cremate him. But as long as his body lies in the village, the Brahmins are not allowed to touch food or water. Yet, who will defile himself by touching Naranappa's sinful, contaminated corpse? As only a Brahmin can cremate another Brahmin, Chandri places all her jewellery at the feet of the leader of the community, Praneshacharya, for the expenses. A young Brahmin scholar, an ascetic in his home where he tends his ailing wife, Praneshacharya is now faced with a moral problem. For, to lay their hands on the gold, and end the pangs of hunger in their bellies, the Brahmins suddenly vie with each other to cremate Naranappa.

Praneshacharya spends a fruitless night pouring over the Scriptures. In his dream he confronts the sneering Naranappa, reliving an encounter in real life, when he had failed to convince the self-proclaimed heretic of the righteousness of following God's path. He prays to Lord Maruti at the temple, but the God gives no answer to his dilemma. Assailed by doubts, weary with starvation, he comes out of the temple to find Chandri waiting for him. When she falls at his feet, a subconscious need for the long denied warmth of a woman's body, and the comfort from it, makes him draw her into a closer embrace. Carried away by the passion of the moment, they make love in the warm night, violating all the codes that have so long held their society together kept them separate.

A group of Naranappa's drunken disciples, resolved to cremate their leader, come to his house the same night, but are frightened away by the rats that infest the place. The whole village is swarming with rats carrying the plague from home to home. Women and children start leaving the village. Praneshacharya's wife dies, and faced now with a personal dilemma, he too leaves the village. On his metaphorical pilgrimage, Praneshacharya befriends the gregarious low-caste, Putta, and comes to terms with the basic hypocrisy of his life. He comes back to the deserted village to cremate Naranappa himself, in an act of expiation.

SAMSKARA won three state awards and the national award for the best feature film of the year. Based on a novel by a well-known young writer of Karnataka, the film was the result of a happy combination of talents. The director, Reddy, is one of the most respected Telugu poets, the first to introduce free verse in Telugu poetry. Girish Karnad, who played the role of the protagonist, Praneshacharya, is a well-known Kannada playwright, whose acting career began on the stage. He went on to direct his own films, and is now a successful screen actor as well. Reddy's talented wife, Snehlata, who played Chandri, took an active part in the theatre movement in Karnataka and was known as a radical intellectual. Imprisoned during the Emergency for her militant opposition to the government, she died of a heart-attack induced by stress. Her prison memoirs are a poignant documentation of those troubled times.

A year before *Samskara* was released, Mrinal Sen's *Bhuvan Shome* had already ushered in what is now called the "new Indian cinema." *Samskara* was another breakthrough. Although it was not a success in the box-office, the film won critical acclaim, and was recognized as one of the major achievements of Indian cinema. The starkness of its presentation, the boldness of its theme of religious hypocrisy, the uncompromising realism of the portrayals, all combined to make it an intensely thought-provoking film. Incidentally, there is an extemely well executed English translation of Ananthamurthy's novel, by the poet A.K. Ramanujan, published by Oxford University Press.

SANKARABHARANAM (The Jewel of Shiva)
colour, 143 min, Telugu, 1979

Production: Poornodaya Art Creations/ Direction, story and screenplay: K. Viswanath/ Camera: Balu Mahendra/ Music: K.V. Mahadevan/ Art Direction: Thota/ Editing: G.G. Krishna Rao
Cast: J.V. Somayajulu, Manju Bhargavi, Allu Ramalingayya, Birmala, Pushpa Kumari, Tulasi Ram, Varalakshmi, Chandra Mohan

SANKARA SASTRY, a revered musician, is known specially for his rendering of the *raga* , Sankarabharanam, which covers the complete musical scale in the ascent as well as the descent. Tulsi, the daughter of a prostitute, who has a great love for traditional classical music, secretly looks upon the Sastry as her *guru*. Her ambition is to dance to his music. But her mother, loyal to her profession, sells Tulsi to a rich landowner against her wishes. Tulsi refuses to give in to what is virtually rape, and struggling to save herself, kills the man with a broken piece of glass. Essentially a humanist, Sankara Sastry provides Tulsi with legal aid, and when she is acquitted, takes her into his own home, flouting the norms of his society. However, when people start avoiding his performances and socially ostracize him, Tulsi quietly leaves the place.
  When she returns as an unwed mother of a boy, ten years have passed. A new generation has grown up in the meanwhile, and traditional music has lost its special place in society. The Sastry, fighting a solitary and losing battle against the invasion of crass modern musical aberrations, has grown old and tired. He no longer has an audience, and, without adequate patronage, is steeped in debt. Tulsi, who has inherited her dead mother's property and is now a rich woman, clears the old man's debts secretly. She even manages to get her son accepted as a disciple. Tulsi now builds an auditorium and names it after her *guru*. Sankara Sastry is invited to inaugurate it, but suffers a stroke in the middle of his performance. Tulsi's son steps in for him, and the old man acknowledges the boy as his true successor before he breathes his last. Tulsi, her dreams fulfilled, now dies at the feet of her master.

SANKARABHARANAM, though not altogether a film in the popular mould, is yet one of the spectacular successes of "commercial" South Indian cinema. If in general the audience in the south seem to have a taste for imitation north Indian fare—the "formula film" with its equal doses of song and dance, love play, comic relief, fights and the chase—they also have an abiding interest in their own musical traditions, much more so than in the north. This is what is the primary attraction of *Sankarabharanam*. (In fact, when Viswanath recently made a fresh Hindi version of the film, with popular local stars, the film made no impact whatsoever.) Of course, he does pander to the popular taste by making the film unabashedly sentimental in approach, with its own share of incredible dramatic incidents. But its charm lies no less in Somayajulu's sincere portrayal as the musician, and Manju Bhargavi's skills as a dancer, than in the rich fare of Carnatic music that it has to offer. Viswanath is concerned about the declining patronage of classical music, and he uses his narrative to emphasize his view that music in its purest form can transcend parochialism and caste, and lead man to the threshold of the divine. Though it may not be easy to whole-heartedly accept this simplistic philosophy, it is no hardship to admit that *Sankarabharanam* is an enjoyable experience for all music-lovers.

SANT TUKARAM (Saint Tukaram)
b&w, 131 minutes, Marathi, 1936

Production: Prabhat Film Company/ Direction: V. Damle, S. Fattelal/ Story: Shivram Washikar/ Camera: V. Avadhoot/ Music: Keshavrao Bhole/ Lyrics: Shantaram Athavale/ Art Direction: S. Fattelal/ Editing: A.R. Sheikh/ Sound: Shankarrao Damle
Cast: Vishnupant Pagnis, Gauri, Pandit Damle, Kusum Bhagavat, Sri Bhagavat, Master Chhotu, B. Nandrekar, Kulkarni, Shanta Majumdar

IN THE VILLAGE of Dehu, Tukaram, a poor householder, spends his days singing devotional songs addressed to Lord Pandurang. In direct contrast to him, is Salomalo, the corrupt Brahmin priest, who makes up in showmanship what he lacks in devotion. In Tukaram's impoverished home, his wife Jijayi toils day and night, looking after her home and the family. Her husband's spiritual involvement annoys her, for he has no time to worry about where the next day's meal is going to come from, or how long a child has been ill. While Salomalo spends his days in luxury, and steals Tukaram's songs to pass them off as his own, Tukaram, finally realizing his duties towards his family, goes looking for a job. A farmer employs him to supervise the workers in his field of sugarcane. Tukaram sits in the field and sings. The crop flourishes, and his employer sends him home with grain and a load of sugarcane. The jealous Salomalo intrigues against Tukaram, and another day, when the crop has grown miraculously to the tune of his songs, Salomalo's men lead a herd of animals into the field. The crop is destroyed. The farmer makes Tukaram sign away his house. Meanwhile, the field flourishes once again, and Pandurang adds to the harvest liberally. The overwhelmed farmer decides to give away all the grain to Tukaram and restore his home to him. Unperturbed by the miracle, Tukaram gives the grain to the poor, watched by an irate Jijayi who knows that the family now faces starvation.

Salomalo sends his mistress to distract Tukaram and steal his songs. Jijayi recognizes her for what she is, and angrily tells her husband. But Tukaram only shows a deep concern for this beautiful young woman who follows a sinful path. Moved by his compassion, the woman refuses to go back to Salomalo, and sings the praises of Pandurang instead. Meanwhile, Rameshwar

Shastri, a much respected Brahmin scholar, comes to the village, and is disturbed to hear the songs of the lowly Tukaram being sung by the common people. But God is the property of the Brahmins alone, and the Shastri orders Tukaram to drown all his books of verse in the river. Tukaram complies, and heartbroken, sits on the river bank praying to his God, refusing to eat or drink. The family starves with him, for Jijayi is no less devoted to her husband. After thirteen days, a goddess appears out of the waters, and returns the books of verse to Tukaram. The villagers watch the miracle, and the Shastri falls at Tukaram's feet.

Stories of Tukaram's saintliness and devotion reach the ears of Shivaji, the Maratha king. He comes in disguise with rich offerings which, to Jijayi's horror, are rejected by her husband. Shivaji is so impressed that he wants to give up his throne and become a disciple of Tukaram. Tukaram sings to him, telling him in his song that the way he must show his devotion is by playing his predestined role as the saviour of his country. The Mughal army attacks the village in the hope of capturing Shivaji. But Tukaram's prayers are answered, and the enemy is bewildered and defeated by the miracles that occur. Shivaji bows to the saint, accepting his advice.

When the time comes for him to leave the earth, a heavenly chariot descends to receive Tukaram. He urges Jijayi to go with him, but Jijayi refuses. The abode of the gods is not for her, and in any case who will look after the household? She will keep the food warm for him till he is back, she says. Tukaram gives his last sermon to his people and bids them farewell. Realizing at last that he will never return, Jijayi rushes to him, but it is already too late, and the divine chariot floats up to the clouds, with Tukaram in it.

LIKE THE Tamil saint, Avaiyyar, Chandidas of Bengal, or Meera Bai of Rajasthan, Tukaram, a poet-saint of the Marathas, also belonged to the Bhakti movement, which released the Hindu religion from the authority of the priests and brought it closer to the people. The songs of Tukaram, composed in Marathi, made full use of the unsophisticated vigour of the language. Almost all the songs in the film are original compositions of the saint. The lyricist Shantaram Athavale's sole contribution to the repertoire in the film was so close to the spirit of Tukaram's own songs, that scholars were said to have mistaken it for the real thing.

An enormous success in the Marathi speaking region, running fifty-seven weeks at one theatre in Bombay, *Sant Tukaram* has been hailed as the first truly cinematic endeavour in India. The film also has the distinction of winning an award as one of the three best films of the year in the Fifth International Film Festival in Venice, the first Indian film to have received such an honour. The simplicity and directness of its appeal is as strong today as it was to the generation for whom the film was made. Devotional films have always been considered a safe bet in India. But unlike many other efforts in the genre, *Sant Tukaram* presents not just a story of a godly man and his miracles, but the fundamental conflict between spiritualism and earthy common sense. Jijayi's contention that the stone idol has little understanding of human beings made of flesh and blood, has almost as much validity in the film, as Tukaram's unwavering faith in his God.

Among the many remarkable characteristics of the film is its acting style. If Bhagavat's Salomalo is a grotesque caricature of the pomp and arrogance of institutionalized religion, Pagnis's and Gauri's portrayals of Tukaram and Jijayi are replete with heart-warming realism. Tukaram's saintliness is based on deep human compassion for his fellow-men, his faith on an understanding of human frailty. The miracles come and go without taking away from his palpable reality as a character. Jijayi, on the other hand, is no stereotype of a shrewish wife. She is a woman who fights for the survival and happiness of her family. She loves Tukaram, but does not consider him a god in the traditional manner of Hindu wives. Hence her anger and her frustration over his divine preoccupations. There are moments of peace and happiness in her life when she can laugh with her children, or bask in the radiance of her husband's love. The rest of the time she strives for a better life with a very human determination. If she covets Shivaji's rich offerings, her pleasure in them is the same as her children's. She displays no vulgar greed, only childlike disappointment when her husband makes her relinquish them. In anger or in happiness, every gesture that Jijayi makes in the film is that of a real woman. There is an amazing lack of theatricality in the film, and a sincerity of expression that was never repeated by the Prabhat team. Pagnis, a stage actor, went on to become the most favourite saint of the Indian screen. But Gauri, who was a menial in the studio, and was picked up to do bit roles in Prabhat's films, never seems to have had another equally important role in which to display her considerable talents as an actress.

SARA AKASH (The Whole Sky)
b&w, 100 minutes, Hindi, 1969

Production: Cineye Films/ Direction and Screenplay: Basu Chatterji/ Camera: K.K. Mahajan/ Music: Salil Chowdhury/ Editing: G.G. Mayekar
Cast: Rakesh Pandey, Madhuchhanda, A.K. Hangal, Dina Pathak, Mani Kaul, Tarla Mehta, Nandita Thakur, Jalal Agha

A TRADITIONAL extended family in the small city of Agra, where the father is the figure of final authority, and marriages in the family are arranged by the elders on the basis of how much dowry the girl will bring. Samar, the younger son, is still at the university, when the family insists on finding him a bride. His sister-in-law is pregnant, and Samar's wife will come useful in the household. Apart from that, the girl they have chosen, will bring a large dowry. Samar's bride, Prabha, is a graduate, but sexually inexperienced. So is Samar. In addition, he is pathologically shy, and did not want to get married in the first place. Not surprisingly, the wedding night is a disaster, and Samar stalks out to sleep on the terrace.

Though Samar is chided by the family, his resistance to his wife is soon accepted by everybody. It is Prabha who bears the brunt of their disapproval for being unable to please her husband. The elder brother's wife resents and envies Prabha's youth, good looks and most of all her education, and expresses her feelings through daily acts of petty cruelty. Only Samar's sister, abandoned by an unfaithful husband, can understands Prabha's predicament. Isolated and ridiculed, Prabha suffers the discipline of the domestic routine in silence.

The elder brother's wife has her baby, and the entire load of the household falls on the inexperienced Prabha. She makes one mistake after another, and finally, when she unwittingly uses holy clay to wash the utensils, Samar slaps her in front of the household. At the suggestion of Samar's sister, Prabha goes away to her parents for a few months. Samar misses the wife he has never accepted, and fantasizes about a reconciliation with her. But when she actually does come back, his feelings remain unexpressed. Prabha picks up her household chores once more in silent defiance. Samar, shy and remorseful, watches helplessly. This time it is Prabha who decides to sleep elsewhere. As she lies weeping alone on the terrace, Samar comes to her. Prabha's unprotesting silence gives way to anger. Suddenly the barriers melt away, and the two young people reach out to each other with passion.

A SIMPLE story, told with touching realism, *Sara Akash* was made the same year that Mrinal Sen's *Bhuvan Shome* ushered in the "new Indian cinema." Part of the same genre, both films have realistic locales, new faces, and an unglamorous setting. Both films found a measure of commercial success that was unusual at a time when the popular cinema, with which they had nothing in common, held tremendous sway over Indian film viewers. For its director, *Sara Akash* was a modest beginning to an extremely successful career that remained at its peak right through the 70s. Basu Chatterji, who was active in the film society movement in Bombay before taking up film making, made over twenty films in that one decade, with a dozen comedies in the three years between 1976 and 1979. He also created space for the common man in popular cinema. *Rajanigandha,* his fourth film made five years later and a stupendous box-office success, established a film career for a rather plain looking young actor, Amol Palekar, in the role of an ordinary, commonplace, middle-class nonentity, daring to fall in love with a pretty girl.

Through the years, Chatterji's films found a cosy niche between the serious parallel cinema and the popular fairytale variety. But none of his later films recalled the simplicity, the gentle compassion and unpretentious realism of *Sara Akash.* Most of them are fun films, with their share of modest fantasy, and some have even used popular stars. Chatterji has been known for his relatively small budgets and his large range of storylines, covering anything from Indian adaptations of *School for Scoundrels* and *My Fair Lady,* to classical period pieces, and hilarious social dramas on the Parsis and the Roman Catholic community of Bombay. In the 80s, his popularity waned, his stories lost their special touch, and the fun was more contrived than spontaneous.

All the same, Chatterji is a survivor, and has now taken up television serials, one of which, featuring the intrepid Rajani, a young middle-class housewife who fights a lone battle against red tape, corruption and every civic problem, has become a modern legend. If the episodes suffered from unbelievably quick solutions and rather wooden acting by its heroine, both her pretty face and her cause found support among millions of TV viewers. An episode criticizing the uncooperative behaviour of taxi-drivers in Bombay resulted in a demonstration by irate cabbies; while the actress, Priya Tendulkar, has become a familiar face in television advertisements as well as other serials.

SARAANSH   (The Gist)
colour, 137 minutes, Hindi, 1984

Production: Rajshri Productions (P) Ltd/ Direction and Story: Mahesh Bhatt/ Screenplay: Sujit Sen, Mahesh Bhatt/ Camera: Adeep Tandon/ Music: Ajit Verman/ Art Direction: M.S. Shinde/ Editing: David Dhawan/ Lyrics: Vasant Deo/ Sound: Hitendra Ghosh
Cast: Anupam Kher, Rohini Hattangady, Soni Razdan, Madan Jain, Suhash Bhalekar, Nilu Phule

YOUNG AJAY was recently mugged and killed, quite senselessly, in a street in New York. Back home in India, his father, B.V. Pradhan, a retired head-master, wakes up at night, goes to his desk, and begins a letter to his son. Then, stirring in the cocoon of his grief, he remembers, and crumples the paper in his hand. With daybreak, life's business carries on. Pradhan and his wife, Parvati, must let out Ajay's room to a paying-guest to augment their meagre income. A young and struggling actress, Sujata, comes to look at the room with her boy-friend, Vilas, son of a powerful municipal corporator, Gajanan Chitre. Sujata is hoping to marry Vilas. But the boy is too afraid of his domineering father to broach the subject. Meanwhile, Sujata will wait in Pradhan's home.

A telegram comes announcing the arrival of Ajay's belongings from America, and his ashes. Pradhan waits in a long queue for hours and coming up against further red tape, finally storms into the room of a senior official, who shamed by the old man's grief and anger, arranges for the urn to be delivered to him. Back home, Pradhan steals a handful of his son's ashes and scatters them in a park nearby, where he sits watching children at play. For him, the cycle of Ajay's life is complete. But Parvati lives in hope: her guru has said, Ajay will soon be reborn, and near them too.

To find a new meaning in his existence, Pradhan decides to look for a job. He attends an interview, but rejects the offer when he realizes that his taking the job would deprive one of his old students, who needs it more than he does. On his way home, Pradhan finds himself in the middle of one of those sporadic riots that are a part of life in the city. He is roughed up by a gang of youngsters, but manages to drag himself home. At night, overwhelmed by his grief and a sense of humiliation, Pradhan attempts suicide. But Vilas, who has stolen into Sujata's room, rushes out to help Parvati save her husband. Shocked and frightened of loneliness, Parvati offers to die with her husband. Only, the night they chose is the same night when Sujata discovers she is pregnant. Vilas wants her to abort the baby rather than face his father. The old couple overhear their quarrel: it is the message Parvati has been waiting for. Ajay will be reborn. She has no time to die now.

Pradhan, who has become fond of Sujata and believes that the girl has a right to the baby, decides to confronts Gajanan Chitre. Chitre, uncouth and unscrupulous, makes his cowering son deny his involvement in the affair and humiliates Pradhan and Sujata. But the municipal elections are round the corner. To stop the indiscretion from becoming public, Chitre now attempts to terrorize Sujata into having an abortion. Parvati protects Sujata with the passion of her faith, but for her husband it is a battle against dehumanization, against the disintegration of all the social values that he has held so dear as an educationist.

That he wins, is an accident of fate, for the minister he finally approaches turns out to be an old student. The siege on the Pradhan household lifts, the nightmare disappears with a few phone calls. To release Parvati from her obsession about her son's reincarnation as Sujata's child, Pradhan arranges for Vilas to take Sujata away. Alone with her husband once again, Parvati reminds him of their suicide pact. Now that her hope is dead, perhaps it is time for them to die as well. But Pradhan now knows that one cannot die for the dead. He takes Parvati to the park at dawn, where, near a lonely bench, his son's ashes have been transformed into wild flowers. As they sway in the breeze, Pradhan and Parvati read in them a final assertion of life.

MAHESH BHATT has had a curious career in the Bombay film industry. Son of a filmmaker of an earlier epoch, he began as a director of "formula films," none of which made as much impact as *Arth*, a film he made in 1982 on the theme of an extra-marital affair in an upper-class home. *Arth* used the two well-established stars of the parallel cinema, Shabana Azmi and Smita Patil, and gave much scope for their acting talents by providing them with roles that were overtly feminist in approach. Stylistically, the film was a tightly knit drama which managed to avoid the obvious sensationalism of the formula film.

The success of *Arth* led Bhatt to investigate other unusual themes that could be popular with his audience without falling into the expected pattern of romance and violence. The result was *Saaransh*. It established Anupam Kher, then in his twenties and prematurely bald, as an actor of considerable talent. His phenomenal success in the role of a retired headmaster did not stop him from becoming a popular villain in Hindi films, and from there moving on to a variety of roles in popular as well as parallel cinema, where his age varies between twenty-eight and seventy. Rohini Hattangady, in real life dimpled, attractive and young, was no surprise as Parvati, having already caught the popular imagination as the aging Kasturba in Attenborough's *Gandhi*. She comes from the Hindi stage, and acts in both popular and parallel cinema, as well as soap operas on Doordarshan. After *Saaransh* its director went on to make his first television feature, *Janam,* drawing upon his personal experiences as an illegitimate child, which fact he publicized with great enthusiasm to the apparent horror and secret glee of his many fans.

SHATRANJ KE KHILARI (The Chess Players)
colour, 133 minutes, Urdu, 1977

Production: Suresh Jindal/ Direction, screenplay and music: Satyajit Ray/
Story: Based on a short story by Munshi Premchand/ Camera: Soumendu
Roy/ Art Direction: Bansi Chandragupta/ Editing: Dulal Dutta
Cast: Amjad Khan, Sanjeev Kumar, Shabana Azmi, Saeed Jaffrey, Farida
Jalal, Richard Attenborough, Tom Alter, Benjamin Gillani

IN 1856, on the eve of the first Indian war of independence, Nawab Wajid Ali
Shah rules the state of Avadh. A product of nineteenth century decadence, the
Nawab is an indifferent ruler, who spends his days as a patron of the arts,
establishing a new genre of court dancing, and humming his own exquisite
Urdu quatrains. In his capital city of Lucknow live two rich landowners,
Mirza Sajjad Ali and Mir Roshan Ali who, as part of the same culture, do
nothing but play chess all day. Mirza's neglected wife, Khurshid, tries to
wean him away from his obsession, but Mirza no longer responds to feminine
charm, and is happy to take refuge in the unreal complexities of the
chessboard. Mir's wife, Nafeesa, on the other hand, enjoys a riotous love life
with her cousin, and would rather have her husband safely immersed in the
game.
 Meanwhile the East India Company, subtle marauders from across the seas,
are playing a bigger game of chess. Lord Dalhousie, the Governor General,
sends General Outram, the British Resident of Lucknow, to present his ulti-
matum to the Nawab. He wants Avadh under British protection and the
Nawab's misrule provides him with the pretext for deposing him. Wajid Ali
Shah, faced with a situation where he must either give up his throne or fight a
battle with the Company, his erstwhile friends, chooses the easier of the two
alternatives. He hands over his jewel studded crown to the British, and
prepares for life-long exile in mocking self-abnegation.
 Mir and Mirza hear that the Company's troops are marching towards Lucknow. Mortally afraid that they may be called up to save the Nawab's throne,
the two friends promptly desert their families and run away to the seclusion of
a remote village where, under the shade of a tree they spread their chess
pieces. The game continues far from the gathering political storm till their
intense rivalry erupts in suspicion and rage. But the antagonism soon dissolves into a silent, shameful acknowledgement of their personal failures and
moral cowardice, the bonds that hold the two friends together. In the shade of
the spreading branches, the game of bloodless combat continues once again as
the British troops march into Lucknow and Avadh passes into the hands of
strangers from another land.

SATYAJIT RAY'S first film in a language other than his native Bengali, *Shatranj ke Khilari* remains a unique cameo in the tapestry of his work. Against a
backdrop of history, the film carries on a gentle, mocking investigation of
humiliation and defeat through a juxtaposition of chess games played in private
lives and politics. Its craftsmanship represents the detailed and intricate orna-
mental patterns of a period when the graces of a civilization were cultivated to

the neglect of political stability. The physical beauty of the film, recalling Mughal miniatures, where an astounding amount of details finds place within a highly restricted visual space, owe a great deal to the artistry of Ray's art director, Bansi Chandragupta. This was Chandragupta's last film with Ray. He died in June 1981, from a heart-attack, on his way to attend the Film India festival in America, where a Ray retrospective was taking place.

"Premchand's story," says Ray, "ends by Mir and Mirza destroying each other while the Company's troops leave Lucknow with Wajid as prisoner. This is an effective juxtaposition but it takes wide liberty with history. Wajid left Lucknow of his own accord and well after the annexation. The idea of the two friends killing each other was abandoned because I felt it might be taken to symbolise the end of decadence. In fact, Nawabi and all that goes with it did not end with the British takeover. The U.P. noblemen kept up their way still well into the present century. Hence the decision to show Mir and Mirza continuing with their game. That they decide to play according to British rules [not the traditional Indian ones] can be seen as a symbol of the acceptance of British domination by Indians."

SHOLAY (Flames of the Sun)
colour, 200 minutes, Hindi, 1975

Production: G.P. Sippy/ Direction: Ramesh Sippy/ Screenplay: Salim Javed/ Camera: Dwarka Divecha/ Music: R.D. Burman/ Lyrics: Anand Bakshi/ Playback: Lata Mangeshkar, Manna Dey, R.D. Burman, Kishore Kumar/ Art Direction: Ram Yedekar/ Editing: M.S. Shinde/ Sound: S.Y. Pathak
Cast: Dharmendra, Sanjeev Kumar, Hema Malini, Amitabh Bachchan, Jaya Bhaduri, Amjad Khan, Satyen Kappu, A.K. Hangal, Iftekhar, Leela Misra, Mac Mohan, Keshto Mukherjee, Sachin, Asrani, Helen, Geeta, Jairaj, Jagdeep, Jalal Agha, Om Shivpuri, Sharad Kumar

THAKUR BALDEV SINGH, once a senior police officer, asks a local jailor to help him find two small-time crooks, Veeru and Jaidev. The Thakur himself had caught them once, and learnt that though they are crooks they are no cowards. Though they are law-breakers, they have not lost their humanity. Escorting them in a goods train two years ago, he had released them when bandits attacked the train. Between them Veeru and Jaidev not only drove the bandits away, but also saved the Thakur's life when they could have escaped, leaving him to bleed to death. Now he assigns the two men the virtually impossible task of bringing the dreaded dacoit Gabbar Singh to him alive. Veeru and Jaidev will be well paid by him, besides getting a reward from the government.

Coming to Ramgarh, the Thakur's estate, the two still think it safer to just break into the Thakur's safe at night and escape with the loot. While trying to open the safe they are seen by Radha, the Thakur's widowed daughter-in-law, who offers them the keys. "At least it will kill the false hopes my father-in-law has put in you," she says. Shamed, the two crooks decide to stay and carry out the Thakur's wishes. Three bandits from Gabbar's gang soon appear to collect from the villagers payment for their safety, but Veeru and Jaidev manage to drive them away. On the day of Holi (a festival of colours ushering in the spring) the bandits strike again. This time Veeru and Jaidev are unprepared and the village takes a beating till, with the help of the spunky carriage driver, Basanti, the two men can retaliate. But it is a very close shave, and when the battle is over for the moment, they confront the Thakur, shocked by the fact that though a gun lay at his feet he made no effort to save them when their lives were in danger.

The Thakur tells them his story: Gabbar Singh had been caught by the Thakur and sent to jail. He escaped soon after and coming to Ramgarh, gunned down the Thakur's entire family. The only one to escape the carnage was the youngest daughter-in-law, Radha, who was away at the temple. Coming home on leave the same day, the Thakur was met with the corpses of his two sons, a daughter-in-law and his little grandson, and the vision of the widowed Radha weeping silently. In a violent rage, the Thakur rode unarmed to the ravines where Gabbar Singh reigned. Finding him helpless, and thinking humiliation a better revenge than death, the bandit hacked off the Thakur's arms which had once held him prisoner.

The horrified Veeru and Jaidev now decide to do the job for free. After all, the government will reward them anyway. While waiting for an opportunity to attack Gabbar, Veeru falls in love with the garrulous but winsome Basanti, while the more serious Jaidev feels drawn to Radha, so young and so alone. Radha too watches Jaidev silently from a distance, and cannot hide her concern when he comes back wounded from another encounter with Gabbar's men, having successfully blown up most of the gang's fresh stock of arms. The game is now in Gabbar's court, and his men waylay and kill young Ahmed, the only son of the blind Imam of Ramgarh.

The villagers, scared for their lives, turn against the Thakur and his two gunmen who have brought things to this pass with their defiance. But the old Imam, much revered in the village, tells them that though he has lost his son, he still prefers death to servility. Veeru and Jaidev attack and kill another three gang members. Meanwhile, the Thakur, whose trust in the two crooks has been vindicated, talks to Radha's father about arranging a marriage between Jaidev and Radha once Gabbar is subdued. Veeru and Jaidev too find themselves dreaming of marrying and leading ordinary lives, perhaps as farmers in Ramgarh itself. When Veeru goes late to a tryst with Basanti, he discovers that the girl has been kidnapped by Gabbar's men. Walking into a trap, he is saved by Jaidev, who gives him cover to get Basanti away from the bandits.

This time it is an all out war, and the men fight it out desperately. Fatally wounded, Jaidev pretends he is mildly hurt, and sends Veeru back to the village with Basanti. He manages to blow up a bridge and kill most of the bandits. When Veeru returns, his friend is dying. Radha's hopes are once again burnt in the funeral pyre, but Veeru will not give up. He corners Gabbar in the ravines, and is about to kill him when the Thakur arrives on the scene. He insists on fighting Gabbar alone, and hits out with his hobnailed shoes. Without the protection of his gang whom he used to terrorize, Gabbar becomes a cowering beast, and his life is saved only when the police arrive and remind the Thakur that he cannot, as an ex-policeman, take the law in his own hands. With Jaidev dead, Veeru decides to leave Ramgarh, but in the empty compartment of the sleepy train he finds Basanti waiting for him.

SHOLAY is one of the all-time greats of Indian cinema. A curry-Western, it successfully brings together the entertainment promised by a typical Indian mainstream film, and the pace, vigour and intensity in the best traditions of the Hollywood Western. With the Indian popular cinema's penchant for borrowing liberally from foreign films, it is quite likely that *Sholay* carries the burden of many such debts. But the sum total is so stunning, so overwhelming, that to be plagiarized in *Sholay* can only be a compliment. Not surprisingly, the film's success was unparalleled. While the mass audience found in it all that they enjoyed most: the laughter, the thrills, the horrors, the pathos, the songs and dances, the fights and the chase; the discerning critic had an equal number of reasons to be impressed. Excellently shot and extremely well-acted, *Sholay* is also equally well-conceived as a screen drama.

The most shattering piece of cinema in the film is the gunning down of the Thakur's family. In the time that it takes for the first body to hit the ground, all the others have been killed as well, and the camera uses freeze and slow-motion along with normal pace to frame that single moment of death. When the Thakur reaches home, there are five bodies swathed in white sheets on the ground. The wind whips the covering off four of them, but the Thakur himself lifts the sheet that covers the little boy. The long moment of silence shows only the Thakur dropping the sheet back; the dead child is never seen, just as the shot that killed him is never shown, its sound drowned by the grinding wheels of the train that brings the Thakur home. The romance between Jaidev and Radha is built on silence too. No words are spoken; only in the night, when Jaidev sits outside his shack playing his mouth-organ, Radha watches him as she slowly crosses the long balcony of her home, turning off the lamps one by one. Watching Jaidev die, she once again silently turns away and hides her face against the Thakur's chest.

Radha's silence is the foil for Basanti's constant happy chatter. Straight out of the fantasy world of Hindi cinema, she drives the only horse-drawn carriage in the village for her livelihood, and falls in love with the hard-drinking, madcap Veeru whose pranks are watched with indulgence by the more sober Jaidev. Humour intervenes almost all through the film, including a homage to *The Great Dictator* in an early prison sequence where the jailor, an amalgamation of Chaplin and Hitler, plays with a globe and trips himself up while Veeru and Jaidev merrily plan their escape. Humour also provides the traditional relief to the tragic background of the story, and Dharmendra, who started his career as a non-actor with a handsome physique, proves himself a tremendous comic performer in *Sholay*.

Salim and Javed, who then worked as a team and produced the screenplays and dialogues for both *Sholay* and Yash Chopra's *Deewar* the same year, became the new stars behind the screen. Just as in *Deewar* they established Amitabh Bachchan as the angry doomed hero of a corrupt urban milieu, in *Sholay* their dialogues became part of the common language of the streets. For years people saw the film over and over again, and anticipated the actors' words every time they opened their mouths on the screen—the ultimate in audience participation.

The greatest hit, however, was the arch villain Gabbar Singh. This was the first screen role of actor Amjad Khan who till then had dabbled in amateur theatricals in Bombay. Amjad Khan created a new kind of villain for the Hindi screen: casual, almost handsome, and with his sudden changes of mood, intensely menacing. His drawling delivery as Gabbar Singh is still imitated by the old and the young, thirteen years after the film's release. Amjad Khan went on to be stereotyped, but has occasionally been allowed roles that have proved his talent as an actor; the best example being that of the arrogant, artistic and weak Wajid Ali Shah, the last Nawab of Avadh, in Satyajit Ray's *Shatranj ke Khilari* (made two years after *Sholay*) which incidentally also featured Sanjeev Kumar, *Sholay's* dynamic Thakur, in a key role.

STREET SINGER
b&w, 135 minutes, Hindi, 1938

Production: New Theatres Limited/ Direction and Story: Phani Mazumdar/ Dialogue: A.H. Shore/ Camera: Dilip Gupta/ Music: Rai Chand Boral/Editing: Kali Raha/ Sound: Loken Bose
Cast: K.L. Saigal, Kanan Devi, Jagdish, Bikram Kapoor, A.H. Shore, Ram Kumari

BHULWA and Manju are two orphan children whom fate brings together. Bhulwa, with his talent for music, trains Manju to sing and dance. In search of a livelihood, they go to the city, where Bhulwa sings on the streets and Manju dances, drawing crowds around them with her charm and grace. Quite by accident, they meet Amarnath, the owner of a theatre who is always looking around for fresh talent. By now Manju has grown into a charming young woman, and her performance on the streets of the city attracts Amarnath's attention. Realizing her potential, he offers to take Manju in his company of players.

The combination of her own talents and Amarnath's intensive training makes Manju into a professional performer. Bhulwa watches her transformation into a successful stage star initially with pride, but soon with growing apprehension. In their years together, their close friendship had inevitably changed to the first stirrings of romance. But it is only now, when Manju's success is drawing her away from him, that Bhulwa realizes what Manju means to him. He begins to feel hurt and neglected while Manju pursues her busy and ambitious career, unaware of Bhulwa's state of mind, taking for granted his affection and his support. When Bhulwa, believing that he no longer has a place in Manju's glamorous existence, decides to leave her, Manju is bewildered. In her innocence, she had never been able to articulate her feelings for Bhulwa, and now finds it difficult to convince Bhulwa of her need for him.

Bhulwa leaves, and Manju, shaken to the core, leaves everything behind to go and look for him. Fame is not more important than Bhulwa's love, nor are riches. When Manju finds him at last, all the unspoken emotions find a voice. They both realize that they can do without the complexities that money and fame invariably bring. Secure in their love for each other, Bhulwa and Manju now go back to being street performers again, back to a life of innocence and simplicity which had brought them so much happiness before.

AN IDYLLIC romance with no pretensions of realism, *Street Singer* is even today a charming experience. Saigal's voice, which has always transcended his less than attractive appearance and his dismal acting capabilities, is in this film pitched against the voice of Kanan Devi, the nightingale of the Bengali screen. Fortunately, Kanan Devi was also a lovely and talented actress, and the combination was devastating for the Indian audience. The film came at a time when the stock of New Theatres was already very high, and displayed once again the ability of its founder, B.N. Sircar, to put the right people together at the right time. His own interest in music had resulted in a collection of extremely proficient performers and composers within New theatres, which included the stars of *Street Singer,* its music director Rai Chand Boral, actor, singer, composer Pankaj Mullick, composer Timir Baran, and the famous blind actor and singer, Krishna Chandra Dey.

SUBARNAREKHA
b&w, 132 minutes, Bengali, 1965

Production: J.J. Films Corporation/ Original Story: Radheshyam/ Story, Screenplay, Direction: Ritwik Ghatak/ Camera: Dilip Ranjan Mukherjee/ Music: Ustad Bahadur Khan/ Art Direction: Ravi Chatterjee/ Editing: Ramesh Joshi/ Sound: Satyen Chatterjee
Cast: Abhi Bhattacharya, Madhavi Mukherjee, Satindra Bhattacharya, Bijon Bhattacharya, Jahar Ray, Gita Dey, Shyamal Ghosal, Abanish Banerjee, Sita Mukherjee, Arun Choudhury, Umanath Bhattacharya

AFTER THE partition of Bengal in 1947, a floating population of refugees takes shelter in clusters of shacks in Calcutta. In one of these settlements, Ishwar and his little sister, Sita, join other uprooted Bengalis, including Haraprasad, an idealistic schoolteacher and his large family. One day Kaushalya, a low-caste woman, comes there with her son, Abhiram. But a local landlord raids the shelter, and Kaushalya is forced to leave without her child. In the fraternity of the dispossessed, Ishwar takes the little boy under his wing. Offered a job in an iron foundry by a rich Marwari acquaintance, Rambilas, Ishwar goes with Sita and Abhiram to Chhatimpur on the banks of the river Subarnarekha. The manager of the foundry is a man old before his time, hovering between sanity and oblivion ever since his only daughter ran away from home. Soon Abhiram is sent away to a boarding school, followed by college, while Sita grows into womanhood in her brother's home.

The old manager retires and Ishwar takes charge of the foundry. Abhiram comes home after graduation. Ishwar wants to send him to Germany for higher studies, but Abhiram wants to stay at home and be a writer. The conflict is further complicated when Abhiram and Sita realize their mutual attraction. They speak of their love in hushed voices, for they know that Ishwar, an upper-caste Hindu and a man of principle, would not tolerate any intimacy between them. Meanwhile, Ishwar is visited by a ghost from the past—one of the idealistic youths of the refugee shelter in Calcutta—now grey and worn out by the daily struggle to live. He brings with him a note for Ishwar, a document of despair and defeat, left by Haraprasad's wife who has committed suicide. Haraprasad himself was last seen begging in the streets.

Soon after this, Rambilas offers Ishwar a partnership, but being a staunch upper caste Hindu himself, makes it quite clear that Ishwar should send Abhiram away. Who knows what caste he belongs to? Abhiram's origins are accidentally revealed when he recognizes a dying low-caste woman at the railway station as his mother. Remembering Rambilas's words, Ishwar asks Abhiram to leave, refusing to consider a marriage between him and Sita. Sita's marriage is arranged elsewhere and her protests harshly silenced. On the night of the wedding, Sita runs away to Abhiram.

The young couple, estranged from Ishwar, live in a Calcutta slum. Abhiram gives up his ambitions and becomes a bus driver, the only job that comes his way in these days of severe unemployment. In Chhatimpur, Ishwar finds that the security and prosperity he had craved for have lost their meaning. Preparing to commit suicide at night, he is startled by the sudden appearance of Haraprasad's ravaged face at the window. Ishwar does not die; instead the two condemned souls go on a bizarre pilgrimage to Calcutta, the city of terrible pleasures.

In the slum, while Sita waits with her son, news comes that Abhiram, involved in an accident, has been beaten to death by an irate mob. To feed her child, Sita is inevitably drawn into prostitution. But her first customer is Ishwar, with his principles and his grief drowned in alcohol. Sita kills herself with a kitchen knife. The blood-spattered Ishwar sees her face through a drunken haze, and states at court that he has killed his sister—the first untruth of his life. After two years of legal wranglings, he is proved innocent and released from prison. Haraprasad brings Sita's son to him. Ishwar goes back to Chhatimpur only to find that the job is no longer his. Led by the little boy who is eager to see his new home, Ishwar moves across the sandy banks of the Subarnarekha once again towards an unknown future.

WITH A COMPLEX storyline, and a carefully woven pattern of coincidences, *Subarnarekha* is perhaps the most artistically consistent of all Ghatak's films. It is also his most powerful indictment of economic and social disintegration in post-Independence India. While tracing the roots of the present malaise in the recent past, Ghatak recalls his own lost dream, not by recreating memories of an idyllic childhood, but by presenting vividly the aftermath of its destruction. The partition of Bengal at the time of Independence, artificially separated a culturally unified people on the basis of religion, and left an indelible mark on the economic and political life of eastern India. Ghatak, who grew up in what is now Bangladesh, expressed his personal emotional trauma of the forced estrangement from his roots again and again in his films. The three films he made at the peak of his career, *Meghe Dhaka Tara, Komal Gandhar* and *Subarnarekha,* all hark back with great nostalgia and anguish to undivided Bengal.

"We were born in a deceived age," he wrote. "The days of our childhood and adolescence saw the full flowering of Bengal. Tagore, with his overpowering genius at the peak of his literary career; the renewed vigour of Bengali literature in the works of the youthful 'Kallol' group; the widespread national movement in schools and colleges, among the youth of Bengal; the villages of Bengal with their folk tales, folk songs and festivals, full to the brim with the hope of a new life. Just then came the war, came famine. The Muslim League and the Congress Party brought the country to ruin by tearing it apart and accepting a destructive independence. Communal riots flooded the country. The waters of the Ganga and the Padma were red with the blood of brothers. These are our own experiences. Our dreams faded. We stumbled and fell, desperately clutching at a wretched, impoverished Bengal. Which Bengal is this, where poverty and immorality are our constant companions, where blackmarketeers and dishonest politicians rule, where terrible fear and sorrow are the inevitable fate of every man!

"In the films I have made in recent years, I have not been able to free myself from this theme. What has seemed to me a most urgent need, is to present to the Bengali people this miserable impoverished face of divided Bengal, to make them conscious of their own existence, their past, and their future."

Ghatak did return to his roots in Bangladesh eight years later to make *Titash Ekti Nadir Naam.* But the experience left him unsatisfied, for history had irrevocably changed a treasured memory. Next year, back in India, he made *Jukti Takko ar Gappo*, his last film, a highly critical analysis of the political ferment in the West Bengal of the seventies. Both films reiterate the betrayal of the partition in different time spaces. The strength and sincerity of his anger, however, remained hidden from the ordinary film viewer, the people he had tried to reach. After his death in 1976, critics finally acknowledged his genius, his highly individual style, the force and the vitality of his message. Today, after many retrospectives abroad, Ghatak has finally gained the recognition that was denied him in his lifetime.

TARANG **(Wages and Profits)**
colour, 171 minutes, Hindi, 1984

Production: National Film Development Corporation/ Direction and Screenplay: Kumar Shahani/ Camera: K.K. Mahajan/ Music: Vanraj Bhatia/ Art Direction: Bansi Chandragupta, C.S. Bhatti/ Editing: Ashok Tyagi/ Lyrics: Raghubir Sehay and Gulzar/ Sound: Narendra Singh
Cast: Smita Patil, Amol Palekar, Dr Shreeram Lagoo, Girish Karnad, Om Puri, Jalal Agha, Rohini Hattangady, Kawal Gandhiok, M.K. Raina, Sulbha Deshpande, Arvind Deshpande, Jayanti Patel

RAHUL, the son-in-law of an old industrialist, and one of the heirs to his fortune, clashes with Dinesh, the industrialist's nephew who is openly unscrupulous. Rahul, for his part, conceals his personal ambition under a cloak of liberalism and encourages indigenous production. In the centre of the conflict sits the wily old man, with money as his sole concern. His tense and elegant daughter Hansa watches him like a hawk, for he is the only man she has ever completely loved.

Outside the palace and its intrigues, are the hovels of the workers in the old industrialist's empire, where Janaki lives. Janaki's dead husband had once led an agitation against the management, and Janaki herself is still considered potentially dangerous. Thrown out of her shack by the industrialist's henchmen, she is picked up from the streets by Rahul and installed in his palatial home as a nursemaid for his child. As Janaki becomes increasingly indispensable, Hansa quietly withdraws, pushing Janaki into a relationship with Rahul.

Having done her duty by producing a son and heir for the family fortunes, Hansa now turns her full attention to her father, her sole obsession. But when the old man falls ill, Rahul keeps Hansa away from her father, and with Janaki's help, contrives to remove the nurse, a secret tippler, often from the sickroom, leaving the old man neglected. One day, the nurse comes back and finds her patient dead. Dinesh, who returns from one of his tours abroad, accuses Rahul of killing his father-in-law, but there is no evidence. With the help of Anita, an old paramour and the old man's erstwhile secretary, Rahul puts Dinesh in a false position with his foreign collaborators. Dinesh's local ally, a crooked trade union leader, is silenced by Janaki and her worker friends. Rahul sends Janaki away to a bungalow in the hills supposedly to protect her from any investigation arising out of the old man's death. Meanwhile he buys the allegiance of a section of the workers, and comes back to tell Janaki that she will be accused of murder. Janaki, betrayed but free, walks back to her old life on the streets.

In Rahul's home, Hansa tries to arouse herself from her grief. After a long time she makes love to Rahul, and wakes up with the promise of a more fulfilling relationship. Yet by the evening she is dead, submerged in the bathtub. Rahul removes his last obstacle by implicating Dinesh in a murder, and takes charge of his empire. Janaki sets fire to the brothel and returns to the shack of a worker friend. As she waits for him to return home, someone throws a lighted cracker in the room. Janaki escapes as the row of shacks goes up in flames.

Perhaps in a dream, on a long and lonely bridge, Rahul approaches Janaki once again with the offer of a life of freedom and equality. Janaki, an ethereal figure of great beauty and sexuality, rejects his offer with supreme indifference. "Go back to your destiny," she says. "I am like the first rays of the sun. I am hard to catch as the wind...."

TARANG, Kumar Shahani's second feature film, is a saga of conflict and betrayal stretching across the boundaries of different worlds. Bridging the gulf between them is Janaki, forever betrayed, forever alone. In the last sequence, where the myth takes over from the real, Janaki's persona extends from the exploited victim of human ambition to a celestial embodiment of freedom. She is desirable, but can no longer be used, for she has the choice denied her in the real world, of going her own way without surrender. Perhaps the polarities will finally converge at the end of the long bridge, perhaps there is hope for a common destination.

One of the brightest alumni of the Film and Television Institute of India, Shahani was greatly influenced by Ritwik Ghatak, the controversial film maker and teacher from Bengal, and D.D. Kosambi, the great Indian polymath. Though he writes rarely, he remains one of the most promising film theoreticians in India today. His films are even more rare, a few shorts and documentaries, and one other feature film, *Maya Darpan*, made in 1972. Very recently, Shahani got together with playwright G. Shankar Pillai and actress Alaknanda Samarth to stage two unusual plays, *Kunti* and *The Human Voice*, which received rave reviews in Bombay. *Tarang*, like his first feature film, is not easy to assess, nor will it ever be received by the general audience with understanding or enjoyment. It is slow, larger than life, and undoubtedly intriguing.

For Shahani, *Tarang* is his exploration of the epic form in cinema. "The epic tradition overcomes the division between the giver and the receiver of art," he says. "It is a pity that societies tend to make museum pieces of art when, in fact, the need for it is as natural and as instinctive in people as eating and drinking." That is probably why *Tarang* comes through to the discerning viewer as a moving experience, even if he is completely unaware of the intricacies of Shahani's personal imagination; unaware that for him, Janaki is the Earth Mother revealing herself as Urvashi, the celestial dancer, seductive and divine, bestower of wealth and fertility; unaware that her last words in the film are a hymn from the Rig Veda.

TAXI DRIVER
b&w, 133 minutes, Hindi, 1954

Production: Navketan/ Direction and screenplay: Chetan Anand/ Story: Uma Anand, Vijay Anand/ Dialogue: Vijay Anand/ Camera: V. Ratra/ Music: S.D. Burman/ Lyrics: Sahir Ludhianvi/ Art Direction: Kakkar, M.K. Burman/ Editing: Jadav Rao/ Sound: R.G. Pushalkar
Cast: Dev Anand, Kalpana Kartik, Sheila Ramani, Johnny Walker, Bhagwan Sinha, Patanjal, Shujju, Kamal Singh, Vernon Corke, Krishnan Dhawan, Rashid, M. A. Latief, Parveen Paul, Hameed Sayani

MANGAL, a taxi driver, saves a young village girl from being molested by two men who had hired his taxi. Driving off to safety with the frightened girl, he learns that she is Mala, an orphan, who has come to Bombay in search of Rattanlal, a music director in the film industry. Rattanlal had come to her village and hearing her sing, promised her a job in the city. Mangal takes her to the address she has been given, but Rattanlal is no longer there. At the end of a long and futile search, Mangal brings her to his room for the night. He will sleep in the taxi, he says, before going off to D'Mello's club where his friends wait for him.

The next day they look for Rattanlal again, but cannot trace him. At the club Mangal comes across the two men from whom he had saved Mala. They pick a quarrel, but are diverted by Sylvie, the girl who dances and sings there and is in love with Mangal. Having heard the men questioning Mangal about a girl, she wants to know more. Mangal's silence makes Sylvie intensely jealous and she taunts him for being a mere taxi driver. Hurt and angry, Mangal decides to break off with Sylvie. Meanwhile an easy friendship springs up between him and Mala. Before they can discuss Mala's future, however, Mangal's sister-in-law comes for a visit. Warned in time, he dresses Mala up as a boy, and with a bit of coaching, turns her into his "cleaner," the foul-mouthed street urchin, Rajput. In all the confusion of his sister-in-law's visit, his friends who know nothing about the girl, accept Rajput as a real boy.

One day Sylvie stops Mangal's taxi and begs him to come and see her again. Mangal ignores her, but that night his room is empty. Mala's note says that she does not wish to come between him and Sylvie. It hits Mangal hard. He spends days refusing passengers and roaming the city in search of Mala. He admits to his friend Mastane that Rajput is actually a girl. Coaxed by Mastane, he picks up a passenger who turns out to be Rattanlal. Meanwhile Mala, after trying several jobs, goes back to surviving as Rajput, cleaning cars. Mastane finds her and brings her to Mangal who drags her into his taxi. "Why did you leave me?" he says drawing her into his arms. As they talk, the ruffians who had tried to kidnap Mala, get into the taxi waving a pistol. They abandon Mangal and Mala at a lonely spot and drive away in the taxi. When they use the taxi to rob a bank, the police ask for Mangal's help as only he and his "cleaner" know what the robbers look like. Threatened by the gang, Mangal takes Mala to Rattanlal who, remembering her talents as a singer, gives her shelter.

The gang have links with the film world, and see Mala in Rattanlal's home. Having met her as Rajput last time, they go unsuspecting with Mala to D'Mello's club to hear Sylvie sing. Noticing her gesturing to Mangal at the club, however, their suspicions are aroused. To ensure their own safety one of them try to knife Mangal while another puts a sleeping drug in Mala's tea. With help from his friends Mangal ties up his antagonist and is dragging the half-asleep Mala away, when the other robber takes out his pistol and shoots at him. Sylvie dances to distract him and throws herself on the main switch. In the darkened room bedlam reigns. Though hurt, Mangal leaps at the gunman. D'Mello calls the police, and the intruders are taken away. Only the gunman, hiding under a table, tries to get Mangal again, but is finally knocked out. As he leaves with Mala, Mangal says he will come to thank Sylvie in the morning, for she has saved his life. Out of the shadows, Sylvie appears in the empty room, dying from a bullet wound. D'Mello finds her and shouts for a doctor. Meanwhile, Mala and Mangal, safe at last and happy, are driven away by their friends.

THE HERO as a common man championing the cause of his downtrodden friends is still a familiar figure in popular Indian cinema. But he has lost his innocence. With the advent of Amitabh Bachchan, Robin Hood has become a dark angel, taking an eye for an eye in a world that has increasingly taken to violence, and where corruption is the rule of the day. When Dev Anand played Mangal, the taxi driver, the brutalization of Robin Hood had not yet taken place. It was a very similar role to the one he had played in Guru Dutt's *Baazi*. The forces of the law were actually with him, and against the evil-doers. So what if he drank a bit or gambled out of frustration once in a while, and had friends who were not quite respectable? He had a large heart, and all he needed was sympathy and love from a good woman to keep him on the right path. Much of the charm of *Taxi Driver* lies in its romantic attitude towards the new working class of the fifties, and the idealism that it embodied.

The film was in many ways a family affair. Produced under their own banner, it was directed by Dev Anand's elder brother, Chetan Anand, who was already an established director of mainstream cinema. The story and dialogue came from the youngest brother, Vijay Anand, who was soon to prove his mettle as a director. The heroine of the film, Kalpana Kartik, who made a most attractive street-urchin, married Dev Anand and retired into domestic bliss.

A part of filmland trivia is the rare appearance of Hameed Sayani in a cameo role as a henpecked magician who employs Mala as a maid and spends his time showing her magic tricks. Sayani, a media man in Bombay, who produced advertising shorts for many years, was an amateur magician, and his neat sleight of hand on the screen is no trick of the camera.

TEESRI KASAM (The Third Vow)
b&w, 159 minutes, Hindi, 1966

Production: Image Makers/ Direction: Basu Bhattacharya/ Story and dialogue: Phanishwar Nath "Renu"/ Screenplay: Nabendu Ghosh/ Camera: Subrata Mitra/ Music: Shankar Jaikishen/ Lyrics: Shailendra, Hasrat/ Playback: Lata Mangeshkar, Asha Bhonsle, Manna Dey, Suman Kalyanpur, Mubarak Begum, Shankar-Shambhu, Mukesh/ Art Direction: Desh Mukherjee/ Editing: G.G. Mayekar/ Sound: Allauddin
Cast: Raj Kapoor, Waheeda Rehman, Dulari, Iftekhar, Asit Sen, C.S. Dubey, Krishen Dhawan, Vishwa Mehra, Samar Chatterjee, Nabendu Ghosh, Keshto Mukherjee

NEARLY caught by the police while carrying blackmarket goods in his cart, Hiraman escapes with his bulls and takes a vow, never to carry contraband again. Transporting bamboo for a trader, he is beaten up by two men when their horse swerves to avoid Hiraman's cart and upsets their carriage. This time Hiraman vows never to carry bamboo again. One night he is asked to carry a woman passenger to a fair forty miles away. On the way, unable to contain his curiosity, he lifts the curtain of his cart. "Lord help me, it's an angel!" he says aloud and wakes up the angel. She is Hira Bai, a Nautanki performer, going to join a new company at the fair. Hiraman's innocence and simplicity charm Hira who is also moved by the old songs that he sings to pass the time. When they stop near a lake, Hiraman tells her in song the legend of Mahua, a beautiful, motherless girl, who falls in love with a stranger near the lake but is sold to a trader by her stepmother. "That is why you must not bathe here, it is bad luck for an unmarried girl," he says, quite oblivious of the the fact that a woman who dances at a fair can hardly be categorized as an innocent, unmarried village belle. But his concern touches Hira's heart, as does his attempt to hide her from all passers-by, as if she is a woman from the inner sanctums of a respectable home.

Hira coaxes Hiraman to spend a few days at the fair and see her dance; she even gives him passes for his friends. Making his friends, the other cart drivers, take a solemn oath that they will keep it a secret from his sister-in-law, Hiraman goes to see the Nautanki, but gets into a fight when he hears a drunkard making insulting remarks about Hira Bai. "What right have you to fight on my behalf?" she says in anger later, and Hiraman, hurt, stays away from the show. But he keeps coming back to the fair, and Hira, calling him into her tent, apologizes and cooks a meal for him. Mollified, and leaving all his earnings in her safekeeping, Hiraman returns to the show, but overhears a conversation between Birju, Hira's agent, and the local landlord, who wants a taste of Hira in private. The worried Hiraman tries to tell Hira to leave a profession where people talk ill of her. "But what else can I do? Besides, I like the heady feeling of dressing up and dancing under the bright lights," says Hira. "Why can't you join the circus? That's a 'company' too," says the innocent Hiraman. On an impulse, Hira goes for a ride in Hiraman's cart. When they return, the landlord appears in her tent and Hira, embarrassed, sends Hiraman away. Suddenly unhappy with her own situation, she firmly refuses the landlord's overtures and incurs his wrath.

Annoyed by the landlord's presence in Hira's tent and by Birju's derisive remarks, Hiraman goes back home, but cannot forget Hira. His sister-in-law asks him for some money, and he promises to go and pick it up for her. But while he is away from the fair, the landlord, egged on by Birju, tries to force himself on Hira who fights him furiously and escapes. In consternation the manager of the company threatens to sack her. But later the entire troupe try to help her solve her dilemma. If she gives up her profession, she will starve. If she does not, she will have to give in to the landlord. Hiraman might think her an angel, but will he be able to accept the truth about her and still admire her?

Hira decides to leave the Nautanki company, for her presence will threaten the livelihood of others; the landlord will not leave them alone. But she cannot live a lie with Hiraman either, and so she sends for him to say good-bye. When Hiraman comes to the fair she has already left for the station. The train is just coming in when he reaches her. She gives him his money, then putting her shawl around him lovingly, says, "I'm going back to my old company. Will you come to see my show at Gulabganj?" Hiraman is silent. "Do not close your heart, Hiraman. You told me the story of Mahua who was bought by a trader. I too have been sold, my friend."

The wind lifts the curtains of his empty cart as Hiraman goads his bulls forward. Mahua's song drifts like a ghost around him. In sudden anger, he turns on his bulls. "Don't stare at me! I vow never to carry a woman from a Nautanki company again!"

TEESRI KASAM is one of those black and white films that one always remembers in colour: the bright yellow light of the summer sun, the shadowed green country roads, the shimmering blue waters of the lake, Hira Bai's swirling skirts of many hues, the sparkling colours of the fireworks in the fair. Along with the visual feast, one remembers the sounds of the film, Hiraman's songs on the road, children singing a wedding song as they chase his cart carrying Hira Bai through a village, the delightfully intimate and occasionally embarrassing Nautanki songs, the song of the cart drivers sitting around a fire at night. And moving through it all is the frail ghost of Mahua of the lake who carries the burden of both Hiraman's innocence and Hira Bai's shame.

There is little of conventional drama in *Teesri Kasam*. The film flows like Mahua's song, sad, beautiful, and eternal. The extraordinary lyricism of *Teesri Kasam* should have made the film one of the phenomenons of Indian cinema. Instead, after a brief moment of glory, it was forgotten by critics and audience alike. Its director, one of the founders of the parallel cinema movement, went on to make other films, none of which reached the same level of sensitivity or artistry. Raj Kapoor, who has played the role of the country bumpkin with a large heart many times before and after, has never played it so well or so realistically.*Teesri Kasam* is also one of the rare films photographed by Subrata Mitra, the cameraman who had contributed so much to the earlier films of Satyajit Ray.

36 CHOWRINGHEE LANE
colour, 113 minutes, English, 1981

Production: Shashi Kapoor/ Direction, story and screenplay: Aparna Sen/ Camera: Ashok Mehta/ Music: Vanraj Bhatia/ Art Direction: Bansi Chandragupta/ Editing: Bhanudas Divakar
Cast: Jennifer Kendall, Dhritiman Chaterji, Debashree Roy, Geoffrey Kendall

VIOLET STONEHAM, a lonely, ageing Anglo-Indian woman, lives in a small apartment in Calcutta and teaches Shakespeare to a class of inattentive school-girls. Though Shakespeare is the one ray of light in her gloomy existence, she is an old-fashioned teacher, making the class more boring than lively. One Christmas morning, walking back from church, she meets an ex-student, Nandita and her boy-friend, Samaresh and invites them home for coffee. The young people, tired of stealing kisses in taxis, persuade her to allow the use of her flat, ostensibly for Samaresh to write his first novel in peace. Soon Miss Stoneham begins to look forward to seeing her young friends who drop in to take her out for a walk, buy her Chinese dinners, coax her to play her old, forgotten records. It is a wonderful new experience. Her days at the school have been dreary for many years, and her only link with the past, a senile older brother, Eddie, awaits death in an old people's home. Yet she has refused her niece's plea to join her in Australia. After all India is her country.

But once Nandita and Samaresh get married, they no longer have any use for Miss Stoneham's friendship, for Nandita's parents present them with a furnished apartment as a wedding gift. In the school too there are winds of change, bringing a younger teacher with a more modern approach to teaching Shakespeare. Miss Stoneham, left to tackle adverbs and past participles, wistfully looks out of the school window for a fleeting glimpse of a sunnier world. She misses Nandita and Samaresh, who with the typical cruelty of youth, forget her in their busy social schedule.

The last link with the past snaps with the death of Eddie. When Christmas comes once again, Miss Stoneham thinks of her young friends. But this time Nandita and Samaresh have other plans, and to avoid hurting her, tell her that they will be out of town. When she takes a home-baked cake to their apartment as a surprise for them to come back to, a party of rowdy youngsters is in full swing. It is a world where Violet Stoneham has no place. She walks away from her humiliation to face her loneliness once more.

ONE OF THE rare examples of an Indian feature film in English, *36 Chow-ringhee Lane* uses the language of our adoption in a manner that makes it our own. Violet Stoneham is an Anglo-Indian, which in India no longer signifies what it did in colonial times—people of British origin who made their homes in India or spent a large part of their lives here. The Anglo-Indian community as it exists today, is a diminishing clan of people of mixed origin, once known as Eurasians, rootless and culturally alienated from the country where they have lived for generations. During British rule, the Anglo-Indians preferred to isolate themselves from Indian society which was in any case too orthodox to accommodate them. The British on the other hand were unwilling to give them an equal status. With independence, some who could afford it, opted to live abroad, but most were forced to make the best of what the nascent republic had to offer them. With their westernized education, one section of the Anglo-Indians had already found permanent professional roles in India. The railways have used them for generations, so have educational institutions; while in business houses they once had a monopoly of the secretarial jobs. With growing social acceptance, the small middle-class Anglo-Indian community mainly settled in Calcutta, have become absorbed in the mainstream of Indian life. But the essential differences still remain in the lower economic levels.

In spite of their prolonged exposure to India, Anglo-Indians use a bastard variation of English as their mother tongue, with sometimes unrecognizable phraseology and always a typical sing-song intonation, not exactly "Indian English," yet borrowing heavily from it. Jennifer Kendall, who so faithfully portrays Violet Stoneham, without mockery (she recites Shakespeare fervently in an unmistakable Anglo-Indian accent) and with great compassion, was herself a British stage actress, married to Shashi Kapoor, a star of popular Hindi cinema. Though highly talented, she was seldom seen on the screen where her husband cavorted round trees chasing nubile young heroines through tortuous plots for years. But she did make rare appearances as in Shyam Benegal's *Junoon*, and Satyajit Ray's latest film, *Ghare Baire*. The Ray film was her last, for she died tragically of cancer soon after. Her father, Geoffrey Kendall, who had for years run a highly successful touring Shakespeare company, gives a cameo performance in *36 Chowringhee Lane* as Violet's irascible and senile elder brother.

Aparna Sen, made her debut as an actress very early in her life in Ray's *Samapti* (one of the three Tagore stories in Ray's *Teen Kanya*), and dominated the Bengali screen for two decades before she took to film making. She continues to be one of the major stage and screen actresses in Bengal, runs a women's magazine in Bengali, and makes films with unusual themes based on her own stories. For her first film, *36 Chowringhee Lane*, Sen won the National Award for best direction, and the Grand Prix at the Manila International Film Festival.

TRIKAL   (Past, Present and Future)
colour, 137 minutes, Hindi, 1985

Production: Blaze Film Enterprises Pvt. Ltd/ Direction, story and screenplay: Shyam Benegal/ Camera: Ashok Mehta/ Music: Vanraj Bhatia/ Art Direction: Nitish Roy/ Editing: Bhanudas Divakar/ Sound: Hitendra Ghosh
Cast: Leela Naidu, Neena Gupta, Anita Kanwar, Soni Razdan, Dalip Tahil, K.K. Raina, Keith Stevenson, Ila Arun, Sushma Prakash, Naseeruddin Shah, Nikhil Bhagat, Kulbhushan Kharbanda

CURIOSITY takes Ruiz Pareira back to a village in Goa where he had spent some days of his youth in the Souza Soares mansion which still stands, hidden behind the uncontrolled wilderness of its once gracious gardens. A decrepit old caretaker opens the door, and Pareira is transported to the magical past.
  A peasant stands with a coffin at the door. Upstairs in a spacious bedroom old Soares lies dead, surrounded by men and women in sombre black. Young Ruiz is there too, the nephew of a family friend, hovering around Anna, the old man's beautiful granddaughter with whom he is madly in love. Soares's wife, Maria, sits silently on her ornate rocking chair in the next room, listening absently to a fado on an old, hand-wound gramophone. People say that Milagrenia, Maria's young companion who plays the gramophone for her, is the illegitimate daughter of old Soares. She is shapely like a deer and young Ruiz lusts after her.
  Sylvia, Maria's eldest daughter, comes to implore her mother to stop listening to music on such a day. With her comes her husband Lucio, his dentures popping out every time he speaks. After the funeral, which Maria attends with grim reluctance, Sylvia tackles her on the subject of Anna's engagement. Senhor Renato and his wife Amalia have been staying in the house in the hope of finalizing the marriage between Anna and their son, Erasmo. But Maria is adamant; she must consult her dead husband before she can cut short the stipulated period of mourning. While Ruiz serenades Anna from the garden, and Erasmo pursues her with doglike devotion, Maria sits with Milagrenia and holds a seance each night. Only, instead of old Soares, she is visited by spirits who come to berate her for the misdeeds of her ancestors who had willingly accepted their foreign masters and their religion.

Meanwhile the Indian government is preparing to take over the little Portuguese colony. Unknown to most of the household, Maria gives shelter to her nephew Leon, a pro-Indian Goan freedom fighter. Anna, who has long been in love with him, finds out where he is secreted, and meets him when the household sleeps. The police come looking for Leon, and though they do not find him, Maria decides that for the safety of the household Leon must leave, and agrees to Anna's engagement with Erasmo. That is when it is discovered that Anna is pregnant. Ruiz's uncle, the family doctor, assumes it is Erasmo's work, but soon realizes that Anna has been keeping him at a distance. He then suspects his nephew and hauls him off to the confessional. But Ruiz has sinned only with Milagrenia who is also pregnant now. Furious, Senhor Renato and Amalia drag the heartbroken Erasmo away.

Maria refuses to marry Anna to Ruiz even if he is more than willing, because he comes from a lower caste. Sylvia is hysterical with worry. Ruiz is packed off home by his uncle, and Anna runs away with Leon. Though Maria is secretly happy with the developments, Sylvia and Lucio, who have spent all their married life in the Soares home, leave in a huff. It was not the kind of alliance they would have wished for Anna.

Suddenly, after many years, the house is empty, but for Maria, Milagrenia, and the servants. Goa is liberated. Maria gets news of Anna and Leon, happily married. New and strange visions assail her in the lonely house. She accepts them as intimations of her own mortality. She knows the old way of life too will soon be swept away by the winds of change.

Twenty-four years later, Ruiz Pareira walks down the overgrown path to the ornate gate, away from the colour and charm of a lost era, into the harsh light of day in modern Goa.

TRIKAL is not one of Shyam Benegal's most successful films. Critics and viewers alike have found it confusing, and alienating in its presentation of a bastard culture which is neither Indian nor fully Western. Yet the film has an undeniable charm. Its nostalgia is palpable and its recreation near perfect. Long before the liberation of Goa, its people had drifted into Maharashtra, in search of livelihood. There is a vast Goan population living in Bombay today, who have never been really absorbed into the Indian milieu. Somewhat in the manner of the Anglo-Indians in Calcutta, they have retained their Western clothes, an odd inflexion in their speech, and their "foreign" religion—Christianity. Yet their dark complexion makes them unquestionably a part of the Indian race, and at a subliminal level, their ethnic identity remains unchanged.

Trikal presents this strange synthesis. It recalls a lost way of life with sympathy and a certain indulgence, laughing gently at the foibles of a dying society which had a relatively brief existence in the long history of civilization in the subcontinent. The warm, glowing colours, the individual nuances of character, the minute details of an opulent multi-cultural lifestyle, provide the ingredients for this little dramatic interlude in the Soares family. Benegal's style is reminiscent of Fellini in Ruiz's youthful and eccentric perception of events: Father Sequeira conducts the funeral service. A sharp wind blows and Anna's skirt flies up, Erasmo's hat blows off, Lucio's dentures pop out of his mouth. In the middle of all the suppressed consternation, Maria keeps her eyes on the coffin. But imitation in Benegal's case is also an acknowledgement of historical and cultural affinity, a placing of his characters in a time and space which had borrowed so much from the alien adventurers who had for a while claimed this small fragment of an ancient land as their own.

22 JUNE 1897
colour, 120 minutes, Marathi, 1979

Production: Nachiket Patwardhan/Direction: Nachiket and Jayoo Patwardhan/ Screenplay: Nachiket Patwardhan/ Camera: Navroze Contractor/ Music: Anand Modak/ Art Direction: Jayoo Patwardhan/ Editing: Madhu Sinha
Cast: Prabhakar Patankar, Ravindra Mankani, Udayan Dixit, Rod Gilbert, John Irving, Sadashiv Amrapurkar

DAMODAR CHAPEKAR, the eldest of the three sons of a singer-priest of Pune, is the leader of a group of militant and fanatic Brahmin youths whose hatred for the British is carried over to a rejection of the colonizers' language as well as their religion. In January 1897 the plague strikes Pune and the city is put under martial law with Walter Rand of the Indian Civil Service in charge. With ruthless efficiency, Rand evacuates and fumigates the affected buildings. The disease is effectively contained, but in the process Rand's aggressive methods earn him the hostility of the Brahmin community. The young men in Damodar's group are already influenced by the strong wave of nationalism that is sweeping across the country. Inspired by the radical teachings of Bal Gangadhar Tilak, and angered by Rand's visible authoritarianism, Damodar plans to kill Rand on the night of 22nd June.
The plan, carefully rehearsed to the last detail, succeeds, and the young revolutionaries escape. But Inspector Brewin of the CID, determined to track down the murderers, leads a massive man-hunt and announces an award of Rs 20,000 for their capture. Brewin leaves no stone unturned, and through Ganesh Dravid, then serving a jail sentence, and his brother Nilu Dravid who had once been a member of Damodar's group, he manages to arrest Damodar Chapekar and extract a full confession from him. In spite of an appeal by Tilak himself, Damodar is sentenced to death.
The second brother, Balkrishna Chapekar, is arrested soon after, and as there is no evidence against him that can be presented at court, Brewin threatens and persuades Vasudev, the youngest brother and a mere boy, to testify against Balkrishna. But before the trial can take place, Vasudev, strengthened in his determination to carry on his brothers' task, avenges Damodar's death by murdering the Dravid brothers with the help of his friend Ranade. The two boys are soon apprehended, and within months, Balkrishna, Vasudev and Ranade are tried by a British court and sentenced to death by hanging.

THE CHAPEKAR brothers were real historical characters, who were followers of Bal Gangadhar Tilak, scholar, mathematician, philosopher and militant nationalist, who laid the foundation of India's independence. A middle-class

Brahmin, Tilak rekindled the Hindu people's pride in their own history, religion and culture, through a renewed interest in the *Vedas,* and in Shivaji, the founder of the Maratha empire in the west and a scourge of the Muslim rulers. Yet, as a political visionary and a pragmatist, in 1916 he signed the historic Lucknow Pact, a Hindu-Muslim accord, with Mohammed Ali Jinnah, the future founder of Pakistan. The pact embodied an ideal of a common Indian nationalism for Hindus and Muslims which might have, but for Tilak's death in 1920, averted the partition of the country.

It is worth considering that if the Chapekar brothers had managed to survive the British, they might have ended up as rabid fundamentalists and instigated communal riots. But then, much of the history of India's freedom movement (as perhaps that of any country) is replete with accidental heroes. Nationalism brought under one umbrella a million motivations and gave them all a unified identity and a destination. The story of the Chapekar brothers has been repeated over and over again in different circumstances in other parts of the country throughout the later years of British rule. The Patwardhan duo, a husband and wife team of practising architects, however, take a leaf out of history more as an exercise in cinema than in patriotism. Being architects, their recreation is not only faithful in every detail, but structurally controlled. Their cameraman is an experienced and highly successful photographer, who has already been initiated in new cinema through Mani Kaul's haunting *Duvidha*. The faces, mostly from the Marathi stage, are powerful in their authenticity. *22 June 1897* is an unusual attempt at bringing a new visual perception into the mechanism of film making. Chiselled faces of grim determination with the firelight dancing on them, rugged stone walls skirting narrow paths, the pillared inner courtyards of traditional dwellings, all fall into place in an intensely moving dramatic experience.

UMBARTHA   (The Threshold)
colour, 135 minutes, Marathi, 1982

Production: Sujata Chitra/ Direction: Jabbar Patel/ Screenplay and dialogue: Vijay Tendulkar/ Story: Based on the novel *Beghar,* by Shanta Nisal/ Camera: Rajan Kinagi/ Music: Hridaynath Mangeshkar/ Lyrics: Vasant Bapat, Suresh Bhatt/Art Direction: Dinanath Chauhan/ Editing: N.S. Vaidya/ Sound: Ravindra Sathe
Cast: Smita Patil, Girish Karnad, Shrikant Moghe, Ashalata, Kusum Kulkarni, Purnima Ganu, Daya Dongre, Shriram Ranade, Satish Alekar, Subhash Godbole, Manorama Wagle, Chanchal Suryavanshi, Aruna Vigar Dive, Nandini Chavre, Swarupa Khopkar, Rani Sabnis, Sandhya Kale, Sushma Deshpande, Manik Bhandare, Jaimala Kale, Sushila Vansale, Surekha Divekar, Sujal Vatve

SULBHA, the wife of a successful young lawyer, Subhash, lives in their spacious home and feels unaccountably restless. The family is not only well-off, but also what could be described as "progressive." Subhash's brother

Mohan runs a flourishing nursing home. Sulbha's mother-in-law is an active social worker and wants Sulbha, who has a degree in social work, to join her organization. Sulbha has no responsibility in her home, as her only daughter Rani is looked after entirely by her childless sister-in-law Maya who also runs the household. Sulbha feels an outsider in her home. Her mother-in-law's mode of social work appears to her more like a power game. She cannot appreciate the dubious legal ethics of her husband, and the appreciative attitude of the entire family towards Subhash when he knowingly wants to prove with false circumstantial evidence that a poor woman with a paralytic husband is of questionable character, to save his client, the doctor who has raped her. Yet her husband would ordinarily be considered a progressive man. He allowed his wife to go away to Bombay to work for her degree. Now he allows her, though reluctantly, to leave home and go and take charge of an institution for deserted and delinquent women in a small town some three hundred miles away. He stands by her when his authoritarian mother opposes the move bitterly; even though he himself cannot comprehend why Sulbha must take a job that will mean living away from her husband.

At the *Mahilashram* (women's home), Sulbha's idealism gets a severe jolt. Her predecessors have established a tradition of corruption and immorality that she finds hard to overcome. The *sari* merchant offers her a bribe. The local legislator rings up to ask for a pretty new girl. The apathy, hypocrisy and greed of the governing body and its upper-class chairperson, Mrs Sampson, shock her deeply. In addition there are internal problems of petty thefts and rackets run within the walls of the institution. A mentally disturbed woman climbs up to the roof and has to be rescued. A woman who had sought refuge from the tortures of her husband, kills her child in the hope of staying on as a criminal, when the governing body rules that she must be sent home. Two lesbians are discovered and humiliated by the other inmates who cannot understand Sulbha's compassion for what they consider immoral even in their own amoral community. Two girls who make a bid for freedom are hauled back like the criminals they are not, and have to be detained in the lock-up against Sulbha's wishes. When they burn themselves to death, Mrs Sampson and the governing body hold Sulbha responsible on all counts. The accusations are many, and a one-man commission is set up to hear the case: a fat, somnolent, indifferent officer, who hardly listens to Sulbha's passionate plea for a radical change in the running of the *Mahilashram*. Sulbha resigns and goes back home in defiance and despair.

Sulbha's mother-in-law responds to her return with cold indifference. Rani no longer knows her mother and reacts with hostility. Only Maya is happy to see her back. Subhash had visited her once in the women's home, and taken umbrage at her spending most of the night at the bedside of a dying girl, rather than with him. Now, after making love to her, he tells her self-righteously that he has taken a mistress whom he has no intention of giving up. Sulbha will, of course, retain the position of his wife at home. Subhash's rejection hits Sulbha like a physical blow. But with it comes freedom. With her inner reserve of strength, she leaves home the next day in search of a life outside its hypocritical, stifling walls.

Bhumika: Shyam Benegal

Saraansh: Mahesh Bhatt

Aadmi aur Aurat: Tapan Sinha

Paar: Goutam Ghose

Pather Panchali: Satyajit Ray

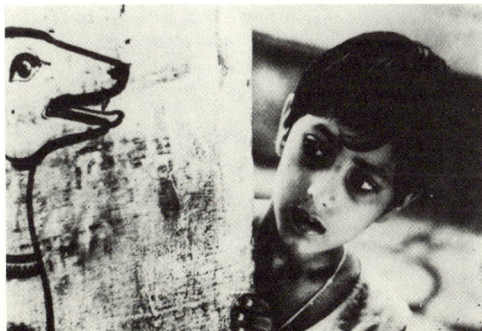

Aparajito: Satyajit Ray

Mukhamukham: Adoor Gopalakrishnan

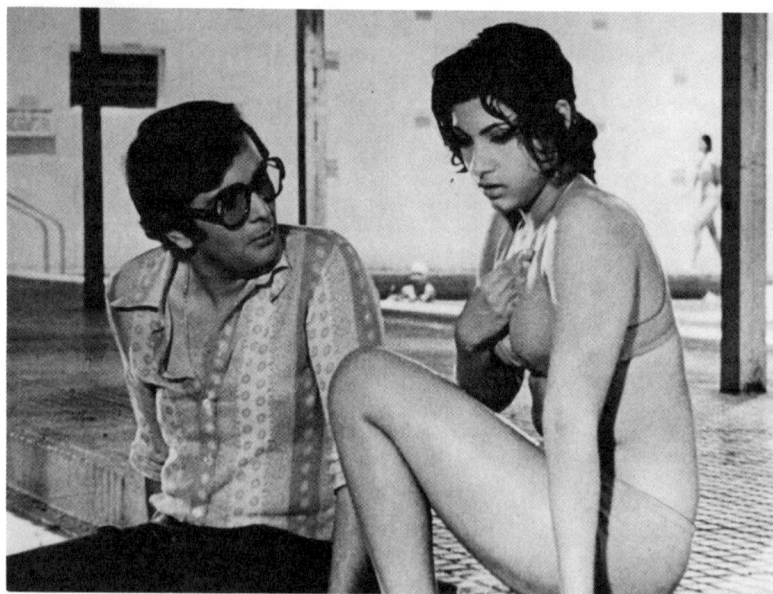

Bobby: Raj Kapoor

Adaminte Variyellu: K.G. George

Maya Miriga: Nirad Mohapatra

Akaler Sandhaney: Mrinal Sen

Apur Sansar: Satyajit Ray

Masoom: Shekhar Kapoor

Bhavni Bhavai: Ketan Mehta

36 Chowringhee Lane: Aparna Sen

Damul: Prakash Jha

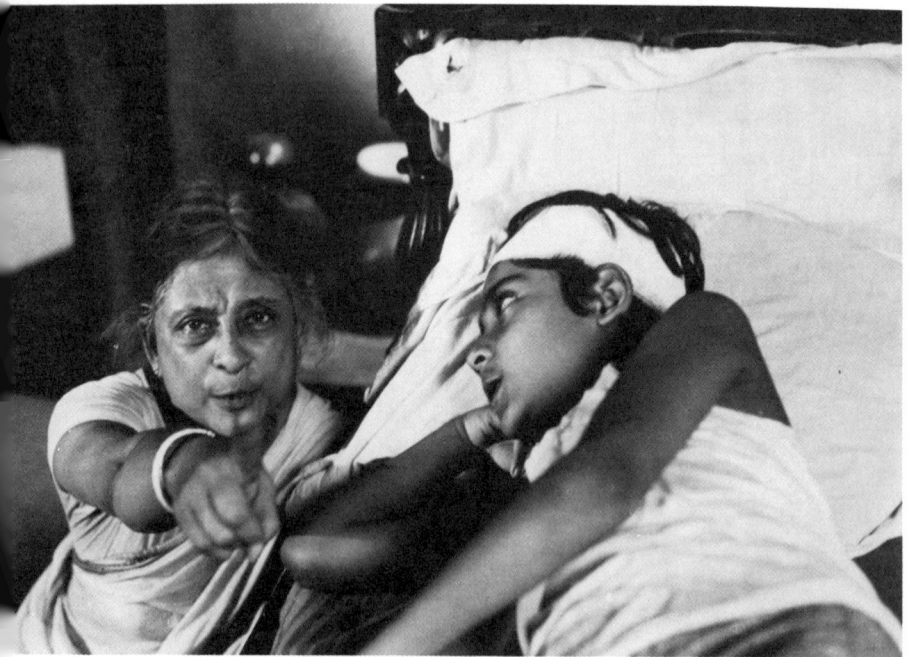

Ek Din Pratidin: Mrinal Sen

Bhuvan Shome: Mrinal Sen

Duniya Na Mane: V. Shantaram

Achamillai Achamillai: K. Balachander

Ghatashraddha: Girish Kasaravalli

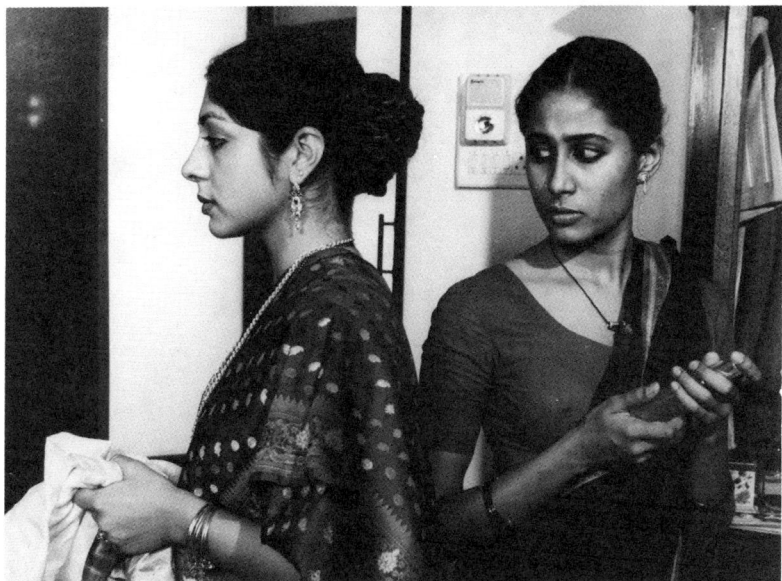

Tarang: Kumar Shahani

22 June 1897: Nachiket and Jayoo Patwardhan

Mudhal Mariyadhai: Bharati Rajaa

Atithi: Tapan Sinha

UMBARTHA is a film for the many Sulbhas of this world who are yet to cross the threshold into freedom. For women like Sulbha, the struggle against hidden corruption and immorality is made more acute by the fact that the real enemies take shelter behind a facade of justice and truth, social respectability and moral self-righteousness. In her own home Sulbha is the outsider, unable to accept the double standards and compromises that form the foundations of middle-class morality. She finds a very similar false morality operating among the community of women who have been ostracized by society for their own deviations. She also discovers the same corruption and hypocrisy among its administrators as she has witnessed in the larger world outside. When Sulbha finally leaves home, she has indeed joined the ranks of the women she had set out to save. But it is a conscious choice which also gives her freedom from the society that she is determined to redeem. *Umbartha* has been perceived as a truly feminist film, for in describing a woman's bid for freedom and individual identity, it places her in a broader human context, where her struggle is against the injustice and untruth that controls contemporary human society at large.

The film's director, Jabbar Patel, is a practising pediatrician, who is also one of the most successful directors of the serious Marathi and Hindi stage. His association with playwright Vijay Tendulkar has been of long standing, and resulted in one of the greatest theatrical triumphs of the decade. *Ghasiram Kotwal,* a play on an unscrupulous Brahmin Minister of 18th century Maharashtra, was first produced in 1972, and still draws huge crowds. Political corruption and social hypocrisy have been the themes of most of Patel's films. His style is grossly non-cinematic, but his acute sense of drama, and the impact of his themes have made him one of the more important film-makers in the country. Patel has no pretensions about being part of the new cinema movement; his films are made for the masses in spite of their serious content. His formula of compromise usually works, for the films run to full houses at least in Maharashtra. *Umbartha* also has a Hindi language version called *Subah* (The Dawn).

UTSAV (The Festival)
colour, 145 minutes, Hindi, 1984

Production: Film-Valas/ Direction: Girish Karnad/ Story: Based on a classical Sanskrit play by Sudraka/ Screenplay: Grish Karnad, Krishna Basroor/ Camera: Ashok Mehta/ Music: Laxmikant Pyarelal/ Lyrics: Vasant Dev/ Art Direction: Jayoo Nachiket/ Sound: Hitendra Ghosh
Cast: Shashi Kapoor, Rekha, Amjad Khan, Anooradha, Shekhar Suman, Kunal Kapoor, Annu Kapoor, Neena Guta, Shankar Nag, Harish Patel, Kulbhushan Kharbanda, Gopi Desai, Anupam Kher

RUNNING away from Samasthanaka, the lecherous brother-in-law of the king, Vasantsena, the most beautiful courtesan of Ujjain, hides in the home of Charudutt, a handsome, impoverished Brahmin whose wife is away from home. Charudutt sends a maidservant with a message to his wife, and mistaking her for Vasantsena, Samasthanaka carries her away. But Aryaka, a revolutionary touring the city in disguise, gives Samasthanaka and his man an unexpected beating and allows the girl to escape. Charudutt is charmed to discover Vasantsena in his home, and the encounter warms into passionate curiosity. When Vasantsena goes, she leaves behind her jewellery, for the roads are unsafe. Charudutt hands the precious bundle to his friend Maitraya when his wife and child return in the morning.

A masseur on the run from his debtors, overhears a conversation about Vasantsena's infatuation for the young Brahmin, and enters the courtesans' dwelling pretending to be Charudutt's emissary. Vasantsena promptly pays off his pursuers. Impressed by the effect one man's name has on his destiny, the masseur decides to abandon worldly desires and become a hermit. Vasantsena's personal maid, Madanika, is in love with Sajjal, the cleverest thief in town. But she is a slave, and to marry her Sajjal needs money to buy her freedom. Wandering into Charudutt's home, he finds Maitreya uncomfortably tossing in his sleep, with the bundle of jewellery under his head. When Sajjal brings the jewels to Vasantsena, Madanika recognizes them and is terrified. But Vasantsena, aware of Sajjal's devotion, accepts the jewels and frees Madanika.

Meanwhile, in Charudutt's home, the theft is discovered and Charudutt's wife, learning of her husband's infidelity, sends Vasantsena her last piece of jewellery and leaves home with her child. Knowing that Charudutt is alone, Vasantsena visits him once again. She wears the stolen jewellery, and Charudutt, relieved to find it safe, makes passionate love to her. Next morning the spring festival begins. Charudutt plans a tryst with Vasantsena in a garden, and promises to send her a carriage. While he is out, his wife returns and meets Vasantsena. A warm friendship springs up between them, and the courtesan decorates her friend with some of her own jewellery, giving the rest to the child to play with. Later, Samasthanaka, who has made a deal with the woman in charge of the courtesans, also sends a carriage to pick up Vasantsena and take her to the same garden. Confusion reigns, and Vasantsena, finding herself in the clutches of Samasthanaka, tries to run away. Infuriated by repeated rejections, Samasthanaka strangles her, then puts the blame on Charudutt who has come looking for Vasantsena in the garden. The soldiers who arrest him, also find the courtesan's jewels in his home and Charudutt is sentenced to death.

The man who was supposed to bring Vasantsena to Charudutt, unknowingly brings Aryaka, the revolutionary who is hiding from the king's soldiers. Now Aryaka and his friends, helped by Sajjal who shows them a secret route, storms the king's fort while the townspeople are busy celebrating the spring festival. At the same time, away from the city, the executioners prepare to carry out the death sentence on Charudutt. Saved by the hermit-masseur, Vasantsena appears just in time to stop the execution. But the executioners are not convinced. They know nothing of Vasantsena; only that Charudutt has killed a courtesan. But Vasantsena insists that Samasthanaka had tried to kill her, and Charudutt has been blamed for her murder. Seeing her alive, Samasthanaka hides behind a rock, while the executioners once again decide that Charudutt must die. Just then, a horseman arrives to announce that the old king has been deposed and the new monarch has pardoned all prisoners. Watching Charudutt embracing his wife in joy, Vasantsena leaves, while the people who had gathered for the execution vent their rage on Samasthanaka. Dusk falls, and Samasthanaka, no longer a powerful courtier, drags his battered and bruised body to the courtesans' dwelling. Vasantsena, putting away her dreams, gently draws him into the house.

IN AN INTERVIEW in *Cinema-India International* (July-September 1984), Girish Karnad talks about *Utsav*: "I have always been obsessed with Sudraka's play *Mrichchakatikam* [*The Little Clay Cart*]. It's an extraordinary work in the context of Indian literature, down-to-earth, funny, irreverent, sensuous. ...*Utsav* was a huge project, and since we wanted to retain the 4th century background, a lot of spadework and considerable research were required. I was lucky in my crew—Ashok Mehta, and my art directors Nachiket and Jayoo Patwardhan....The film has no message, political, social, or of any other kind. The basis is the Sanskrit theory that a work of art should create a *rasa*, a mood, an evocation of emotion—not preach. What I hoped to do was to revive the two qualities which ancient Indian literature had, but which we seem to have lost in the course of the last thousand years—sensuousness and humour. Not sex, but sensuousness, the poetic, tactile quality of it."

Though shown in the Indian Panorama section of the International Film Festival in Delhi, *Utsav*, produced by Shashi Kapoor, with its large cast, lavish sets and costumes, was a financial disaster. Not even its English version, made specially for a foreign audience, made money. But it remains a unique experiment in Indian cinema. Rekha, the reigning star of popular films at the time, is at her sensuous best, and Shashi Kapoor, erstwile popular hero, with his handsome face hidden behind a drooping moustache, excels as the disgusting yet pathetic Samasthanaka. The film is a rousing celebration of life, and every character, from the svelte Madanika and the fleet-footed Sajjal to the effeminate Charudutt and the masseur turned hermit, finds a special place in this narrative of another age. Even the extraneous Vatsyayana (played by Amjad Khan), busily instructing the courtesans on the spiritual aspects of sex, and prying on their activities with their clients to add it all to his famous *Kama Sutra*, sets the mood of the times.

Sudraka, on whose play the film is based, is one of the unknowns of history, though most probably he did live in the 4th century, before Kalidasa appeared on the scene. The *Kama Sutra* was supposed to have been written between the 1st and 4th centuries A.D., and Vatsyayana certainly does not appear as a character in Sudraka's play. But history is not the purpose behind *Utsav*. Presented in the tradition of the picaresque, this tale of pimps, prostitutes and pickpockets, retains the earthy, bawdy humour of the marketplace, and a certain emotional pragmatism that allows Vasantsena to relinquish Charudutt and accept the now powerless Samasthanaka in the end.

GENERAL INDEX

A

A Throw of Dice 14
Aadmi aur Aurat 9-10
Aag 47
Aakrosh 10-12
Abbas, K.A. 15, 42, 53, 73, 74, 75, 79, 80
Abbas, Khwaja Ahmad *see* Abbas, K.A.
Abraham, John 20, 28, 29, 30
Achamillai Achamillai 12-13
Achhut Kanya 13-15, 111
Achrekar, M.R. 42, 105
Adaminte Variyellu 15-17
Adi Shankaracharya 17-19
Agashe, Mohan 10, 139
Agha, Jalal 87, 127, 161, 166, 172
Agnisnaan 19-20
Agraharathil Kazhuthai 20-22
Ajantrik 4, 22-24
Akaler Sandhaney 24-25, 75
Akash Kusum 52
Akram, Shaikh 127
Alam Ara 1
Albert Pinto ko Gussa Kyon ata Hai 102, 124
Alekar, Satish 183
Allauddin 42, 46, 53, 176
Alter, Tom 165
Alvi, Abrar 105, 153, 154
Aman 127
Aman, Zeenat 98
Amar Akbar Anthony 25-28
Ambat, Madhu 17, 150
Amjad Khan 118
Amma Ariyan 28-30
Amrapurkar, Sadashiv 37, 182

Amrit Manthan 30-31
Amrohi, Kamal 126, 140, 142
Anand, Chetan 174, 176
Anand, Dev 44, 45, 94, 95, 174, 176
Anand, Jagmohan 123
Anand, Uma 174
Anand, Vijay 94, 95, 174, 176
Ananthamurthy, U.R. 90, 156, 158
Anarkali 128
Andaz 31-33
Ankur 6, 140
Ankush 10
Annadata 73
Annadurai, C.N. 3, 126
Anooradha 185
Anthony, P.J. 135, 136
Aparajito 33-35, 36
Appu, M.N. 15
Apte, Shanta 30, 31, 80
Apur Sansar 35-37
Aravindan, G. 7, 51, 63, 64, 137, 138, 139
Ardh Satya 6, 37-38
Arjun, C. 103
Arth 164
Arunavikas 114, 150
Arvind Desai ki Ajeeb Dastan 124
Arya, Ishan 87
Ashalata 183
Asher, Ramesh 48
Asif, K. 120, 126, 128
Athavale, Shantaram 80, 159, 160
Atithi 38-39
Attenborough, Sir Richard 164, 165
Aurat 39-41

Ávadhoot, V. 79, 80, 159
Avaiyyar 41-42
Avashesh 91
Awara 42-44
Azmi, Kaifi 87, 105, 140
Azmi, Shabana 11, 25, 114, 139, 140, 164, 165
Azmi, Shaukat 87

B
B.R. Films 98
Baazi 44-46, 176
Babbar, Raj 98
Babi, Parveen 25, 68
Babu, Ramachandra 15, 20, 135
Babu, Surendra 137
Baby Shakuntala 155
Bachchan, Amitabh 5, 25, 68, 69, 70, 93, 166, 168, 176
Badayuni, Shakeel 126
Bakshi, Anand 25, 166
Balachander, K. 12, 13
Balamurali Krishna, M. 17
Bali, Geeta 44
Bandyopadhyay, Bibhutibhushan 33, 35, 36, 148, 150
Bandyopadhyay, Kanu 33, 148
Bandyopadhyay, Karuna 33, 107, 148
Banerjee, Ajit 92
Banerjee, Ajitesh 38
Banerjee, Durgadas 56
Banerjee, Kali 22, 145
Banerjee, Partha 139
Banerjee, S.D. 17
Banerjee, Satya 83
Banerji, Bibhutibhushan *see* Bandyopadhyay, Bhibhutibhushan
Banks, Louis 133
Bansal, R.D. 60
Bapat, Vasant 183
Barnouw, Eric 80
Barsaat 46-48, 54

Bartley, Marcus 62, 146
Barua, P.C. 71, 73, 154
Barua, Pramathesh Chandra *see* Barua, P.C.
Barve, Bhakti 100
Basak, Gonesh 77
Basrur, Krishna 136, 185
Basu, Gangapada 22, 145
Baswani, Ravi 100
Bedekar, Vishram 156
Bedi, Rajinder Singh 61, 112, 114, 131, 132
Beena 28
Begum, Mubarak 176
Begum, Shamshad 127, 131
Benegal, Shyam 6, 11, 50, 51, 140, 179, 180, 181
Bhaduri [Mitra], Tripti 74
Bhaduri, Jaya 92, 93, 166
Bhagavat, Sri 159, 161
Bhaktavatsalam, P. 65, 136
Bhargavi, Manju 158, 159
Bhaskar, Vijaya 89
Bhatia, Vanraj 50, 100, 123, 172, 178, 180
Bhatt, Mahesh 6, 163, 164
Bhatt, Pravin 114
Bhatt, Suresh 183
Bhattacharya, Abhi 170
Bhattacharya, Basu 176
Bhattacharya, Bijon 73, 121, 170
Bhattacharya, Himadri 83
Bhattacharya, Manoranjan 56
Bhattacharya, Nikunja 19
Bhattacharya, Radhamohan 24, 111
Bhattacharya, Satindra 22, 121, 170
Bhattacharya, Umanath 24, 83, 170
Bhatti, C.S. 11, 37, 172
Bhatvadekar, Harishchandra Sakharam 1
Bhavani, Adoor 62

Bhavni Bhavai 48-49
Bhoge, Bejoy 143
Bhole, Keshavrao 30, 80, 159
Bhonsle, Asha 68, 98, 176
Bhonsle, Vaman 118
Bhopali, Kaif 140
Bhumika 50-51
Bhupinder 68
Bhushan, Bharat 17, 103, 118
Bhuvan Shome 4, 5, 51-53, 157, 162
Biggs, C.E. 58
Bilgrami, Madhosh 123
Billimoria, Dinshaw 112
Bimal Roy 71, 73
Bimal Roy Productions 112
Bir, Apurba Kishore 136
Biswas, Anil 39, 109
Biswas, Chhabi 107, 108, 111
Biswas, Samita 38
Bobby 53-55
Bombay Film Society 4
Bombay Talkies 14, 15, 47, 109, 110
Boral, R.C. 56, 152, 169, 170
Boral, Rai Chand *see* Boral, R.C.
Bose, Debaki 56, 57
Bose, Kamal 77, 131
Bose, Kartick 9
Bose, Loken 169
Bose, Mukul 56
Bose, Nitin 56, 152
Burman, M.K. 174
Burman, R.D. 68, 114, 166
Burman, S.D. 94, 105, 153, 174

C
Calcutta Film Society 4
Cartaw, Steven 156
Cawas, John 75, 77
Chakra 55-56
Chakraborty, S. 87
Chakravarty, Tulsi 22, 145, 146, 148

Chanda, Samir 133
Chandavarkar, Bhaskar 116, 136, 137, 143
Chander, Krishen 73
Chandidas 56-58
Chandra, Suresh 83
Chandragupta, Bansi 24, 33, 35, 55, 60, 61, 107, 145, 148, 165, 166, 172, 178
Chandralekha 3, 42, 58-59, 129
Chandramohan 30, 31
Chandru 58
Charulata 60-61
Chaterji, Dhritiman 24, 178
Chatterjee, Anil 22, 107, 121, 139
Chatterjee, Ravi 22, 121, 170
Chatterjee, Satyen 9, 22, 121, 170
Chatterjee, Shekhar 51
Chatterji, Basu 162
Chattopadhyay, Soumitra 35, 36, 60
Chaturvedi, B.K. 98
Chauhan, Dinanath 183
Chauhan, Y.G. 44, 105, 153
Chemeen 62-63
Chhinnamul 3
Chidambaram 63-64
Chitnis, Leela 42, 94
Chomana Dudi 65-66
Chopra, B.R. 98
Chopra, Dharam 98
Chopra, Prem 53
Chopra, Vinod 100, 102
Chopra, Yash 68, 168
Choudhary, Jehangir 96
Choudhuri, Ranjit 55
Choudhury, Supriya 121
Chowdhury, Salil 24, 62, 77, 112, 114, 131, 132, 161
Chughtai, Ismat 87
Contracter, K.M. 75
Contractor, Navroze 82, 182
Cowan, Tom 156

D

D'Cruz, George 92
Dakhal 140
Damle, G. 155
Damle, Shankarrao 159
Damle, V. 30, 31, 80, 156, 159
Damul 66-67
Dana Veera Sura Karna 148
Das Gupta, Bijohn 114
Das, Robin 100
Das, Shanti 98
Dasgupta, Chidananda 4, 61, 146
Dasgupta, Uma 148
Date, Keshavrao 80
David 74, 109, 131
De, Dipankar 24, 143
Deewar 68-70, 168
Deo, Vasant 163
Desai, Gopi 48, 185
Desai, Leela 152
Desai, Manmohan 25, 27, 28
Desai, Nimesh 48
Desai, S.N. 46
Desai, Vasant 79, 92
Deshpande, Arvind 10, 172
Deshpande, Sulabha 50, 172
Detha, Vijaydan 82
Dev, Vasant 185
Devadas 15, 85, 129, 137
Devarajan 63
Devatha 70-71
Devdas 15, 71-73, 154
Devi 112
Devi, Aparna 148
Devi, Chunibala 148
Devi, Kanan 169, 170
Devi, Ranibala 145
Devi, Reba 148
Devi, Saraswati 13
Dey, Krishna Chandra 56, 71
Dey, Manna 42, 68, 103,131, 166, 176
Dhaibar, K. 30

Dhaimade, Das 92, 131
Dharamvir 127
Dharmaraj, Rabindra 55, 56
Dharmendra 92, 93, 98, 166
Dharti ke Lal 73-75
Dhawan, David 163
Dhawan, Prem 73
Dholakia, Rajat 96
Diamond Queen 75-77
Divakar, Bhanudas 50, 55, 178, 180
Divecha, Dwarka 166
Dixit, Udayan 182
Do Bigha Zameen 77-79
Dongre, Daya 183
Dr Kotnis ki Amar Kahani 79-80
Dubey, Satyadev 50, 67
Duniya na Mane 80-82
Dutt, Guru 3, 4, 44, 45, 105, 106, 153, 154, 176
Dutt, Sunil 40
Dutt, Utpal 51, 52, 53, 92, 139
Dutta, Dulal 33, 36, 60, 108, 145, 148, 165
Duvidha 82-83, 183

E

Ek Chadar Maili si 61
Ek Din Pratidin 83-85
Ek Duje ke Liye 13
Elippathayam 85-87
Elkunchwar, Mahesh 10, 11, 96

F

Farida Jalal 165
Fattelal, S. 30, 31, 80, 155, 156, 159
Fearless Nadia 75, 77
Film and Television Institute of India 5, 16, 23, 24, 49, 91, 117, 124, 137, 174
Film Finance Corporation 5
Film Institute *see* Film and Television Institute of India

Films Division 2

G

Gaekwar, S.R. 75
Gajbar, Bal 79
Gandhi 164
Gandhi, Sanjeev 96
Gandhiok, Kawal 172
Ganesan, Sivaji 124, 126
Ganga, P. 129
Gangadhar 89
Garam Hava 6, 87-88
Gaulbert, Lawrence 20
Gauri 159, 161
Gejje Pooje 89-90
Gemini Pictures 41, 42, 58
Gemini Studios 3, 59, 148
George, K.G. 15, 16, 62
Ghantasala 146
Ghare Baire 36, 179
Ghasiram Kotwal 185
Ghatak, Ritwik 4, 22, 23, 24, 29,
    85, 112, 114, 121, 122, 131, 132,
    170, 171, 172, 174
Ghatashradhha 90-91
Ghosal, Smaran Kumar 33
Ghose, Goutam 139, 140
Ghosh, Bhupen 148
Ghosh, Hitendra 114, 163, 180,
    185
Ghosh, Kamal 58
Ghosh, Nemai 3
Gillani, Benjamin 48, 165
Gita 87, 166
Gokhale, Mohan 48, 123
Gopalakrishnan, Adoor 7, 85, 86,
    129, 130, 131, 136
Gopi 15, 63
Goswami, Malaya 19
Goswami, Tarun 19
Gowarikar, Asutosh 96
Great Dictator, The 168
Guddi 92-93
Guha Thakurta, Mrinal 22
Guha, Anita 103

Guide 94-96
Gulzar 92, 93, 114, 116, 118, 120,
    133, 172
Gulzar, Rakhee 143
Gupta, Anubha 107
Gupta, Dilip 112, 169
Gupta, Dinen 22, 121
Gupta, Neena 100, 180, 185
Gupte, Amol 96
Guru Dutt Films 105, 153
Gurudutta 118

H

Habibullah, Shama 11
Hangal, A.K. 67, 92, 133, 161, 166
Hansraj, Jugal 114
Harikumar 63
Harishchandra 104
Hattangady, Rohini 123, 163, 164,
    172
Helen 25, 166
Holi 96-98
Human Voice, The 174

I

Inamdar, Shafi 37
Indian Peoples Theatre Association
    (IPTA) 3, 73, 74, 88, 132
Indira, M.K. 90, 150, 151
Insaaf ka Tarazu 98-100
IPTA *see* Indian Peoples Theatre
    Association
Irani, Aruna 53, 67
Irani, Faredoon A. 32, 39
Iyer, G.V. 17, 18
Iyer, Ganapathy Venkataramana
    see Iyer, G.V.

J

Jaane bhi do Yaaro 100-102
Jabanbandi 73
Jadav 44
Jaffrey, Saeed 114, 165
Jafri, Ali Sardar 73

Jagirdar, Gajanan 155, 156
Jai Santoshi Ma 6, 103-105
Jaikishen 46, 176
Jain, Jainendra 53
Jain, Nemichand 73
Jain, Ravindra 98
Jaipuri, Hasrat 42, 46, 176
Jairam, Vani 92, 118
Jalaja 85
Jalal, Farida 53, 165
Jalsaghar 36
Jambulingam 146
Jamuna 71, 73
Janakiram, M.S. 41
Janam 164
Javed 68, 166, 168
Jayashree 79
Jeevan 25
Jeevan Naiya 110
Jha, Prakash 66, 67
Jhanak Jhanak Payal Bajey 4
Joshi, Ramesh 22, 121, 170
Jukti Takko ar Gappo 172
Junoon 179

K
Kadri, Shamsudin 32, 39
Kaghaz ke Phool 105-106, 154
Kakkar 174
Kalpana 89
Kalyanpur, Suman 176
Kamalakar 25
Kanagal, S.R. Puttana 89
Kanchanjungha 106-109
Kannan, B. 124
Kanwar, Anita 180
Kapadia, Dimple 53, 54
Kapadia, Jamnadas 73
Kapoor, Annu 66, 185
Kapoor, Kunal 185
Kapoor, Mahendra 25, 98, 103
Kapoor, Pankaj 100, 123
Kapoor, Prithviraj 42, 44, 127
Kapoor, Raj 3, 4, 15, 32, 33, 42,

44, 46, 47, 53, 54, 176, 178
Kapoor, Rishi 25, 53, 54
Kapoor, Shammi 118
Kapoor, Shashi 68, 133, 178, 179, 185, 187
Kapoor, Shekhar 114
Karamana 85, 129
Karanth, B.V. 18, 50, 65, 83, 85, 90, 150
Karanth, Prema 150, 151
Karanth, Shivarama 65
Kariat, Ramu 62, 63
Karmakar, Radhu 42, 53
Karnad, Girish 18, 50, 65, 136, 137, 156, 157, 172, 183, 185, 187
Kartik, Kalpana 44, 174, 176
Karunanidhi, M. 126
Kasaravalli, Girish 90, 91
Kaul, Mani 82, 161, 183
Kaushik 32
Kaviyoor Ponnamma 135
Kay Gee 67
Kendall, Geoffrey 178, 179
Kendall, Jennifer 178, 179
Khan Ashish 9
Khan, Ali Akbar 22, 111, 112
Khan, Amjad 123, 165, 166, 169, 185, 187
Khan, Bahadur 87, 170
Khan, Bare Ghulam Ali 126
Khan, Hammu 82
Khan, Mehboob 31, 39
Khan, Ramzan 82
Khandhar 140
Khanna, Vinod 25, 118
Kharbanda, Kulbhushan 50, 55, 133, 180, 185
Kher, Anupam 163, 164, 185
Khote, Durga 53, 127, 131
Kinagi, Rajan 183
Kiron, Usha 131
Kismet 109-111
Kittoo, M.R. 12
Kolhapure, Padmini 98

Komal Gandhar 172
Kosambi, D.D. 174
Koshal, Kanan 103
Kothari, Rajen 65
Krishnakant "Pummy" 48
Krishnamoorthy, P. 17
Krishnamurthy, Lakshmi 156
Krishnan, A. 146
Krishnanunni 28
Krishnaswamy, S. 80
Kshudhita Pashan 111-112
Kulkarni, N.B. 140
Kulkarni, Umesh 90
Kumar, Ajit 90
Kumar, Ashish 103
Kumar, Ashok 14, 15, 109, 110,
 111, 140
Kumar, Dilip 15, 32, 33, 73, 112,
 114, 127, 131, 133
Kumar, Kishore 25, 68, 131, 132,
 166
Kumar, Raaj 140
Kumar, Sanjeev 165, 166, 169
Kumari, Kamlesh 152
Kumari, Kusum 14
Kumari, Meena 140, 142
Kumta, Padma 65
Kunku 81
Kunti 174

L
Lachchu Maharaj 127
Lagoo, Shreeram 96, 98, 118, 172
Lakhia, Meera 48
Lankesh, P. 156
Laxmikant 25, 53, 185
Light of Asia, The 14
Lucknavi, Shams 31
Ludhianvi, Sahir 44, 68, 98, 153,
 174

M
Ma Bhoomi 140
Madhu 62

Madhubala 127
Madhuchhanda 161
Madhumati 112-114
Mahadevan, K.J. 58
Mahadevan, K.V. 158
Mahajan, K.K. 24, 51, 83, 161,
 172
Mahal 142
Mahanagar 93
Maharashtra Film Company 31
Mahendra, Balu 158
Majumdar, Sreela 24, 66, 83
Malati 147
Malini, Hema 118, 166
Mammooti 15
Manaswini 116
Mandi 140
Mane, B. 98
Mangeshkar, Hridaynath 55, 183
Mangeshkar, Lata 25, 31, 42, 127,
 131, 140, 166, 176
Mangeshkar, T.R. 68
Mangeshkar, Usha 103
Mani 146
Mani, M. 85, 129
Manimala 116
Mankani, Ravindra 182
Marathe, Anant 155
Masoom 114-116
Master, Madhulal D. 75
Master, R.P. 75
Masud, Iqbal 104
Mathew, Joy 28
Mathur, R.D. 126
Maya Darpan 174
Maya Miriga 116-118
Mayekar, G.G. 42, 46, 161, 176
Mazumdar, Phani 169
Meena 90
Meenakshi 155
Meera 118-121
Meghe Dhaka Tara 121-123, 172
Meher, Sadhu 51
Mehta, Ashok 178, 180, 185, 187,

143
Mehta, Ketan 48, 49, 51, 96, 97
Mehta, Kumud 83
Mehta, Tarla 161
Menon, Ravi 82
Mera Naam Joker 54
Mirza, Saeed Akhtar 102, 123, 124
Mirza, Vajahat 38, 127
Mishra, Binod 116
Mishra, Raj Gopal 116
Mishra, Sudhir 100, 102, 123
Misra, Leela 42, 103, 153, 166
Mistry, Fali 94
Mistry, Jal 46
Mistry, Keshav 32
Mistry, Pestonji D. 75
Mitra, Durgadas 33, 36, 83
Mitra, Shambhu 74
Mitra, Subrata 33, 35, 60, 61, 107, 108, 133, 145, 148, 176, 178
Mitter, Subodh 71
Modak, Anand 182
Moghe, Shrikant 183
Mohammed, Ghulam 140
Mohan Joshi Haazir Ho! 123-124
Mohanam 12
Mohapatra, Nirad 116, 117
Mohapatra, Sampad 116
Moitra, Jyotirindra 121
Mother India 40
Mudhal Mariyadhai 124-126
Mughal-e-Azam 120, 126-129
Mukesh 25, 31, 42, 176
Mukhamukham 129-131
Mukherjee, Arun 83, 107
Mukherjee, Arundhati 111
Mukherjee, Barun 55
Mukherjee, Bimal 111
Mukherjee, D.N. 92
Mukherjee, Desh 118, 176
Mukherjee, Devika 24
Mukherjee, Dilip Ranjan 38, 170
Mukherjee, Gyan 109
Mukherjee, Gyanesh 22, 121

Mukherjee, Hrishikesh 62, 77, 92, 112, 114, 131, 132
Mukherjee, Keshto 92, 131, 166, 176
Mukherjee, Madhavi 60, 170
Mukherjee, Parthasarathi 38
Mukherjee, S. 15
Mulay, Suhasini 48, 51, 53
Mullick, Amar 56
Mullick, Pankaj 152, 170
Mumtaz Shanti 109
Munshi Premchand 165, 166
Murthy, V.K. 105, 153
Musafir 114, 131-133
Music Room, The 108

N
Nabanna 73
Nadira 25, 140
Nag, Anant 50
Nag, Shankar 136, 137, 185
Nagaiah, V. 70
Nagarik 4, 23
Naidu, Keshav 11
Naidu, Leela 180
Naik, Pandurang 155
Nair, Balan K. 85, 129
Nair, Chandran 137
Nair, M.T. Vasudevan 135, 136
Nair, Rajam K. 15, 85
Namboodiri 137
Narasimhan, V.S. 12
Narayan, R.K. 94
Narayanan 70
Nargis 32, 33, 40, 42, 44, 46, 47
Naseeruddin Shah 10, 11, 37, 48, 50, 51, 55, 96, 100, 102, 114, 123, 139, 140, 180
Naskar, Gangadhar 24, 51, 83
National Film Archive of India 5, 109
National Film Development Corporation 17, 100, 132, 172
Naug, Biren 153

Naushad 32, 126, 140
Naval, Deepti 66, 96, 123
Navketan 44, 45, 94, 174
Naya Sansar 75
Nayak 108
Nayek, Kamal 9, 19
Nedumudi Venu 137
Nene, Raja 156
New Delhi Times 133-134
New Theatres 15, 38, 56, 57, 71, 73, 152, 169, 170
Nigar Sultana 127
Nihalani, Govind 6, 10, 11, 12, 37, 38, 50
Nimmi 46
Nirmalyam 135-136

O
Om Prakash 42
Ondanondu Kaladalli 136-137
Oridath 137-139
Osten, Franz 13, 14

P
Paar 139-140
Padamsee, Raisa 82
Padmanabhan, A.M. 66, 96
Pagnis, Vishnupant 159, 161
Pai, Dattaram N. 109
Paigankar, Anjali 55
Painter, Baburao 31
Pakeezah 140-143
Pal, D.N. 140
Palekar, Amol 9, 50, 162, 172
Palnitkar, V.H. 39
Pandey, Rakesh 161
Pandya, Chandrakant 39
Parama 143-145
Paranjape, Shakuntala 80
Parasakthi 126
Parash Pathar 36, 145-146
Parashar, Deepak 98
Pareenja, R.D. 109
Parthasarathy, M.D. 41

Party 11
Parvez, Yunus 87, 98
Patala Bhairavi 146-148
Patankar, Prabhakar 182
Patel, Hirabhai 103
Patel, Jabbar 6, 183, 185
Pathak, Dina 48, 118, 123, 161
Pathak, S.Y. 166
Pathak, Supriya 114
Pathare, Jayant 92
Pather Panchali 4, 34, 36, 108, 148-150
Patil, Smita 10, 11, 24, 37, 48, 50, 51, 55, 56, 63, 164, 172, 183
Patwardhan, Jayoo 123, 136, 137, 182, 183, 185, 187
Patwardhan, Nachiket 123, 136, 137, 182, 183, 185, 187
Phalke, Dada Saheb 1
Phaniyamma 150-152
Phukan, Biju 19
Phule, Nilu 163
Pillai, G. Shankar 174
Ponnamma 129
Prabhat Film Company 30, 31, 80, 155, 156, 159, 161
Prabhat Studios 4, 45
Pradeep 103, 109
Pradhan, Binod 100
Pran 25, 28, 53, 112
Prasad, V.R.K. 17
Premnath 46, 53, 54
President 152-153
Pudovkin, V.I. 4
Puri, Amrish 37, 50
Puri, Om 10, 11, 37, 38, 48, 96, 100, 133, 139, 172
Pushalkar, R.G. 140, 174
Pyaasa 106, 153-154
Pyarelal 25, 53, 185

R
R.K. Films 42, 46, 53
Radha 124

Radha, M.K. 58
Rafi, Mohammad 25, 31, 42, 127, 140
Raghavan, K. 135
Raha, Kali 169
Rai, Himanshu 13, 14, 15, 110
Raina, M.K. 133, 172
Raj, Prayag 25
Raja, Ilaya 124
Rajaa, Bharathi 6, 124, 126
Rajagopal, U. 62
Rajanigandha 162
Rajesh 12
Rajkamal Kala Mandir 79
Rajkumari, T.R. 58
Rama Rao, N.T. 3, 147, 148
Ramachandra, S. 65, 90
Ramachandran, K. 15
Raman, S.V. 105
Ramanathan, S.P. 12, 124
Ramani, Sheila 174
Ramanujan, A.K. 158
Ramesh 28
Ramnoth, K. 70, 71
Ramshastri 155-156
Ranade, Rahul 96
Rangraj, A. 25, 53
Rani, Devika 14, 15, 110, 111
Ranjeet 25
Rao, Akkineni Nageswara 73
Rao, Akshata 136
Rao, G.G. Krishna 158
Rao, L.V. Sharada 17, 150, 151
Rao, M.V. Narayana 17
Rao, M.V. Vasudeva 65
Rao, S. Rajeswara 58
Rao, Vijay Raghava 51
Ratra, V. 44, 174
Ravi 20
Ray, Satyajit 4, 23, 33, 35, 36, 51, 60, 61, 78, 85, 93, 107, 108, 112, 145, 146, 148, 150, 165, 166, 169, 178, 179, 180
Raza, S. Ali 31

Razdan, Soni 163, 180
Reddi, B.N. 70, 71
Reddi, Bommireddi Narasimha *see* Reddi, B.N.
Reddy, K.V. 146
Reddy, Pattabhi Rama 63, 156, 157
Reddy, Snehlata 156, 157
Rehman 153
Rehman, Waheeda 94, 95, 105, 106, 153, 176
Rekha 185, 187
Rizvi, Ahsan 127
Roy Chowdhury, Mahua 9
Roy Chowdhury, Reba 24
Roy Chowdhury, Sajal 24
Roy, Alaknanda 106
Roy, Bimal 3, 71, 73, 77, 79, 112, 114
Roy, Debashree 178
Roy, Nirupa 25, 68, 77, 131
Roy, Nitish 133, 180
Roy, Pijush Kanti 19
Roy, Shobhendu 103
Roy, Soumendu 165
Roy, Subodh 9, 38, 111
Roy, Sudhendu 112, 114, 131

S
Sabnis, Rekha 136
Sagar 54
Sagar, Ramanand 46, 47
Sahib Bibi aur Ghulam 106
Sahni, Balraj 44, 74, 77, 78, 87, 88
Sahni, Bhisham 12, 123
Sahni, Damyanti 74
Sahu, Kishore 94
Saigal, K.L. 71, 73, 152, 153, 169, 170
Saigal, Kundan Lal *see* Saigal, K.L.
Saikia, Bhabendra Nath 19, 20
Saini, Virendra 123
Salim 68, 166, 168
Saluja, Renu 37, 100, 123, 133

Samapti 180
Samarth, Alaknanda 174
Samskara 18, 63, 156-158
Sandhyaraag 20
Sankarabharanam 158-159
Sant Tukaram 104, 105, 159-161
Sanyal, Pahari 107
Sapru 140
Sara Akash 161-163
Saraansh 163-164
Sarada 85
Sardar Akhtar 40
Saritha 12
Sathe, Ravindra 183
Sathe, V.P. 42, 53, 74, 79
Sathyan 62
Sathyu, M.S. 6, 87, 88
Satpathy, Bansidhar 116
Satpathy, Bibekanand 116
Satyam Shivam Sundaram 47
Sayani, Hameed 174, 176
Sayed, M.K. 127
Sazaye Maut 102
Sehay, Raghubir 172
Sehgal, Subhash 96
Sekar, A.K. 41, 58, 70
Sen, Aparna 143, 145, 178, 180
Sen, Gautam 66
Sen, Gita 24, 83
Sen, Mrinal 4, 5, 24, 25, 51, 52,75, 83, 85, 140, 157, 162
Sen, Suchitra 73, 131, 132
Sen, Sujit 163
Sengupta, Pinaki 33
Sengupta, Robin 133
Seth, Raghunath 66
Shah, Archana 48, 96
Shah, Kundan 100, 102
Shahani, Kumar 23, 51, 122, 172, 173, 174
Shaikh, Farouque 87
Shaikh, M.A. 68
Shailendra 42, 46, 77, 94, 112, 114, 131, 132, 176

Shaji 63, 64, 137
Sham, Munshi 75
Shankar 46, 176
Shankar, Mamata 83
Shankar, Ravi 33, 35, 73, 118, 120, 145, 148
Shankar-Shambhu 176
Shantaram, V. 4, 5, 30, 31, 79, 80, 81, 156
Sharada, L.V. *see* Rao, L.V. Sharada
Sharar, Dewan 79
Sharma, K.R. 41
Sharma, Mukul 143
Sharma, Ramesh 133, 134
Sharma, Vijay 103
Shatranj ke Khilari 140, 164-166, 169
Sheela 62
Sheikh, A.R. 159
Sheikh, Babu 94
Shinde, M.S. 163, 166
Shiraz 14
Shivpuri, Om 98, 118, 166
Sholay 6, 27, 104, 166-168, 169
Shrikanth, S.V. 89
Simhasan 6
Singh, K.N. 42, 44, 46, 74
Singh, Manohar 66, 133
Singh, Narendra 172
Singh, Neetu 25, 68
Singh, Shailendra 25
Sinha, Madhu 182
Sinha, Mala 153
Sinha, Tapan 9, 10, 38, 111, 112
Sinha, Vidya 118
Sippy, Ramesh 27, 54, 166
Sirkar, B.N. 2, 57, 73, 170
Sivan 85, 129
Sivan, Papanasam 41, 58
Somayajulu, J.V. 158, 159
Spreti, Karl von 13
Sreenivasan 137
Sreenivasan, M.B. 15, 20, 85, 129

Sreevidya 15
Sridhar, K.S. 150
Srinivasa Kalyanam 3
Street Singer 169-170
Subah 185
Subarna, K.V. 90
Subarnarekha 170-172
Subbalakshmi, M.S. 120
Subbu, K. 41, 42, 58
Subbu, Kothamangalam *see* Subbu, K.
Suhasini 15
Sultanpuri, Majrooh 31, 140
Suman, Shekhar 185
Sundaram, G.O. 15
Sundarambal, K.B. 41, 42
Sunitha 28
Suratwala, Essa M. 118, 131
Surendra 40
Suryakumari, T. 70
Swaminathan, Venkat 20
Swapnadanam 16
Swayamvaram 136

T
Tabarana Kathe 91
Tagore, Sharmila 35, 36, 133
Tandon, Adeep 163
Tanuja 114
Tarafdar, Rajen 24
Taranath, Rajeev 156
Tarang 172-174
Taxi Driver 174-176
Teen Kanya 180
Teesri Kasam 176-178
Tendulkar, Vijay 10, 11, 37, 183
Thakur, Dinesh 118
Thakur, Nandita 161
Thilakan 15, 129, 137
36 Chowringhee Lane 178-180
Timir Baran 71, 170
Titash Ekti Nadir Naam 172
Trikal 180-182
22 June 1897 182-183

Tyagi, Ashok 172
U
Umashashi 56
Umbartha 183-185
Urs, Sundar Krishna 136
Utsav 185-187

V
Vacha, Savak 13, 109
Vaidya, N.S. 183
Vaijayantimala 73, 112
Vaikunth, K. 118
Vairamuthu 12
Vamsa Vriksha 18, 65
Vande Mataram 71
Varma, Ravi 85, 129
Vasan, S.S. 3, 42, 58, 59
Vasu 156
Vasudev, S.G. 156
Vauhini Pictures 70, 71
Veena 105, 140
Verman, Ajit 37, 163
Vijaya Productions 146
Vishrambhai, D. 73
Viswanath, K. 158

W
Wadia Movietone 75, 77
Wadia, Homi 75, 77
Wadia, J.B.H. 75, 77
Wadia, Jamshed *see* Wadia, J.B.H.
Wadkar, Hansa 51
Walker, Johnny 105, 112, 127, 153, 174
Wirsching, Joseph 140

Y
Yagnik, Apurwa 66
Yakub 40
Yedekar, Ram 166

Z
Zaidi, Shama 50, 87

CHRONOLOGICAL INDEX

YEAR	TITLE OF FILM	TRANSLATED TITLE	
1932	Chandidas	Chandidas	56
1934	Amrit Manthan	The Churning of the Oceans	30
1935	Devdas	Devdas	71
1936	Achhut Kanya	The Untouchable Girl	13
1936	Sant Tukaram	Saint Tukaram	159
1937	Duniya na Mane	The Unexpected	80
1937	President	President	152
1938	Street Singer	Street Singer	169
1940	Aurat	Woman	39
1940	Diamond Queen	Diamond Queen	75
1941	Devatha	Divinity	70
1943	Kismet	Fate	109
1944	Ramshastri	Ramshastri	155
1946	Dharti ke Lal	Children of the Earth	73
1946	Dr Kotnis ki Amar Kahani	The Journey of Dr Kotnis	79
1948	Chandralekha	Chandralekha	58
1949	Andaz	*Beau Monde*	31
1949	Barsaat	Rain	46
1951	Awara	The Vagabond	42
1951	Baazi	A Game of Chance	44
1951	Patala Bhairavi	The Goddess from below the Earth	146
1953	Avaiyyar	Avaiyyar	41
1953	Do Bigha Zameen	Two Acres of Land	77
1954	Taxi Driver	Taxi Driver	174
1955	Pather Panchali	Song of the Road	148
1956	Aparajito	The Unvanquished	33
1957	Musafir	Traveller	131
1957	Parash Pathar	The Philosopher's Stone	145
1957	Pyaasa	Thirst	153
1958	Ajantrik	Pathetic Fallacy	22
1958	Madhumati	Madhumati	112
1959	Apur Sansar	The World of Apu	35
1959	Kaghaz ke Phool	Paper Flowers	105
1960	Kshudhita Pashan	Hungry Stones	111

1960	Meghe Dhaka Tara	The Cloud Capped Star	121
1960?	Mughal-e-Azam	The Great Mughal	126
1962	Kanchanjungha	Kanchanjungha	106
1964	Charulata	Charulata	60
1965	Atithi	The Runaway	38
1965	Chemeen	Wrath of the Sea	62
1965	Guide	The Guide	94
1965	Subarnarekha	Subarnarekha	170
1966	Teesri Kasam	The Third Vow	176
1969	Bhuvan Shome	Bhuvan Shome	51
1969	Gejje Pooje	The Mock Marriage	89
1969	Sara Akash	The Whole Sky	161
1970	Samskara	Funeral Rites	156
1971	Guddi	Darling Child	92
1971	Pakeezah	Pure Heart	140
1973	Bobby	Bobby	53
1973	Duvidha	In Two Minds	82
1973	Nirmalyam	The Offering	135
1975	Chomana Dudi	Choma's Drum	65
1975	Deewar	Wall	68
1975	Garam Hava	Hot Winds	87
1975	Jai Santoshi Ma	In Praise of Mother Santoshi	103
1975	Sholay	Flames of the Sun	166
1977	Agraharathil Kazhuthai	A Donkey in a Brahmin Village	20
1977	Amar Akbar Anthony	Amar Akbar Anthony	25
1977	Bhumika	The Role	50
1977	Ghatashraddha	The Ritual	90
1977	Shatranj ke Khilari	The Chess Players	164
1978	Ondanondu Kaladalli	Once Upon a Time	136
1979	22 June 1897	22 June 1897	182
1979	Ek Din Pratidin	And Quiet Rolls the Day	83
1979	Sankarabharanam	The Jewel of Shiva	158
1980	Aakrosh	Cry of the Wounded	10
1980	Akaler Sandhaney	In Search of Famine	24
1980	Bhavni Bhavai	A Folk Tale	48
1980	Chakra	The Vicious Circle	55
1980	Insaaf ke Tarazu	The Scales of Justice	98
1980?	Meera	Meera	118
1981	36 Chowringhee Lane	36 Chowringhee Lane	178
1981	Elippathayam	The Rat Trap	85
1982	Phaniyamma	Phaniyamma	150
1982	Umbartha	The Threshold	183

1983	Adaminte Variyellu	Adam's Rib	15
1983	Adi Shankaracharya	Adi Shankaracharya	17
1983	Ardh Satya	Half Truth	37
1983	Jaane bhi do Yaaro	Who Pays the Piper...	100
1983?	Masoom	Innocent	114
1983	Maya Miriga	The Mirage	116
1984	Aadmi aur Aurat	Man and Woman	9
1984	Achamillai Achamillai	Fearless	12
1984	Damul	Bonded until Death	66
1984	Holi	The Festival of Fire	96
1984	Mohan Joshi Haazir Ho!	A Summons for Mohan Joshi	123
1984	Mukhamukham	Face to Face	129
1984	Paar	The Crossing	139
1984	Saraansh	The Gist	163
1984	Tarang	Wages and Profits	172
1984	Utsav	The Festival	185
1985	Agnisnaan	Ordeal	19
1985	Chidambaram	Chidambaram	63
1985	Mudhal Mariyadhai	A Matter of Honour	124
1985	New Delhi Times	New Delhi Times	133
1985	Parama	Parama	143
1985	Trikal	Past, Present and Future	180
1986	Amma Ariyan	Report to Mother	28
1986	Oridath	Somewhere	137

INDEX OF ENGLISH TITLES

Adam's Rib (Adaminte Variyellu)
15
Adi Shankaracharya (Adi
Shankaracharya) 17
Amar Akbar Anthony (Amar
Akbar Anthony) 25
And Quiet Rolls the Day (Ek Din
Pratidin) 83
Avaiyyar (Avaiyyar) 41
Beau Monde (Andaz) 31
Bhuvan Shome (Bhuvan Shome)
51
Bobby (Bobby) 53
Bonded until Death (Damul) 66
Chandidas (Chandidas) 56
Chandralekha (Chandralekha) 58
Charulata (Charulata) 60
Chess Players, The (Shatranj ke
Khilari) 164
Chidambaram (Chidambaram) 63
Children of the Earth (Dharti ke
Lal) 73
Choma's Drum (Chomana Dudi)
65
Churning of the Oceans, The
(Amrit Manthan) 30
Cloud Capped Star, The (Meghe
Dhaka Tara) 121
Crossing, The (Paar) 139
Cry of the Wounded (Aakrosh) 10
Darling Child (Guddi) 92
Devdas (Devdas) 71
Diamond Queen (Diamond Queen)
75
Divinity (Devatha) 70
Donkey in a Brahmin Village, A
(Agraharathil Kazhuthai) 20

Face to Face (Mukhamukham)
129
Fate (Kismet) 109
Fearless (Achamillai Achamillai)
12
Festival of Fire, The (Holi) 96
Festival, The (Utsav) 185
Flames of the Sun (Sholay) 166
Folk Tale, A (Bhavni Bhavai) 48
Funeral Rites (Samskara) 156
Game of Chance, A (Baazi) 44
Gist, The (Saraansh) 163
Goddess from below the Earth, The
(Patala Bhairavi) 146
Great Mughal, The (Mughal-e-
Azam) 126
Guide, The (Guide) 94
Half Truth (Ardh Satya) 37
Hot Winds (Garam Hava) 87
Hungry Stones (Kshudhita Pashan)
111
In Praise of Mother Santoshi (Jai
Santoshi Ma) 103
In Search of Famine (Akaler
Sandhaney) 24
In Two Minds (Duvidha) 82
Innocent (Masoom) 114
Jewel of Shiva, The
(Sankarabharanam) 158
Journey of Dr Kotnis, The (Dr
Kotnis ki Amar Kahani) 79
Kanchanjungha (Kanchanjungha)
106
Madhumati (Madhumati) 112
Man and Woman (Aadmi aur
Aurat) 9
Matter of Honour, A (Mudhal

Mariyadhai) 124
Meera (Meera) 118
Mirage, The (Maya Miriga) 116
Mock Marriage, The (Gejje Pooje)
 89
New Delhi Times (New Delhi
 Times) 133
Offering, The (Nirmalyam) 135
Once Upon a Time (Ondanondu
 Kaladalli) 136
Ordeal (Agnisnaan) 19
Paper Flowers (Kaghaz ke Phool)
 105
Parama (Parama) 143
Past, Present and Future (Trikal)
 180
Pathetic Fallacy (Ajantrik) 22
Phaniyamma (Phaniyamma) 150
Philosopher's Stone, The (Parash
 Pathar) 145
President (President) 152
Pure Heart (Pakeezah) 140
Rain (Barsaat) 46
Ramshastri (Ramshastri) 155
Rat Trap, The (Elippathayam) 85
Report to Mother (Amma Ariyan)
 28
Ritual, The (Ghatashraddha) 90
Role, The (Bhumika) 50
Runaway, The (Atithi) 38
Saint Tukaram (Sant Tukaram)
 159
Scales of Justice, The (Insaaf ka
 Tarazu) 98

Somewhere (Oridath) 137
Song of the Road (Pather Panchali)
 148
Street Singer (Street Singer) 169
Subarnarekha (Subarnarekha) 170
Summons for Mohan Joshi, A
 (Mohan Joshi Haazir Ho!) 123
Taxi Driver (Taxi Driver) 174
Third Vow, The (Teesri Kasam)
 176
Thirst (Pyaasa) 153
36 Chowringhee Lane (36
 Chowringhee Lane) 178
Threshold, The (Umbartha) 183
Traveller (Musafir) 131
22 June 1897 (22 June 1897) 182
Two Acres of Land (Do Bigha
 Zameen) 77
Unexpected, The (Duniya na
 Mane) 80
Untouchable Girl, The (Achhut
 Kanya) 13
Unvanquished, The (Aparajito) 33
Vagabond, The (Awara) 42
Vicious Circle, The (Chakra) 55
Wages and Profits (Tarang) 172
Wall (Deewar) 68
Who Pays the Piper... (Jaane bhi
 do Yaaro) 100
Whole Sky, The (Sara Akash) 161
Woman (Aurat) 38
World of Apu, The (Apur Sansar)
 35
Wrath of the Sea (Chemeen) 62